COLD WAR OR DÉTENTE?

THE SOVIET VIEWPOINT

**Georgi A. Arbatov
Willem Oltmans**

Zed Books Ltd., 57 Caledonian Road, London N1 9BU.

Cold War or Détente? The Soviet Viewpoint was first published in the
United Kingdom by Zed Books Ltd., 57 Caledonian Road, London
N1 9BU in 1983.

Cover design by Jacque Solomons
Printed by The Pitman Press, Bath

Not available in the United States of America

British Library Cataloguing in Publication Data

Arbatov, Georgi
   Cold War or Détente?
   1. World politics–1975-1985
   2. Soviet Union–Foreign relations–1975-
   I. Title   II. Oltmans, Willem
   327'.09171'3   D849

   ISBN 0-86232-205-7
   ISBN 0-86232-206-5 pbk

Publisher's Note

These interviews were conducted in English. They were translated into Russian, Japanese, German and Dutch and published originally in Europe soon after the Carter-to-Reagan transition early in 1981. Since then, Mr. Oltmans and Professor Arbatov have updated major sections of the interviews to cover events during the first twenty-one months of President Reagan's administration, including the imposition of martial law in Poland, the growth of the antinuclear movement in Europe and the United States, and the overtures prior to the revival of talks between the Soviet Union and communist China.

Clearly, few of Professor Arbatov's statements are extemporaneous. Most were carefully formulated in response to Mr. Oltmans' written questions and further elaborated during their discussions. Whether or not Professor Arbatov's views reflect a consensus of opinion among the Soviet leadership, his positions as chief Soviet expert on American affairs, Member of the Central Committee, and advisor to the late President Brezhnev, make him well qualified to speak to people in the West on issues of extreme importance to both the Soviet Union and the United Kingdom. This is especially true in light of the fact that he has worked as a consultant to Soviet leader Yuri Andropov.

It is hoped that the U.K. edition of *The Soviet Viewpoint* will serve as a useful reference point for people in the West in their analyses and discussions of how to perceive the policies and intentions of the Soviet Union, and how to respond to them.

Contents

About the Authors

Georgi Arkadyevich Arbatov is the director of the Institute of United States and Canadian Studies in Moscow. He is a Doctor of History, and has been a Full Member of the Soviet Academy of Sciences since 1974. At the Twenty-sixth Party Congress in 1981 he was elected a Full Member of the Central Committee. He is a deputy of the USSR Supreme Soviet and has been a member of the Commission on International Affairs of the Supreme Soviet's Council of Nationalities since 1974. His decorations include the Order of Lenin, the Order of the October Revolution, the Order of the Red Star, two Orders of the Red Banner of Labor, and the Badge of Honor.

Georgi Arbatov was born on May 19, 1923, in the Ukrainian city of Kherson. He entered military school in June 1941, and took part in World War II as an officer of a rocket-mortar unit. Demobilized in 1944, he went on to the Moscow Institute of International Relations. He graduated in 1949 and began work as a journalist and editor at the Foreign Literature Publishing House, then on the staffs of the journals *Kommunist* and *Problems of Peace and Socialism.* From 1962 to 1964 he was a department head at the Institute of World Economy and International Relations. In 1964 he became a consultant to Yuri V. Andropov, then one of the Secretaries and now the General Secretary of the Central Committee of the Communist Party of the Soviet Union, and in 1967 began his present job as director of the Institute of United States and Canadian Studies.

Mr. Arbatov is the author of a number of works, including *The Fundamentals of Marxism-Leninism* (coauthor, 1958), *Ideological Struggle in*

International Relations Today (1970), *USA: Modern Management Methods* (1971), *The Nixon Doctrine* (1972), *USA: Scientific-Technological Revolution and Foreign Policy Trends* (head of research teams, 1974), and *US Global Strategy in the Age of Scientific-Technological Revolution* (1979).

A participant of the Pugwash Conference since 1967, the Dartmouth Conference since 1969, the Independent Commission on Disarmament and Security Issues (the Palme Commission) since 1980, and the 1973 Soviet-American summit, Mr. Arbatov has long been actively involved in parliamentary contacts between the United States and the Soviet Union. He is married and has a son.

Willem Oltmans, the noted Dutch journalist and author, was educated at Yale University and spent twelve years as a United Nations correspondent. On the basis of the M.I.T.-Club of Rome project *Limits to Growth*, Oltmans conducted a series of 120 interviews with some of the world's leading thinkers on the subject of population growth and resource exhaustion. These interviews were published in two volumes entitled *On Growth* (G. P. Putnam & Sons, 1974–75).

After many years of political reporting, Willem Oltmans is now specializing in scientific subjects. In the summer of 1981 he completed a series of twenty-four interviews with Dr. Philip Handler, president of the National Academy of Sciences from 1969 to 1981, a few months before Dr. Handler's death.

Foreword

In the years following World War II, my family left the Netherlands and emigrated to South Africa because we sincerely believed that a Soviet invasion of Western Europe was imminent. At Yale University, where I studied international relations in the class of 1950, Arnold Wolfers, master of Pierson College, where I lived, stressed that the most important outcome of World War II was not the crushing of the Nazis, but the rise of the Soviet Union to superpower status.

Only in 1971 did I first journey to the USSR. I was preparing for National Dutch television a documentary on the subject "Limits to Growth," then published by the Club of Rome and put together by a team of scientists at M.I.T. using methods designed by Jay W. Forrester. For this project I interviewed and filmed both Georgi A. Arbatov, director of the Institute of United States and Canadian Studies, and Dr. Jermen M. Gvishiani, vice chairman of the Committee on Science and Technology of the USSR Council of Ministers.

During the following twelve years I made dozens of additional reporting trips to the Soviet Union, and whenever his schedule permitted I would sit down with Professor Arbatov to exchange views on the United States and the world. Each time I became more convinced that, aside from his occasional interviews in selected media or leading articles in *Pravda,* an effort should be made to let a wider public be aware of Dr. Arbatov's views and thoughts about U.S.-Soviet relations.

I prepared a folder with 150 basic questions and submitted them to Professor Arbatov. In preparation, I had visited numerous USSR specialists in the United States, from the National Academy of Sciences to research centers at Harvard and Stanford, to such insiders as the Rostow brothers, Paul Nitze, Admiral Elmo Zumwalt, Major-General Keegan, Richard V. Allen, and others. In principle, Professor Arbatov agreed late in 1979 to prepare this book, and we immediately started working on it. The events in Iran and Afghanistan, and the overall deterioration of the international situation, naturally, became subjects of discussion, adding new dimensions and a new significance to our dialogue.

Among the questions I asked, there were quite a few unpleasant ones, implying criticism of Soviet life and the policies of the USSR. Professor Arbatov did not take them as unfriendly, realizing that those questions were really on the minds of many people in the West. I think our work itself confirmed that peaceful coexistence is possible. On many questions we remained in disagreement, and yet the work went on in an atmosphere of goodwill, mutual understanding, and the desire of both sides to make the book as useful as we could.

A vacuum in information no doubt prevails. Seldom do we see ourselves as others see us or as we really are. Therefore, I hope this comprehensive summary of the views of a foremost specialist from the other side will contribute to a more accurate view of how the United States, and maybe all of us in the West, are being looked upon and considered in the capital of the largest country in the world. It is a most incomplete contribution; many more questions will be on the minds of readers, as they were on mine. But projects like this are bound by certain limits, and it is hoped, nevertheless, that a modest addition will be made to a deepened and extended understanding between two great peoples, as well as to those whose principal interests are bound by history to either superpower.

I am obliged to stress that part of this manuscript was completed early in 1981. Since then, Professor Arbatov and I have managed to update many of the questions and answers to cover events in the first half of the Reagan administration, including the imposition of martial law in Poland. There are still some accents on the Carter administration, Afghanistan, and other matters that might have receded into the background had I been able to complete the interviews a year later. Perhaps it is better that certain earlier events remain in focus—they are often the foundation on which present and future relations are constructed.

While working on this book, I came into contact with several staff members of the Institute of United States and Canadian Studies of the Academy of Sciences in Moscow. We were a cooperative team, and I would like to thank them for their assistance and encouragement.

Willem Oltmans
New York, 1982

Introduction to the British Edition by the Rt. Hon. Michael Foot, M.P.

Nothing could be more dangerous for the future of mankind than a further intensification of the nuclear arms race. Yet that is the real peril facing us.

It is in this atmosphere that any contribution to the understanding of relations between the superpowers is most important. While this book obviously stresses the Soviet position, it significantly illuminates areas of agreement which might have been possible had the West fully comprehended their attitudes.

We know from the past history of the Cold War that there have been "hawks" and "doves" on both sides. Georgi Arbatov could be said to fit into the latter category although he may not thank anyone for saying so. What has been so extraordinarily dangerous is that any attempt to seek out and understand the position of the "doves" on the Soviet side has been condemned by some irresponsible statesmen in the West as being "soft on communism". Those in the West who have altered their position in the light of the evidence – George F. Kennan and Paul Warnke are two of the most prominent Americans who spring to mind – have been derided and condemned as well.

So the history of the Cold War has mostly been written from the standpoint of the "hawks" on both sides, when what was most vitally needed was a comprehension of the fields of agreement which those who really sought them on both sides were trying to inject into the negotiations.

Britain has, unfortunately, been the mute bystander in the negotiations between the superpowers in the last few years. Those of us who have tried to make value judgments on their relative positions on the basis not of what is immediately "good" for the contending alliances but on what might carry the world away from the nuclear brink have had far too little positive information on which to make them.

So I welcome the publication of this book in Britain. It is inevitably a one-sided judgment but if we ignore all that motivates those who negotiate for the Soviet Union there is no chance of an agreement of any sort whatsoever. In the present state of the nuclear arms race that is unthinkable.

Introduction by
The Honorable
J. William Fulbright

This book is about the most dangerous and controversial issue confronting the United States and its allies. It presents an in-depth analysis of Soviet-American relations by an important official of the Soviet government. Professor Arbatov is the director of the Institute of United States and Canadian Studies in Moscow, a full member of the Central Committee, and a deputy of the USSR Supreme Soviet.

Professor Arbatov's views about the purposes, the intentions, and the actions of the United States and the Soviet Union will surely attract the interest of all students of foreign affairs, in and out of government, and I hope will inspire a process of introspection and self-examination by our political leaders.

For over thirty years, two schools of thought regarding Soviet-American relations, the cold-war school and the détente school, have competed for the allegiance of the American people. The critical question is whether the Soviet Union is an inveterate antagonist of the United States or a potentially reliable collaborator in trade, arms control, and in restraining regional conflicts.

Professor Arbatov, a strong supporter of the détente school, gives his analyses of not only the United States, but also China, Japan, Europe, Poland, Afghanistan, colonialism, human rights, and peace generally. Granting that Professor Arbatov presents Soviet actions and policy in the best possible light, nevertheless, his observations should be the subject of serious study and evaluation by the Congress, the administration, and the public. To understand the Russians, their purposes and their abilities, and decide how we should treat them is the most critical problem facing the nations of the West.

In his memoirs, Lord Grey, the foreign minister of Great Britain during World War I, wrote: "The lesson of European history is so plain. It is that no enduring security can be found in competing armaments and in separate alliances; there is no security for any power unless it be a security in which its neighbors have an equal share. . . . Nations are always making mistakes because they do not understand each other's psychology."

Coming at this particular time, as a major escalation of the arms race is getting under way, this book should prompt a serious effort to understand the psychology of the Soviets and to find the means to give both our countries an equal share in the security that we seek. The urgency of our need to make this effort was reflected in Admiral Rickover's recent farewell statement before Congress, in which he warned that we are in danger of arming ourselves into oblivion.

To understand the psychology of the Soviets, it is essential that we comprehend thoroughly the consequences of their conviction that the United States requires as a condition of normal relations that they change the basic structure of their society. In a significant passage in Professor Arbatov's statement he says: "[I]n some key American foreign policy documents, like NSC-68, basic changes in our internal structure were put forward as a sine qua non for peaceful coexistence. Many actions in U.S. foreign policy in recent years reflect those guidelines. More than that— somewhere deep in the American political conscience there still lives the thought that we are something illegitimate, created not by God but by the Devil, and that our existence in its present form should be ended somehow."

This belief of the Russians finds its counterpart in the often asserted view of the cold-war school in America that Russia is determined to destroy the American government and dominate the world. These mirror-image views of each other accelerate the escalation of the arms race to an irrational magnitude and threaten the survival of both countries. Under these conditions, each of the great powers is likely to be mistaken about the psychology of the other, and the result may be a nuclear catastrophe, which neither desires.

This unusual treatise presents serious and responsible Americans with the Soviet point of view. It is vitally important to our future that we make no mistake in understanding it.

J. William Fulbright served as senator from Arkansas from 1945 through 1974. He was chairman of the Senate Foreign Relations Committee from 1959 through 1974. He is now counsel to the law firm of Hogan & Hartson in Washington, D.C.

Preface

Books on contempory international relations have one common quality, as I have found out: work on them never ends. Events follow each other so fast that by the moment you seem to have completed the work, you feel an almost irresistible urge to add something. But there ought to be a final full stop at some point. There were several such points during the work on this book, and then each time I would yield to the temptation to try and add yet another final touch. My latest attempt of this kind resulted in this short preface to the American edition written in late December of 1982.

I would like to begin by mentioning the latest important events.

On the tenth of November my country suffered a great loss: the death of Leonid Brezhnev, whose presence in this book will be felt by the reader through my many references to his words. I am aware that many people around the world, including many Americans, are wondering what Soviet foreign policy will be like after he is gone. The answer to this question was given in the very first statements by the new General Secretary of the Central Committee of our Party, Yuri Andropov. He has emphasized the continuity of the Soviet foreign policy, stressed that peace and cooperation will remain its overriding goals, and expressed unequivocally our attitude toward détente as a permanent value that will ultimately triumph. Our position on Soviet-American relations was also made clear enough: we want normalization of those relations, successful talks on arms limitation and reduction, development of cooperation on the basis of equality, reciprocity and absence of preconditions.

In particular, I would like to draw the reader's attention to the new proposals on nuclear disarmament unveiled by Yuri Andropov in his speech on the occasion of the sixtieth anniversary of the formation of the USSR, December 21, 1982.

He stated that the proposals put forward by the Soviet Union at the talks in Geneva envision substantial cuts in all categories of nuclear weapons now in the possession of the two sides. We are ready to reduce our strategic nuclear arms by more than 25 percent, that is, by hundreds if the United States agrees to cut its arsenals accordingly, so that the two sides would have equal numbers of strategic delivery vehicles. We also propose that the number of nuclear warheads be substantially lowered and that improvement of nuclear warheads be maximally restricted. After such an agreement is reached, the Soviet Union will be ready for still larger mutual reductions of the strategic arsenals. And, as stressed by Andropov, while the talks are in progress, it would be wise to freeze the existing arsenals of strategic weapons.

Concerning nuclear weapons in Europe, Yuri Andropov has reiterated that we are prepared for an agreement to remove all types of them from this continent, which would, in effect, make Europe a nuclear-free zone. As a step toward this goal, he stated Soviet readiness to agree to retain in Europe only as many medium-range missiles as are kept there by Britain and France. This means that the Soviet Union would reduce hundreds of missiles, including dozens of SS-20s. Along with it there must also be an accord to reduce to equal levels the numbers of Soviet and NATO medium-range nuclear delivery aircraft in Europe.

I would like the American reader to understand correctly our position on these issues. We are prepared to go very far down the road of arms reductions and seek mutually acceptable solutions. But it is important that people in the West also understand that no American arms buildup will ever force us into unilateral disarmament. Confronted with attempts to win a military superiority over the Soviet Union, we will have to counter this challenge not with new concessions, but development and deployment of corresponding weapons systems of our own.

We would hate the events to take such a course. But if Washington's policy makers consider their new weapons as their "trumps" at the talks, let them know that these "trumps" are false.

As a matter of fact, there should be no reason why one should ask questions about the main content of the Soviet foreign policy, even in connection with such an event as the change of the General Secretary of our Party.

Peaceful coexistence, disarmament, and international cooperation have been and remain the fundamental objectives of Soviet foreign policy. I cannot imagine a Soviet official who would say that the West should choose between changing its system and war, or that a nuclear war between the USSR and the United States would kill "only" 10 percent of the population, and "if there are enough shovels to go around, everybody's going to make it." Such statements are absolutely unthinkable in my country, if only because her people and her leaders do know what war is all about, and they know it not only from movies and novels, but from their own experience. For such a people, peace is the highest value and the top national priority. And here (this subject is also discussed in our book) is one of the main asymmetries between the Soviet Union and the United States. This asymmetry does color the approaches of both sides to vital problems of today's world. And past years have shown that such asymmetries can play a serious negative role.

I hope that this and other asymmetries can be overcome. Today, it is difficult to be optimistic about the near prospects for Soviet-American relations. And yet, I do not exclude a possibility that the U.S. policy may become more realistic soon. After all, life must teach people something, must it not?

I am fully aware that some lessons may at first enrage. I am referring to the two biggest upsets Washington seems to have suffered in the last year or two. One has to do with Poland. Some people in America hoped for the most dramatic turn of events in that country (a civil war, appearance of Soviet troops, etc.). I can see why, and the reader will find discussion of this subject in the book.

The other upset has to do with the change of leadership in my country. It was widely expected in Washington that this change would produce a political crisis in the Soviet Union that might be taken advantage of. And I can bet that quite a few contingency plans for this event had been prepared long ago. But they had to remain on paper.

Thus, neither of the two expectations materialized, which was a blow to the extremists in Washington. I do not expect them to turn into moderates as a result, but in broader policy-making circles and among the public at large more realistic attitudes might have been strengthened.

There are quite a few things that awake hope. After all, everything in this world tends to change—people, their views, and governments. And these changes may help everyone understand that without peace, development of normal relations, and disarmament, humanity has no future. Sooner or later we all shall have to recognize this truth in all its fullness. And it is vitally important that we do it soon enough—before it is too late. The goal of survival demands efforts by each and every one of us.

Half a century ago, talented Soviet writer Bruno Yasenski, who witnessed the tragic world events of the twenties and thirties, gave very wise advice:

Do not be afraid of enemies—at worst they may kill you.

Do not be afraid of friends—at worst they may betray you.

Beware of the indifferent—they do not kill and they do not betray, but it is only by their silent consent that murder and treachery exist on Earth.

Indifference. . . . We cannot afford it in the nuclear age.

Georgi Arbatov
Moscow
December 1982

List
of Acronyms

ABM   antiballistic missile
ACDA   Arms Control and Disarmament Agency
CPSU   Communist Party of the Soviet Union
ERW   enhanced radiation warhead (neutron bomb)
ICBM   intercontinental ballistic missile
INF   intermediate nuclear forces
IRBM   intermediate-range ballistic missile
MBFR   Mutual and Balanced Force Reductions
MIRV   multiple independently targetable reentry vehicle
MRBM   medium-range ballistic missile
MX   Missile, Experimental
NSC-68   National Security Council Paper No. 68
PD-59   Presidential Directive No. 59
SLBM   submarine-launched ballistic missile

Chapter 1 | On the Ordeal of Détente and the Value of Accurate Perceptions

The 1970s were the decade of détente. Are the 1980s to become the decade of Cold War II?

Let us not be so fatalistic that we write off a whole decade. But for now one has to face the fact that the overall international situation has deteriorated seriously over the last several years. Not too long before that, it seemed that the world had found a way out of the hostilities and stupidities of the Cold War, that détente had been established as a normal condition. Yet now, to some people, détente is beginning to look like a temporary, if welcome, aberration from the grim normalcy of distrust, enmity, and confrontation that prevailed in international relations in the first two decades after World War II.

What then would be the real "normal" condition?

I would like to be quite unequivocal about it and say that what we see now is a deviation from normalcy, the norm being a relaxation of international tension, the development of cooperation, and progress in arms control. But I am hesitant to do so, at least before we define the precise meaning of "normalcy." If we talk about some natural condition, like a body's normal temperature, suggesting that the body is healthy and nothing threatens its health, then I am sure détente is the normal state of affairs, while the Cold War is not. But one can also understand "normal" as "usual," as a condition so natural that it does not even need any special efforts to sustain it.

1

It's normal, say, for a piece of cork to float on the surface of water. If you want to bring it down to the bottom or raise it up in the air, you must make an effort; once the effort is stopped, the cork is back to "normal." In this sense, détente, alas, has not yet become a normal condition of international relations. It still takes a special effort to maintain it, while all you have to do to bring back tension is sit on your hands.

In other words, détente got into trouble because efforts to maintain it proved insufficient?

No, I wouldn't go along with this. Sure, some people worked harder for détente than others; but it was not just inertia that détente was up against. What really tipped the scales was a strong countermobilization of those who saw détente as a dangerous heresy. Specifically, détente was undermined by the shift in U.S. foreign policy in the late 1970s and the early 1980s.

American readers will be furious reading this, because they are convinced that the decisive factor for the present deterioration was Afghanistan.

I am well aware that our actions with regard to Afghanistan were used to spark a whole storm of emotions and denunciations in the West. But political judgments should be based on facts, not emotions. The official American argument that the reason for the current deterioration lies in events in Afghanistan holds no water, if only because the principal decisions shaping the basics of the new U.S. policy, a policy understood here in the Soviet Union as a big step backward to the Cold War, had been taken well before those events.

What decisions do you have in mind?

The NATO decision to increase military budgets annually for a period of fifteen years (Washington, May 1978), the U.S. president's decision on a "five-year plan" for more military programs and unprecedented arms spending (November 1979), and the highly dangerous NATO decision to build and deploy in Europe new medium-range American missiles (Brussels, December 1979). Also, prior to events in Afghanistan, the United States froze, for all practical purposes, the arms-limitation talks. Ratification of the SALT II treaty was already in considerable doubt in September-November 1979. At about the same time Washington attempted a hasty rapprochement with China. In the late fall of 1979 the United States sent to the Persian Gulf a swarm of its warships with planes and nuclear weapons. It was difficult for us to believe that this was done just to free the hostages in Tehran and was not part of an overall change in American foreign policy and military posture. Therefore, it was understood in the

Soviet Union as early as mid-December 1979 that the United States was making a sharp turn in its policies.

In other words, American policies influenced Soviet actions in Afghanistan?

They were an important factor.

Do you mean that if détente had developed normally, and the difficulties you cited had not occurred, the Soviet Union would not have sent its troops to Afghanistan?

Quite possibly so. But please, understand me correctly: the sending of troops was not a "punishment" of the United States or of the West for bad behavior. It had more to do with our new assessments of threat, of the situation created by the United States and NATO. As President Brezhnev put it in his interview with *Pravda*, the decision to send a limited military contingent to Afghanistan had not been easy for us to make.[1] The Afghan government repeatedly requested our assistance long before the eve of 1980, but we held back. By the end of 1979, however, the situation in Afghanistan inevitably had to be viewed in the context of rapidly increasing international tension in the world at large and in that particular region. In that context, the threat to the postrevolutionary regime in Afghanistan, as well as the threat to our own security, assumed a much greater dimension than would have been the case under conditions of détente.

Events in Afghanistan truly alarmed Americans and their allies because they became confused over Soviet intentions. President Carter emphasized that he was not prepared to gamble on Soviet intentions.[2] So maybe the change in U.S. foreign policy that you referred to earlier was caused by what was interpreted as an increasing Soviet threat, confirmed later by the events in Afghanistan.

Frankly, when I hear talk about the "Soviet threat," not from a brainwashed man in the street, but from responsible politicians and experts, it occurs to me that they have in mind not so much the Soviet Union, its power and intentions, as the United States, its policy and military posture, and the American role in the world. They have full knowledge of the military, economic, and political realities, and the existing balance of power. It is simply more convenient to make the most fantastic claims and demands in American foreign and military policies, while making the Soviet Union seem as if it had provoked the Americans into action. We do not see things this way. As we see them, no one has provoked America into hardening its foreign policy. Rather, for quite some time, the United States has been heating itself up methodically, until it has reached its present state of mind over its relations with the USSR and the outside world in general.

But you cannot deny that the Soviet Union has increased its military power tremendously over the years.

Yes, our power did increase. We had good reasons to take care of our defense. And many of those who complain so loudly about the Soviet military threat know that our efforts have been for defense rather than for aggressive purposes.

But NATO keeps stressing that the Soviet buildup goes beyond legitimate defense requirements.

"Why beholdest thee the mote in thy neighbor's eye, and considerest not the beam in thine own eye?" I often wonder how American politicians and generals would have sized up their legitimate defense requirements if there had been stationed about one million Warsaw Pact troops and about a thousand nuclear launchers north of Michigan, while Texas bordered not on Mexico but on a country of a billion people, armed with nuclear weapons, with which they had very complicated relations, to say the least.

If there is no Soviet threat, as you say, what then do you see to be the true reasons for the latest American hard line?

There are, in my opinion, two sets of reasons: those that have worked to change the mood and the balance of forces in the American power elite, and those that have created a political atmosphere in the country that allow these changes to be translated into practical policy. As far as the elite is concerned, the main causes of change are, I think, connected with the difficulties of adaptation to new realities of the world situation. These realities have certainly created problems for the United States, demanding a very substantial reorientation of U.S. foreign policy. They called for breaking with the guidelines, notions, and standards of political behavior characteristic of an entire epoch—an exceptional epoch, at that, in terms of the situation America found itself in immediately after World War II, emerging from it as the wealthiest and most powerful nation, having experienced neither any devastations nor major sacrifices. That situation created an impression at the time that the world was headed directly into something called an "American Century," and that the United States could buy almost anything and anybody, and suppress or destroy by its superior might those it could not buy. That historical situation was unique and transient. But many Americans came to regard it as the natural and eternal order of things.

Wouldn't you agree that many Americans have done away with such illusions?

Some have, others have not. Parting with such illusions turned out to be tremendously difficult. I think the 1980 election campaign was quite revealing in this respect, demonstrating that the mood of nostalgia for the "American Century" was quite strong.

Coming back to the shifting moods in the power elite, I would stress another point—apprehension in those circles that the relaxation of world tensions would somehow undermine the American political will. I'd like to recall one episode from 1972, when the first summit meeting had just ended, and the American president returned to Washington. What was uppermost on the minds of American policy makers? As Kissinger testified in his memoirs, it was neither joy nor satisfaction, but rather fear and concern that from then on it would be more difficult to mobilize public support for military programs, that many other old policies would be harder to pursue.[3]

In general, it turned out that U.S. policy makers conceded to take part in détente only with great difficulties, apprehensions, and numerous qualifications. They had to take part, because by the late sixties and early seventies the old policies had thoroughly exposed themselves as senseless and dangerous. However, those old policies were not uprooted, and pretty soon began reasserting themselves with increasing strength as brakes on détente, trends toward a resurrection, to some extent or other, of the Cold War, to an acceleration of the arms race and a breakdown in negotiations.

Are you saying that the American power elite has become disenchanted by détente over the last few years and thus decided to go back to the Cold War?

This would be an oversimplified view of the problem. For one thing, I don't think that the American power elite has ever been enchanted by détente. As we Marxists see it, détente, improvement of relations and greater cooperation with the USSR, not to mention disarmament and renunciation of the use of force, are neither the most typical nor the most habitual features of the policies and political views of that elite. But we do see a differentiation within that elite, different groupings that have differing approaches to problems. And what is most important, the objective course of events, objective realities, can sometimes even compel people with established opinions to change their attitudes. But this does not mean that such changes come easily or that they are irreversible. The old, the habitual, that which is almost the second nature of the most influential strata of the ruling class, tends to come back to the fore at the slightest provocation. As to the very influential groups pushing for the most conservative, most militaristic, and most irresponsible policies, they opposed the turn to détente even before it took place, trying desperately to prevent it. And after the turn did take place, they spared no effort to reverse the events.

You have referred to the difficulties of adaptation. What has proved for the United States the most difficult to adapt to?

I believe the most difficult thing to adapt to was the loss of American military superiority over the USSR and the establishment of parity between the two powers. It was also very difficult for the United States to get used to the contraction of the sphere of the usability of force, to the fact that even such a strong military power as the United States cannot afford to do in the world whatever it likes, even if it concerns much weaker states, like Iran or Nicaragua. I would also refer to the growing independence of allies.

Then there is the fact that the American economy is now dependent on other countries. When that became evident, the talk about the coming benefits of "interdependence" was easily drowned out by the yells about intolerable "vulnerability."

Talking of the pains of adaptation, I would also mention illusions that played a part in producing the drift to a new cold war, like the illusion that the United States is able to restore its former preeminence and its special position in the world.

Right after his inauguration, President Reagan started persuading Americans that they have a right "to see the boldest dreams."

That may be, but those dreams should not include the notion that the problems facing the Soviet Union will "weaken" it so much that the United States will gain a capability to exert a strong influence on Soviet policies. I'd like to return to this question somewhat later; for now, let me just remind you that such forecasts about the USSR have been made repeatedly over the last sixty-odd years, only to be proven wrong.

I would also point out an important domestic American factor that contributed to the change in U.S. policy.

The election campaign?

We can talk about the 1980 campaign too, but the factor I have in mind is of a longer-term character. I mean the growing complaints of the American establishment about the "ungovernability" of America: lack of consensus, fragmentation of political institutions, an overload of social demands on the political system, "too much" democracy, and so forth. It is not forgotten that during the Cold War the United States was a more "organized" and "disciplined" society, which simplified the task of governing. I suspect that many of those who have grown desperate over this "ungovernability" expect a more tense international situation to make Americans more doc-ile. All these factors combined produced, in my opinion, a consensus among significant parts of the U.S. power elite that the way to increase American power and influence in the world, as well as to reduce domestic instability, was to turn to a tougher policy, to build up American military might and be ready and willing to use it more freely. In addition, American economic strength is to be exerted more directly and with fewer scruples, suppressing some and intimidating others. Of course, this is a very rough outline of the situation. The real picture is more complex.

That sounds like a qualification.

Well, I wouldn't like to oversimplify the situation and assume order and organization where both are lacking. Actually, I could mention two princi-pal qualifications. One is that the processes of consensus building and decision making in the U.S. power elite are such that a president may not need a very solid consensus. In some respects, it may be easier to lead a more fragmented and disoriented elite than a more tightly knit and self-assured one. The other is that, despite the consensus that seems to have emerged at the top of the American political system, there remain, I think, serious doubts about this new U.S. foreign policy. It is doubted because many fear that it won't work and will be very dangerous to the United States itself.

What changed the political atmosphere in that country?

First I would mention a conscious and consistent effort by traditional opponents of détente. American public opinion was very strongly in favor of détente. But it was also extremely frustrated over some foreign-policy developments during the last decade, especially in Indochina. The hard-liners, with their "Soviet threat" and "you can't push America around" propaganda, have been rather successful at channeling those frustrations in the direction they desired.

A sudden upsurge in patriotism was perhaps a result of the Iranian hos-tage crisis.

Please do not understand this as a justification of what was done to the American embassy and U.S. diplomats in Tehran, but the American reac-tion looked to me more like chauvinism and jingoism.

Don't Russians love their country?

Yes, we do. We also respect and value patriotism in other nations. We think it's a strong moral force that can play a decisive role at a time of national crisis. But true patriotism also means a rational attitude toward one's own nation and a critical attitude when one's nation does wrong. Incidentally, that's how Lenin understood patriotism. It has to be distinguished from nationalistic fervor, which has so often led countries astray. It was this latter variety that the nineteenth-century English lexicographer Samuel Johnson had in mind when he called patriotism "the last refuge of the scoundrel."

Do you see still other reasons for the U.S. policy change?

The policy of détente was never given a real chance in America. It's fashionable now among the hard-liners in Washington to deride détente for sapping America's will and resolution in her dealings with the world. But if there was any area where American will and resolution were really lacking, it was in Washington's attitude toward relaxation of tensions, arms control, and confidence building.

And then arrived the 1980 presidential election. Even prominent analysts, like Colonel Jonathan Alford, deputy director of the International Institute for Strategic Studies in London, told me it was "very, very sad indeed" that the entire world stops and has to wait until the presidential election circus ends in America. Alford added, "This is not only immensely sad but potentially rather dangerous."

Indeed, election time in America is a bad time for good policy and a good time for bad policy. It's understandable, to some extent. Prior to becoming an excellent president or a disastrous president, one must first become president. In order to become president, the candidates often stop at nothing. But sometimes one wonders why, almost every time around, candidates seem to join in a veritable conspiracy to foster the arms race and to promote anti-Soviet feelings. Well-known American scientist Jerome Wiesner said at the end of the last election campaign, in an article in the *New York Times,* that "during each presidential election campaign we are subjected to a bombardment of hysterical, frightening estimates of impending Soviet strategic superiority, accompanied by calls for a major buildup of our nuclear forces."[4] And he traces the history of this dangerous tradition to 1948. There have been quite a few campaigns since then that were bad indeed in this respect. But the 1980 campaign was a real international disaster. Almost no debates on the real issues facing America took place. There were no attempts to reevaluate the national interests and work out rational means of promoting them. Instead,the world heard deafening saber rattling, a fierce competition in demands for increased military expenditures, and the announcement of a new, rather dangerous, nuclear doctrine. Then, there was the commando raid on Iran. The country was in a state of artificial crisis, and some Americans thought it was because President Carter regarded the crisis as his only salvation from electoral defeat.

What could have been the alternative?

As an ideal—though I find it too good to believe myself—an election campaign that serves as a means of political education, as an instrument for initiating suggestions for corrections in government policies. But the mechanisms of the political process did not work for those democratic purposes. I think Senator Edward Kennedy was right when he said that the U.S. political process had been taken hostage in 1980.

Well, we do seem to be drifting toward a new cold war.

The point is that the second edition of the Cold War could be much more dangerous. A return to unrestricted animosity and confrontation would occur at a new level in the development of means of destruction, making a military confrontation more probable and its consequences more disastrous. Furthermore, the cold-war whirlwind in the eighties would suck in a much larger number of countries than before. The greater the number of participants in an international conflict, the greater the risks, especially if some of the participants are prone to playing reckless and irresponsible games in the world arena.

Besides, a return to the Cold War would make the proliferation of nuclear weapons practically unavoidable. There is another important matter. In the coming decades, global problems like the depletion of natural resources, environmental pollution, and hunger will be still more acute. Détente, arms control, and international cooperation would increase chances for their solution, while in conditions of cold war these problems may become intractable.

Patrick Caddell, the Carter White House pollster, once said in an interview in Playboy, *"Oh, a little war does a lot for your rating in the polls. But the absence of war does not translate into political points. Any president can force the country to rally around him with decisive martial action. Eisenhower had Korea and Lebanon, Kennedy had Cuba and Vietnam; Johnson, Nixon and Ford had Vietnam . . ."*[5]

Quite an example of the "moral" presidency: war is discussed as an acceptable means to prevent another routine change of guard in Washington. Doesn't Mr. Caddell's statement indicate some serious deficiencies in a political system that turns war into a welcome contribution to political success?

*Caddell may sound cynical, but do you think such behavior has been
demonstrated in the past?*

Yes, it's a long-standing feature of American politics that in difficult times
politicians find it more profitable and secure to gravitate to the Right, to
play tough. For some reason, such a position is still considered more
patriotic, even though in the nuclear age it is precisely this position that
can invite the greatest trouble upon a nation. For some reason, such a
position is regarded as more realistic, even though the worst illusion today
is to try to achieve security through an arms race and use of force. The
cowboy shooting from the hip does remain a popular symbol in America,
but there must be more important psychological reasons for such a state
of affairs. One of them could be an inertia of thinking, an inability to shake
off the burden of old perceptions, inherited from the Cold War. These
perceptions remain strong because of their inviting simplicity.

What do you mean by simplicity?

In a cold-war environment, everything moves on the level of a cheap
western. You have a concrete enemy who is the source of all evil. You have
a crystal-clear goal—to bring this enemy down. The more damage you
inflict on the other party, the better off you are. And you have established
and tested the means to do it without any pangs of conscience. You can
appeal to such atavistic feelings as jingoism, suspicion, and hostility toward folks who live differently, and yearn for national superiority. You
find yourself in a two-dimensional world of black and white, and quite
importantly, you can describe your political platform in one minute of
television prime time.

The philosophy of détente is much more sophisticated and difficult to
grasp. One has to be broad-minded and tolerant enough to understand the
possibility and the desirability of coexistence and cooperation between
nations that are vastly different in their social systems, political institutions, values, sympathies, and antipathies. One would have to realize that
relations between them aren't a zero-sum game in which one side wins
exactly as much as the other loses, and that despite all differences and
difficulties they still might have overwhelming mutual interests.

What is even more difficult to understand is that the source of trouble
is not always "the other guy," but often one's own mistakes and wrong-
doings, or even forces and events nobody controls. And one has to realize that qualities like restraint, moderation, readiness for compromise,
even though they require not only more wisdom but greater political
courage as well, are preferable to self-righteousness, arrogance, and the
inclination to play tough. Finally, one should try to understand the other
side. How does your policy look to them? What are their perceptions of
your policy?

Are you disappointed? Has détente proven too sophisticated for the broad public to understand?

You see, it's a process. In the 1950s, the intricacies of modern international politics were understood by very few people. In the 1960s, the numbers of those who understood began to grow rapidly. In the 1970s, certain truths about the modern world penetrated the minds of millions. I am still hopeful that the ideas of détente will triumph in the 1980s.

There have been some developments in Europe and America that give grounds for such hopes.

You mean the antinuclear movement that started in 1981?

Yes.

You said that it takes a strong effort to sustain détente, while tension is self-generating. Did you mean the intellectual and psychological complexity of détente as compared to the dangerously simplistic formulas of the Cold War?

Yes, but not only this. The force of inertia is important. Détente is just a few years old, while the Cold War that preceded it lasted for several decades. Those decades have left behind not only a lot of preconceptions and prejudices, but also some built-in mechanisms. I mean the mechanisms of the arms race, the existing military and political alliances, as well as other parts of the huge infrastructure created in the service of the Cold War, such as the bureaucracies and organizations for psychological warfare, covert operations, and similar activities. All these mechanisms seek to ensure their own survival. This means that they have to generate international tensions, spur military rivalry, and sow distrust and hatred of the external enemy. These mechanisms are made still stronger in the United States by certain "transmission belts" that link them with important parts of the economic system and very influential vested interests.

Will there ever be a stable détente?

Détente has a lot going for it. It has a great vital force. The main argument for détente is that it has no acceptable alternatives if we are to avoid doomsday.

What exactly does the USSR mean by détente?

Let me quote the most authoritative definition, which came from Leonid Brezhnev: "Détente means, primarily, the overcoming of the Cold War and a transition to normal, smooth relations among states. Détente means a willingness to resolve differences and disputes not by force, threats, or saber rattling, but by peaceful means, at the negotiating table. Détente means a certain degree of trust and the ability to reckon with each other's interests. This, briefly, is our understanding of détente.''[6]

Chancellor Bruno Kreisky of Austria told me that he feels the signing of the Austrian Peace Treaty in 1955 was the very beginning of the policy of détente in Europe.

The signing of the Austrian Peace Treaty was by its very nature and consequences undoubtedly an act of détente. But I am not certain whether we can single it out as the very beginning of this political process.

International politics are getting ever more complex. Nevertheless, U.S.-Soviet relations continue to play a crucial role and remain a central axis for the whole world system.

You are right. Even though it would be a mistake to look at every world development through the prism of those relations, one cannot overestimate their importance for humanity. Let me put it this way: while an improvement of relations between Moscow and Washington is not a panacea for all troubles, unrestrained hostility between the two can lead to the extinction of our civilization.

I asked Harvard psychologist B. F. Skinner what he considered the top priority of our day. "Survival!" he shot back.

As simple as that. The overwhelming mutual interest between the USSR and the United States is indeed survival. It makes peaceful coexistence between us imperative. Whether one likes it or not, we are chained to each other on this planet. Neither side can leave the globe. We are here. Americans are here. We've got to learn to live in peace. If we succeed, we will not only survive, but may be able to establish relations that could bring benefits to each other and to the world as a whole. Our well-being and the world's well-being depend to a large extent on whether we spend more on peaceful endeavors or continue to squander our resources through the arms race. There could be tremendous benefit for all humanity in the cooperation of the two biggest economic and scientific-technical potentials in the world. Finally, we are faced with growing global problems that can only be tackled in a peaceful atmosphere.

If we allow ourselves to slide down into uncontrollable hostility, we can expect, at best, a quite drab and bleak existence, and, at worst, a nuclear incineration of life on this planet. True, the task of improving relations between the two most powerful nations in the world, who have been antagonists for decades, is a tremendous challenge. But it is required by the realities of the nuclear age.

Expectations of improved relations are constantly dashed. That leads to despondency and cynicism.

Unfortunately, this is so. It is unfortunate since there are obvious dangers in having negative attitudes about the possibility of lessening tensions. If such attitudes persist, many people will assume as a fact of life that there is nothing to expect but hostility, an unlimited arms race, and political or even military confrontations. Such desperate moods can turn into self-fulfilling prophecies.

After the events of the last few years, people can hardly be blamed for harboring those feelings.

But it's wrong. Those events hardly prove that confrontation is inevitable, or that a resumption of the Cold War is unavoidable. Rather, what we have seen is that processes aimed at improving our relations and easing international tensions can be halted, that a deterioration can be readily provoked, and that much of what was built carefully during the last decade with intensive effort and hard work on both sides can be all too easily destroyed. In other words, we've seen that it's not enough to build better relations, but that we must also learn to keep and safeguard them. This is a conclusion we are drawing in the Soviet Union.

There is a lot of talk now about rivalry between the United States and the USSR. High U.S. officials refer to this rivalry as the main source of the problems. Their view is that the rivalry will continue under any conditions, though it may be combined with limited cooperation.

Indeed, this is the official American position. Over the last two or three years it has evolved from "competition plus cooperation" to "mostly competition." Both elements are certainly present in our relations, but we ought to see that the relative weight and importance of each of these two elements—competition and cooperation—in our relations, can differ substantially under different political conditions. Paraphrasing the well-known statement by Clausewitz, détente is not a continuation of the Cold War by other, more cautious and safer, means. It is a policy that, by its nature and objectives, is opposed to the Cold War, and is aimed not at gaining victory in conflicts by means short of nuclear war, but at the settlement and prevention of conflicts, at lowering the level of military confrontation, and at the development of international cooperation.

*Former American ambassador to Moscow Malcolm Toon once said—and
this is a view widely shared in Washington—that no millennium of friendship and mutual trust would arrive "without a basic change in Soviet
philosophy and outlook." Sovietologist Richard Pipes, while on the staff
of Reagan's National Security Council, went further, suggesting that unless the Soviet Union changed its ways there might ultimately be no
alternative to war between East and West.*

You would have to be in an overoptimistic mood to expect a millennium
of friendship and mutual trust anywhere around the world in the near
future. It would be ideal, of course, to create such a millennium, but for the
moment we should be concerned with more elementary problems, like
plain survival. Meanwhile, suggesting that a significant improvement of
relations is possible only if there is a basic change in Soviet philosophy
and outlook is a sure prescription for greater tensions. That is precisely the
approach that has been practiced by the United States over and over again
for more than half a century. The only result has been to prevent our two
nations from putting their relations on a normal basis. Neither side has
benefited from it. The gist of peaceful coexistence is that we can live side
by side, have normal relations, even good relations, while remaining different from each other and not demanding that the other side become like
ourselves.

*But existing deep philosophical differences will continue to have an ad-
verse effect on relations.*

Well, they can have such an effect, but one should not exaggerate the
potential for international conflict inherent in those differences.
   Let's imagine a hypothetical situation where, instead of the Soviet
Union, there is another superpower facing the United States, absolutely
similar to it, a carbon copy of the United States—a superpower with the
same philosophy and outlook, the same economic and political systems,
the same political habits, including those connected with elections; with
a similar Congress inhabited by quite a few trigger-happy politicians, with
the same Pentagon, military-industrial complex, and mass media; a superpower with the same energy-wasting way of life and very similar interests
in the Persian Gulf, and in oil and other mineral resources around the
world. Imagine that this United States II is just as egocentric, self-righteous, and full of messianic aspirations as its prototype, just as itching to
reform the entire world to its liking, to build a Pax Americana of its own.
Would our planet be better off and a safer place to live than at present,
with the United States and the Soviet Union being as different from each
other as they are?

Wait a minute. Do you mean that the basic differences between the United States and the USSR are actually furthering the cause of peace?

No. But I mean that such differences don't make war inevitable or even probable. And I firmly believe that the policy of the Soviet Union helps further the cause of peace.

And what if we had a USSR I and a USSR II?

I think we would be able to find peace with our alter ego much more easily. But let me continue.

World War I, as well as countless smaller wars, were in fact clashes between states that had similar philosophies and socioeconomic systems, similar aims and outlooks. In World War II capitalist countries were fighting each other, some as allies of the USSR. As to the Soviet-American competition, I don't think it need necessarily create dangers to peace. It can remain a natural competition as long as we control military rivalry, avoid unnecessary or artificial conflicts, and remember the overriding common interests that call for cooperation.

How would you define "natural competition" between the two superpowers?

It is not so much a competition between superpowers as a competition between differing social systems. Natural competition between the two different social systems means that each system demonstrates, not only to its own people but to the world at large, what it is able to achieve in economic and social development, in quality of life, culture, ideas, and so forth. Such competition is inevitable, but it should not necessarily lead to political and military conflicts between states.

Much more of the current misunderstanding, as well as willful misinterpretation, of this matter stems from different ideas of competition. Soviet-American competition is often portrayed in America as a struggle between good and evil, with the Americans, of course, as the good guys. Many people who assume they are being objective may think in terms of competition between two empires, where each is trying to grab as much of the cake as possible and achieve control over the world. But I would not agree with such imperialistic thinking.

The United States, in 1945, did hold the fate of the world in its hands, but it seems to have dropped it.

In our view, Washington did have strong imperial and hegemonistic aspirations after World War II. The United States was predominant economically and had a huge strategic superiority based on a nuclear monopoly. It felt it could shape and reshape the world according to its liking.

It has come a long way from that position.

Yes, but the United States did not let go of what it held because of goodwill. The world simply changed immensely, and the United States now occupies a more modest, though very prominent, place on our planet. But it has proved to be tremendously difficult for Washington to learn to live with these changes, to get rid of old illusions, misperceptions, and unfounded claims. Lately, it has looked as if these old pretensions have again begun to guide Washington's foreign policy.

Why should we not suspect the USSR of wanting to replace the United States in its paramount position?

Such an idea would be totally alien to our philosophy and outlook. It should also be borne in mind that the Soviet economy does not need foreign expansion for its growth. But even if one should disregard all this, there would still be very solid practical grounds for not wanting to imitate the United States in this respect.

The costs of maintaining empires nowadays are growing, while the benefits are shrinking. Look at all the troubles America has been having in the last decade and a half because of her worldwide involvement. And the present imperial drive can only worsen America's problems. In today's world, imperialism is a losing proposition. It just does not work.

How would you evaluate U.S.-Soviet relations at this point?

The more I study the United States, the more cautious I become in my evaluations. Sometimes, when I'm asked about Soviet-American relations, I recall the wise man who, when he was asked, "How is your wife?" responded, "Compared to what?" Only if you place relations in a comparative perspective can you avoid both excessive pessimism and overblown optimism.

In answer to your question, I would say that there have been worse times in Soviet-American relations, but there have been much better times as well. To be more exact, so much has been done by the Americans lately to spoil our relations that they are at the lowest point in perhaps a decade.

That is a rather gloomy evaluation.

I'd very much prefer a different one, but what else can I say after what was done in the last year of Carter's presidency and the first years of Reagan's? A great deal of what had taken so much pain and effort to build was broken and smashed in a rampage of destruction. It looked as if some people had been dreaming of this orgy for a long time, barely holding themselves back. Arms-control talks were damaged, if not derailed. Economic relations were almost entirely discontinued. Consular ties were undermined. The agreement on direct air links was violated, and many cooperative activities in science have been broken off. An atmosphere was created that virtually incited criminal acts by anti-Soviet hate groups. Alas, to destroy is so much easier than to build.

Mr. Reagan started his presidency with a series of harsh verbal attacks on Soviet leaders. That hardly helped U.S.-Soviet relations.

Yes, since the very first days of the Reagan administration, its leading spokesmen have missed no chance to make abusive charges against the USSR, like the charge that the Soviet Union supports international terrorism, uses chemical or bacteriological weapons, and so forth. The bully-boy rhetoric was supplemented by corresponding policies—primarily, by whipping up the arms race. I think that an important motivation of such rhetoric and policy was an intention to provoke the Soviet Union into changing its policies, and thus justify a return to cold war.

The Twenty-sixth Congress of the CPSU demonstrated the failure of these attempts. It put forward a constructive program on major international issues, including Soviet-American relations. President Brezhnev repeated from the Congress's podium that we continue to regard normalization of those relations as a matter of great importance.

But not everything depends on us alone. Just like in personal situations, it takes one side to start a quarrel, while peace can only be based on the mutual agreement of all participants.

But even if there were the will in Washington to improve relations with the Soviet Union, there remain endless roadblocks.

Yes, there have always been roadblocks. But I think recent history has shown that it is possible to remove them, provided both sides understand that such efforts are demanded by their overwhelming mutual interests. I believe those interests make it worthwhile to keep trying.

We are talking of coexistence. But doesn't Khrushchev's famous phrase "We will bury you!" still adequately reflect the Soviet attitude?

That expression became an object of feverish speculation at the time it was made, some two decades ago. I will not defend the rhetorical merits of that particular phrase, but let me point out that its meaning was far from aggressive or warlike. The idea was to convey confidence in socialism's historical advantages over capitalism, which, in our conviction, will make a worldwide triumph of socialism inevitable in the long run. Of course, victory is understood in the sense that people in capitalist countries will choose socialism themselves, without any pressure or coercion from our side. We communists believe so. Otherwise we would not be communists. Just as the supporters of capitalism, or the free-enterprise system, or whatever else they may call it, believe, I assume, in the advantages of their social system, expecting that sooner or later all nations of the world would prefer it. But we don't think that our different beliefs and expectations should prevent us from coexisting.

In the West we believe that communists do not deal with questions of socialist revolution simply as spectators. You consider it your international duty to assist revolutionaries. This is what leads to trouble, creating situations where there is no room for peaceful coexistence.

This reasoning looks plausible only on the surface. We are not indifferent to the outcome of struggles for socialism in other countries, nor do we conceal our sympathies. But we hold that the only way to help socialist revolution abroad is by means of our example, by building a better society in our own country, by solving successfully the problems that still exist. We are against imposing socialism on other nations, against what is called "the export of revolution."

At the same time, we are opposed to any export of counterrevolution; that is, attempts at restoring prerevolutionary regimes by means of outside interference. History has shown that the export of counterrevolution remains a rather common practice, so the enemies of socialism are not indifferent spectators by any standard either.

Sorry, but this sounds like pure propaganda.

No, we do treat these matters very seriously. As a matter of fact, the first serious discussion within our party following the 1917 Revolution was devoted to this very question, since some in the party—the ultraleftists, the Trotskyites—insisted that we should spread the revolution beyond our borders by means of a revolutionary war. The overwhelming majority of the party resolutely rejected this idea. Lenin maintained that pushing a foreign country toward revolution would be "a complete break with Marxism."

There was, it seems, a similar conflict between Moscow and Beijing.

You are right. It was one of the main issues during the first stage of the split between us in the late fifties and early sixties. Mao and his group declared that peaceful coexistence was a "betrayal of the revolution" and kept repeating that "power comes from the barrel of a gun." It was the same unacceptable concept Lenin fought against.

But what about Afghanistan? Has the Soviet Union not imposed its will on a small neighbor since 1978, gradually escalating its interference up to a point where it's virtually running that country now? It seems to be a classic case of exporting communism by the force of arms.

We did not "export" the April 1978 revolution to Afghanistan. Anyone familiar with the situation there is aware of this fact. We first heard of the revolution from Western news media.

As a matter of fact, no one needed to export a revolution to Afghanistan: conditions in that country had reached a point where a radical change of the political and social systems became for the Afghans the only way out of a deep crisis. Don't forget that Afghanistan is one of the poorest and most backward countries in the world. It is sorely in need of economic development, social and cultural progress, and meaningful democracy for its seventeen million people. Some timid reforms were tried there prior to the revolution, but they failed to solve the social and economic problems of the country. Modernization by evolution just didn't work, while pressures for change were growing.

By the way, the uprising that took place in April 1978 was provoked by an attempt of the old regime to stage a coup and eliminate the Afghan Left —the labor unions, the student unions, and the National Democratic Party. Responding to a series of murders and arrests, the National Democrats took up arms and deposed the old regime. It was a purely internal Afghan development.

But the Soviet Union strongly sympathized with the revolutionaries.

Yes, it did. The aims of the revolution were very noble and reflected the real needs of the people: to give land to those who till it, to eliminate hunger, to stop discrimination against women and ethnic minorities, to educate a nation where 90 percent of the people can't read or write—in short, to provide for basic human rights and social justice. We have significantly increased our economic and technical assistance to Afghanistan since the revolution.

As well as military assistance?

Certainly. The revolution needed to defend itself. The old ruling elite that lost its power, its land, and its privileges as a result of the revolution has been doing everything it can to regain power. It has been actively supported by the United States, China, Pakistan, Saudi Arabia, and Egypt. The new government in Kabul has been up against a formidable array of hostile forces. You have to keep in mind that some of the Afghan frontiers are virtually open because of migrations back and forth by nomadic tribes. Almost from the first days of the April revolution, Afghanistan has been subjected to foreign intervention. Our military assistance was aimed not at imposing our will on Afghanistan, but at helping its government withstand outside interference.

Let's return to Afghanistan later. We have deviated from the subject of peaceful coexistence, which depends to a large extent on Soviet perceptions of the United States, and, of course, vice versa. How do you view the United States from Moscow?

This is a very complex question. America is a subject of great interest in the Soviet Union. Lots of books and articles have been written. It is quite a challenge to give a short but substantive picture of our perceptions. Let me try, although I will have to be sketchy.

I'd like to repeat that people in the Soviet Union take a lively interest in America. I refer to the broadest strata of our people, regardless of age, education, or the kind of work they do. I think there's a definite asymmetry here as compared to American interest in the USSR. We in the Soviet Union view the United States as a very strong country, both economically and militarily. U.S. foreign policy is seen by our people as characterized by imperial designs, especially pronounced at this stage. And I must say that Soviet people can only interpret the current American policy vis-à-vis our country as very hostile.

In other respects, the United States is a country that is never dull to watch, though I would add that it sometimes makes you mad. Our people are very interested in American culture, literature and cinema, music and architecture. The best American works in these fields are widely known here. Our specialists are well acquainted with the achievements of American science, technology, industry, medicine, and agriculture. There's an interest and sometimes even enthusiasm, particularly among youngsters, for such features of the American way of life as pop music, jeans, chewing gum, Pepsi-Cola and Coca-Cola, the Wild West, and so forth.

At the same time, the Soviet public is well informed of the growing problems facing America. First, I have in mind the economic problems—inflation, unemployment, energy problems, and so forth. I mean also the social problems, like the conditions of black Americans, Indians, and Spanish-speaking ethnic groups; the growing troubles of the old urban centers like New York or Cleveland; the problems of crime, drug addiction, access to health care for a majority of Americans; and many others. Finally, I have in mind the political and spiritual problems besetting American society. We are convinced—and the whole stream of historical events strengthens this conviction—that ultimate power in the United States, and the last word in its affairs of state, belongs to the corporate elite. This conviction, to a very serious degree, determines our view of American democracy and American ways of life.

How did Watergate strike people in the USSR?

As very unusual. But apparently it looked rather strange even to Americans themselves. Nothing like it ever happened in American history before. I must say that several researchers at our institute won their bets on the Nixon resignation at the time. The same number lost, however, so I would not boast of our foresight.

Let me ask you about the Institute of United States and Canadian Studies. I must say you have quite an elegant eighteenth-century mansion here, less than a mile from the Kremlin. What do you and your colleagues do?

Well, we do not spend all our time betting on political events in America, to be sure. Our institute is one of many research centers organized by the Academy of Sciences of the USSR.

When was it established?

In 1968.

What are the principal spheres of study here?

American and Canadian economic problems, domestic and social problems, political parties, the electoral processes, and so forth. We also study American military policy, not the U.S. military establishment as such, but the impact of military expenditures and programs, doctrines and postures on American foreign policy, including, of course, American-Soviet relations. We also study problems of arms control. A special department does research on problems of U.S. foreign policy in various regions, such as Europe, the Far East, the Middle East, and in developing nations. There is a department that studies American public opinion, ideology, and culture.

You have a large staff?

About 350, plus twenty to thirty postgraduate students. We pass on doctoral degrees. A large number of our staff have been trained right here.

Where do your publications go?

Books are our main product. Among our recent works are such monographs as *Modern U.S. Foreign Policy Concepts, U.S. Foreign Economic Policy, Canada on the Threshold of the Eighties, Modern American Political Consciousness, U.S. Economy: Problems and Contradictions,* and *U.S. Congress and Foreign Policy.* We also have a monthly publication. Our specialists are in great demand for broad educational activities, like lectures, writing articles for the media, TV appearances, and the like.

Surely the reports of the institute go to the government?

Well, if we have any bright ideas, we have no problem bringing them to the attention of the government. The main thing is to have the bright ideas in the first place. If people in the government ask us questions in the fields that we are familiar with, we have no secrets. But I would like to emphasize that our institute has not been created for a day-by-day service in foreign policy. That is the business of the Ministry of Foreign Affairs and our embassy in Washington. Our task is to study long-term problems and trends, and to develop fundamental research that can contribute to understanding more deeply and reliably the countries we study.

You must have American counterparts.

There are no exact counterparts, but there exist a lot of smaller centers for the study of the USSR at universities, or at Pentagon-sponsored organizations like the Rand Corporation or the Institute for Defense Analysis. There are other centers as well, like the George Kennan Institute at the Smithsonian Institution in Washington.

Do you have regular contacts with American scholars?

Yes, we do have many working contacts with universities, the Council on Foreign Relations, the Brookings Institution, the Stanford Research Institute, and other centers. With some of them we carry out joint research projects.

You also exchange scholars?

Yes. Our people go there, and we invite scholars, public figures, prominent businessmen, and others to visit us. Besides, many Americans call on us while visiting Moscow. Unfortunately, steps taken by the U.S. government in the last year or two to sharply curtail scientific and other exchanges between our countries have affected our institute's ties, as well.

Could you name a few of the Americans who have visited the institute?

Certainly. Walter Mondale lectured here when he was a senator. Edmund Muskie paid a visit, and former ambassador W. Averell Harriman visited the institute a couple of times. We have hosted such leaders of the Communist Party USA as Gus Hall, Henry Winston, and Angela Davis. Who else? The list is quite lengthy. Senators Kennedy, Baker, Garn; Congressman Vanik; Cyrus Vance; Zbigniew Brzezinski; Harold Brown and Marshall Shulman; Michael Blumenthal; Arthur Burns; John Kenneth Galbraith; George Kennan; Robert Pranger; Leslie Gelb; Harold Agnew of the Los Alamos Laboratory; Paul Doty and Stanley Hoffman of Harvard; William Kintner; David Rockefeller; Bank of America President A. Clausen; Roy Ash and the late Tex Thornton from Litton Industries; Paul Austin from Coca-Cola and Don Kendall from Pepsi-Cola; Chief Justice Warren Burger; Retired General James Gavin and Retired Admiral Gene La Rocque; William F. Buckley, Jr. and his brother James Buckley; and almost the entire Armed Services Committee of the U.S. House of Representatives.

From talking with all these visitors, and from your own journeys to the United States, didn't you gain the impression that Americans often tend to advertise and exaggerate their problems? Do you think there is a kind of masochistic streak in the American mind?

You see, each society has its own criteria for judging what is a problem and what is not. These criteria change with the times. Yes, Americans usually tend to be quite open about some of their problems, and I consider it their strong point. I don't think it's masochism. We communists call it self-criticism and think that it only helps a society to move ahead. At the same time, American self-criticism shouldn't always be taken at face value. We note some peculiarities here. Americans, for example, have a special gift for "exorcising" their problems, or talking them away, if I may say so. They often seem to believe that it's enough to raise a problem, to discuss it, even to spotlight it, to denounce it—and then forget all about it, moving the spotlight on to another sore spot. That works like letting off steam from a boiler.

Another trait that amazes an outsider is the American ability to "deodorize" the evils of their society and put up with them. Americans are well aware, for instance, that the police in some of their cities are corrupt; that the casinos are controlled by the Mafia; that advertising is full of lies; that politicians often cheat to get elected and, once elected, take it easy on their campaign promises; and so forth. But there's no real public indignation. Far from it: it looks as if some people regard these episodes as good entertainment or good sports, and some even envy the adroitness of the players.

As to this talk of masochism, such complaints are indeed heard more and more in the United States. I don't think it is incidental. In recent times, one observes a definite trend away from self-criticism and toward national self-congratulation, and a weakening of the desire to confront problems head-on.

What do you mean precisely?

Many opinion leaders in the United States have been trying to persuade Americans that they've never had it so good, or that the causes of American difficulties lie beyond the American shores, or that Americans can solve their problems quite easily just by regaining their faith in themselves, in America, and in the current administration and its programs. This sort of intellectual cowardice and scapegoating looks to me like one of the serious spiritual-political problems in America today. It is truly a serious problem because it frustrates the search for rational solutions precisely when such solutions are urgently required. And it increases the possibility of the nation making serious mistakes.

You don't think the time for self-criticism has passed in the United States?

No, I do not, if only because the search for solutions to the numerous problems facing the country is far from completed. My colleagues and I think that American society has been living through a protracted, multifaceted crisis involving many spheres of American life. It is becoming increasingly clear that, unless some very serious and rational attempts are made in the United States to adapt its policies, including its foreign policy, to changing realities, America is in for a series of very strong shocks, possibly stronger than at any time in her history.

A revolution?

Rest assured, we don't foresee the collapse of American social and political institutions in the immediate future.

No communist takeover by 1984?

If things go in the direction some people have predicted, a few of Orwell's predictions about the Big Brother state may come true by 1984, but it surely would be an anticommunist Big Brother.

Wouldn't you welcome exacerbation of American problems as a plus for the Soviet Union in its historic competition with the United States?

Well, anyone receives some intellectual satisfaction from a confirmation of his political views and theories. Marxists are no exception in this regard. This is anything but gloating. It is very well understood in the USSR that it is not Wall Street that suffers from urban blight, unemployment, or crime in the street, but the average American. How can we rejoice over these problems? If you analyze the reports about Western social problems in our news media, you'll notice that the tone is not one of glee or hand rubbing. We don't drink toasts to the automobile lines at American gas stations or stage a party rally each time an American city goes bankrupt.

More sophisticated people here are even concerned about the exacerbation of certain American problems—not because they like the present American system, but because they are aware that a national crisis may be deeper than the public understanding of its causes and its possible solutions. You see, people may be very unhappy about the status quo, but misguided about the real reasons for their unhappiness. They may listen to false prophets or support pseudosolutions. This is what happened in Italy in the 1920s and in Germany in the 1930s. After all, the same Great Depression that brought Franklin Roosevelt to power in the United States and led to New Deal reforms made Hitler the German fuhrer and led to World War II.

Yes, we do want to win the historic competition with capitalism, but we don't want to celebrate our victory on heaps of radioactive rubble.

According to some American figures, socialist governments now control 39 percent of the surface of the world, while 42 percent of the world population is following Marxist ideology.

These figures can be corrected somewhat, but it is obvious that socialism and communism have become a foundation of life on a very substantial part of our planet.

How then do you explain former President Carter's remark in his Annapolis address, that communism was becoming "increasingly unattractive to other nations, even to those of Marxist-Leninist coloration"? Or President Reagan's statement that we are witnessing the beginning of the end of communism?

We can only interpret such statements as wishful thinking on the part of the White House. They are refuted by the figures you just mentioned, illustrating the basic thrust of world development nowadays away from capitalism.

Do you think the events in Poland give support to such a view of socialism?

No, I do not. No system is guaranteed against mistakes and difficulties. Capitalism is certainly no exception in this regard. Neither is socialism, which undertakes far more complex social and political tasks.

Naturally, no historical process, no revolution ever develops smoothly. Socialist countries have had their share of disappointments as well. But if you analyze objectively what goes on in the world as a whole, I think U.S. presidents should be more cautious in their forecasts.

But the economic situation in many socialist countries, including the USSR, is far from rosy, indeed.

We have some economic problems that are openly and intensely discussed. But name me a country that does not. And you cannot ignore the fact that our country continues to grow at a steady pace. Our growth rates are at a level considered at least normal by Western standards. We haven't had a single economic recession in our history. In the 1970s, real per capita income in the USSR was increased by half, while 40 percent of our population has moved to new and better apartments.

It all sounds rather optimistic. Didn't the growth rates of both your GNP and your industrial production sharply decrease in the seventies?

They did decrease somewhat, even though they were still almost twice as high as in the United States.

How about agriculture? It's often described in the West as a complete disaster.

This is simply not true. We still have serious difficulties in our agriculture. To some extent they are caused by our hard weather and climatic conditions less favorable than in most Western countries. But this is one of the branches of our economy that is in the process of especially fundamental and rapid development. In the last five years we have invested 172 billion rubles in agriculture, or about 25 percent of the overall budget. The output of main agricultural products has been increasing steadily, even if slower than we'd like.

You don't think a revolution is around the corner for the United States. But in general, do you consider it possible that a radical change may sooner or later come about in that country?

Why not? Believing in a socialist future for all peoples, I don't see anything that would make the United States exceptional in this regard. Perhaps not in the near future, but ultimately there will be a socialist transformation of American society. It's up to the American people alone to decide about the kind of system that best suits their interests. When the time comes for a socialist America, it might be quite different from other socialist countries. American socialism will bear a label: "Made in USA."

In 1933, the Americans opted for a radical solution, while the Germans embarked on the way toward doom. Do you think that the Americans may blunder into a similar crisis in the future?

Hopefully not, and there are reasons for this hope. If anything, I have observed that Americans have wisened up considerably during the past decades. Stormy times usually are better educators than sleepy times. Aside from an enrichment in historical experience, we witness definite progress in mass education. Americans are reading more now. There is a veritable reading boom in the United States. Many Americans are now probably less susceptible to official propaganda and more inclined to make up their own minds and form independent judgments.

But this progress toward a more realistic perception of the world has been rather slow, I am afraid. There is still a lot of ignorance and gullibility in the country. The situation both in America and abroad is much more complex now than in 1933, while mass-manipulation techniques have made a giant stride. Those who are trying to mislead the nation have become more sophisticated. Therefore, the possibility of choosing a wrong option at a moment of crisis, in spite of all the increased enlightenment of the average American citizen, cannot, in my opinion, be ruled out.

Indeed, in Europe it is often felt that Americans, unlike Europeans, simply refuse to face the fact that empires have become obsolete.

I agree. There are many lessons to be learned, many new realities to be understood. For instance, Americans have grown accustomed to a sense of absolute security, because this was instilled over two centuries by the insurmountable barriers of two oceans. The strategic preponderance the United States enjoyed in the first postwar decades must have contributed to this feeling of absolute safety. Now the situation has drastically changed. America finds herself not only at rough military parity with the USSR, but absolutely on a par with us and all other countries in terms of vulnerability to a holocaust should a war break out. This is a novel psychological experience for Americans. It is certainly not easy to get used to it or to get along with it. It nurtures a climate for more panicking about the "Soviet threat" and creates a permanent temptation to follow those who promise an act of magic—a return to past invulnerability if only a sufficient number of dollars are allocated and an adequate number of weapons systems produced.

And then one has to see that United States remoteness, self-sufficiency, and isolationism did not encourage much interest in the outside world. That is why Americans are not particularly given to scrutinizing the intricacies of the international scene. This also helps sustain a situation in which foreign policy so often falls prey to domestic politicking.

What is your impression of the attitudes of average American citizens to the USSR?

Well, I've encountered a lot of ignorance, inaccurate perceptions, misunderstanding, mistrust, and so on. But I've almost never felt hatred of our country or of the Russians. The average American—at least this is my impression from my own encounters—is willing to listen and learn. I also think the natural friendliness and open-mindedness of most Americans are helpful here.

In 1979, the Foreign Relations Committee of the U.S. Senate issued a book on U.S.-Soviet relations. You, among others, contributed to it. I would like to deal with some of the questions you discussed there. One was whether the American public had an accurate perception of the Soviet Union, its people, and its leaders.

I don't think it does—even on the problems that are of high importance to the United States itself. Inaccuracy of many American perceptions of the Soviet Union is hardly surprising given the fact that there may be no other country in the world of which U.S. perceptions have for such a long time been formed on the basis of such one-sided and distorted information. That is why they are so tinted with strong biases and prejudices.

There was also the following question: on the basis of what information, and as a result of what psychological, social, and political forces, is American public opinion toward the Soviet Union shaped?

My answer was as follows: the bulk of information the Americans get about the Soviet Union is secondhand, delivered to the American public through American intermediaries—journalists, experts, politicians, reports by the CIA and other governmental and private organizations. To a certain extent this is probably the case with any other country. But in informing the American public about the Soviet Union, these American intermediaries very often display a particular bias. This is the result of personal ideological prejudices characteristic of many of them, and of direct or indirect pressure of those who have vested interests in creating a distorted picture of the Soviet Union.

The United States is hardly comparable to any other country in the world in terms of the extent to which special interests affect national policy and the concepts that underlie it. Among those vitally interested in the distortion of the American perception of the USSR are the military-industrial complex, the ultraconservative elements, groups benefiting from the Cold War, organizations representing anticommunist emigration from Eastern Europe, the Israeli lobby, and others.

Does American public opinion, in your view, have any real influence on U.S. foreign policy?

Without doubt, American public opinion affects official policy. This influence at certain times and under specific circumstances—on the eve of elections, for instance—can be substantial, indeed. However, in my opinion, normally the president and the Congress tend to respond not so much to public opinion as to the sentiments of well-organized pressure groups. And of course, in many instances, instead of echoing public sentiments, the U.S. government and groups wishing to influence its policies may attempt to change public moods in a desired fashion.

Does American public opinion differ significantly from the views of U.S. experts regarding the Soviet Union?

It probably does, but one should bear in mind that there are great differences between the opinions of the U.S. experts themselves. For a long time, a majority of them held a position of utmost hostility to the Soviet Union. This is probably accounted for by the fact that Soviet studies flourished in the time of the Cold War, the interests of which many of those experts served. A disproportionately high share of emigrés from Eastern Europe among the U.S. experts on the Soviet Union was also a factor. Their attitudes toward the Soviet Union might have been tainted by highly negative personal emotions connected with the changes that took place in their countries after World War II. The situation has been changing to a certain extent over the past few years. The United States has produced a "national cadre" of experts on the Soviet Union, differing widely in their personal outlook, but reflecting a wide range of American political interests and opinions. Younger people in Soviet studies, whatever their outlooks, were not brought up as cold warriors. And, of course, among the older generation there are notable exceptions—people possessing not only outstanding knowledge, but great integrity and a clear understanding of the importance of normal relations with the Soviet Union. But with new-type or old-type experts, U.S. policy makers can find confirmation of practically any desired viewpoint.

None of this is meant as a call to distrust the experts. I only think that, first, even with the experts available, personal competence of the political leaders is essential, and second, those who are inclined to rely on the advice of these experts should become expert themselves in deciding which of the experts are likely to provide an objective and thorough analysis.

How about the political elite? Do you think it is sufficiently enlightened to construct effective policy?

We face another paradox here. One cannot help but notice that U.S. foreign policy has traditionally been served by a very big concentration of brains—maybe the biggest in the world. The administrations have regularly tried to draft the best and the brightest to serve the government. A host of research centers, both inside and outside the universities, has been scrutinizing on a day-to-day basis everything worth attention, and even many things patently unworthy of attention. The Pentagon, the CIA, the State Department, and other offices have been spending huge sums on conducting analytical research to assist in policy making. The elite is constantly enlightened and educated about the intricacies of world politics and about ways to solve military, economic, and political problems. But once you observe the practical results of this voluminous activity, you begin to wonder about cost-benefit ratios. The entire intellectual potential of U.S. policy making proved unable to save America from a series of very bad miscalculations and mistakes, which may have been even bigger than those made by other countries.

How do you account for this paradox?

Well, I don't think that the policy makers just don't listen to the researchers and analysts. They may not listen enough in some cases, and sometimes the specialists may not be very good. But the reasons for these policy failures go deeper than this. One has to take into account certain domestic political mechanisms that push the policy makers to wrong or even irrational decisions. The leadership-selection process in the United States might be such that in some cases the qualities of leaders aren't up to the tasks they have to perform. But the most important reason is the existence of certain strong vested interests that contradict and negate the demands of logic and reason.

Stanley Hoffman once said that the causes of U.S. foreign policy failures have to do not with muscles, but with brains. This is certainly true. But if we are witnessing a new wave of political body building, it's not just because some people are too stupid to understand the situation. The system itself must be curbing and circumscribing reason with a very narrow and stiff framework, indeed.

What aspects of American foreign policy give you the greatest headaches?

Some of them we have already touched on—such as an inclination to shun the most complex problems of security in a nuclear age by escalating military spending and piling up mountains of weapons. Another one is the predominance of political leaders' domestic concerns over a steady course in foreign policy. Just look how it works in the case of the U.S. Middle East policy.

Then, there is a lack of continuity that makes the United States such an unstable partner, even in the most important endeavors like arms control agreements. Take the sad story of SALT II. We started negotiating it with

President Nixon, but then had to begin almost from scratch with Ford, then again with Carter. And now President Reagan wants to change everything once again, or drop it altogether.

I would also refer to some very tangible remnants of American messianism.

What precisely do you mean by that?

Well, here's an illustration: "I have always believed that this land was placed here between the two great oceans by some divine plan. It was placed here by a special kind of people.... We built a new breed of human called American."[7] That's Ronald Reagan in 1980. It may look like the heritage of a Calvinist past. Back in those times, Pilgrims, if only for survival's sake, just had to believe they were founding a new and chosen land, free of the old world's sins. Eventually, that defensive feeling evolved into an offensive one in the form of "Manifest Destiny," then over to the "American Century," and so on. Although by now this messianism has lost much of its former elan, the almost instinctive yearning to teach others by sermon if possible, or by force if necessary, still persists in full strength. Recently, we have witnessed a revival of this zealotry. Worst of all, it constantly belies double standards. All this strongly interferes with the maintenance of normal relations between the United States and other countries.

If you have in mind human rights, we'll return to them. Let's for the moment stay with American foreign policy.

Then let me mention another feature typical of U.S. foreign policy, though America is hardly unique in this: a tremendous respect for strength. As far as I understand American attitudes, a weak country is no partner for them. It's only the strong that they respect, and this should be regarded as a fact of life, at least for the time being. Though the main American complaint about the Soviet Union today centers around our strength and even our alleged superiority, I think that our weakness wouldn't have provided for better Soviet-American relations. Quite to the contrary. Our country in such a case would have been far worse off in its relations with the United States than now. The same, by the way, can be said about many other countries that gained their independence and freedom of action just because the Soviet Union emerged as a counterweight to overwhelming American power. Saying this, I don't mean to picture America as a nation inherently aggressive. This is simply not so, if we take Americans as human beings. But though the United States likes to attribute this exclusive respect for strength to other countries, it's mostly applicable to the United States itself. We have more than once felt it on our own skins.

But your becoming strong hasn't turned your relations with the United States into a romance, either.

No, it hasn't. I only want to stress that our weakness would have made these relations worse. It would have increased false hopes for remaking us according to American standards. Stating this, I'm nevertheless hopeful that the situation will change; that in due course considerations of power will play a lesser role both in United States policy and in international relations throughout the world.

During the twenty years that I lectured to American audiences from Corpus Christi, Texas, to Sheboygan, Wisconsin, I was never able to explain the meaning and the fear of war, as we knew it during the Nazi occupation of Holland.

Gunnar Myrdal once observed that "the U.S. citizen's lack of a firsthand memory of the horrors of a war constitutes a danger for the U.S. as well as for the rest of the world."[8] Indeed, the two world wars that ravaged Europe and profoundly changed European attitudes toward the smell of gunpowder made America richer. In World War II, when fifty million people died, the American losses were about 2 percent of ours. The Piskarev Memorial Cemetery in Leningrad alone contains more war dead than the total of American casualties in World War II. To our country, that war meant the tremendous destruction of economic potential, while the same war pulled America out of the depression. I'm certainly not denouncing America for sacrificing much less than others at the altar of war, nor am I calling on them to sacrifice more. From the moral viewpoint, however, one could expect from Americans a much less cavalier attitude toward war than the one epitomized by former Secretary of State Haig's pronouncement that there are things more important than peace. As to the practical aspect, I agree with Myrdal that an important safety check is lacking in the American mind as a result of some gaps in their historical experience.

As a European student of the United States for the past thirty years I would say that all this is closely tied to American egocentrism.

I think you're right. I've observed many times how difficult it is for Americans to put themselves in other people's shoes, or even to imagine the consequences of American actions for others. Sometimes I think that it is not only the dubious intentions and vested interests of some Americans that cause some of the problems that are of foremost importance today, but also this inability to look at life through the eyes of the other side. We have already discussed, for instance, how the United States, in evaluating Soviet military power, ignores the real threats faced by the Soviet Union and then shouts about the "Soviet threat."

I don't think the United States fully understands its own allies, either; in particular the fact that, for Europeans, Europe is not an advanced outpost guarding the American heartland, nor a faraway theater for some tactical operations, but their one and only living space. Therefore, Europe may have a different attitude toward détente and toward the development of peaceful relations with the USSR. I heard from my West German friends that it took Jimmy Carter almost his entire term to realize just what Ostpolitik truly meant to West Germans.

I wonder how long it will take the current U.S. administration to realize what détente means to all Western Europeans.

In September 1981, during an interview for a Dutch television program, I asked ACDA Director Eugene Rostow if he realized that we, in Europe, were becoming more afraid of Washington than of Moscow, since the Reagan administration was behaving like a bull in a china shop in its foreign affairs. He was clearly taken aback by the question.

Naturally, because the Reagan people came to Washington certain that cold-war policies would not only get broad support in Europe, but would make Europeans more loyal to the United States. And when the antinuclear movement shook Western Europe their first reaction was to blame it on Russian propaganda.

American ignorance about the Third World is even greater. I don't think Americans have any awareness of how the Third World peoples live, how they feel, or what they want—including America's closest neighbors, like the peoples of El Salvador, Nicaragua, Guatemala, and Panama, or the whole of Latin America.

It often occurs to me that the Americans have been exclusively fortunate in their history, perhaps too fortunate, to be capable of fully understanding and harboring genuine sympathy toward nations with more difficult histories.

But what about American charity and giveaway programs?

Yes, there are many charitable institutions, some of which assist the alleviation of poverty and further other humane causes. As to charity, I don't want to repeat the trivial accusation that this is just a way to allay pains of conscience and to obtain greater pleasure from one's own satiety. In some cases, motives are quite different, sometimes noble. But most charitable activities are a far cry from any ideal of selfless and pure Christian sharing. They are largely oriented to the economic and political interests of the American establishment.

Take the 1980 events in Kampuchea. The United States created obstacles to the shipment of relief supplies to the Kampuchean government, which controlled most of the country's territory and was engaged in a desperate attempt to save that ill-fated nation from death and degradation brought on by the barbarian rule of Pol Pot. At the same time, the United States was loudly insisting on its right to give "charitable aid" to the remnants of Pol Pot's army near the Thai border. And, to add insult to injury, the U.S. government was charging the Kampuchean government with indifference to human suffering.

There's no way to explain American behavior here as a manifestation of humanitarian concern. But everything begins to look logical once you recall U.S. geostrategic interests in this area. And it is often forgotten in the heat of righteous indignation that the lion's share of the blame for the Kampucheans' ordeal lies with the United States. Having committed military aggression against Cambodia in 1970, having interfered in her internal affairs and facilitated the overthrow of the neutralist government of Prince Norodom Sihanouk, the Americans actually paved the way for Pol Pot.

Returning to Soviet-American relations, do you feel that a pluralistic, disorganized, and at times wild society can truly coexist with an orderly and centralized one?

When a society goes wild, it's difficult for anyone to coexist with it. But let's put aside cases of national hysteria as exceptional situations. As to American pluralism, blaming it for setbacks suffered by détente in recent years would be tantamount to scapegoating. We know that American society is complex, heterogeneous, and in some aspects decentralized, and we are fully prepared to coexist with that society as it really is.

But wouldn't it make sense if the U.S. Congress were more disciplined and could support the president on urgent matters like SALT II?

It certainly would. But we have to be realists. The Congress plays an important role in the American political system, and now, with all our experience in dealing with it, we understand the existing political procedures in Washington well enough. Of course, I have to confess that we sometimes have questions about the wisdom of procedures under which a few senators, representing a small minority of the population, can block a treaty of vital, even crucial, importance to the whole nation. For example, according to the polls, the SALT II treaty was supported by a majority of more than 70 percent of the American people, while 10 to 15 percent were against it. But we put such questions aside, understanding that these procedures are a constitutional matter that can be decided only by the Americans themselves.

And then, we firmly believe that détente could withstand an honest political debate in Washington. If anything, such a debate would only strengthen it. It was, in our opinion, not the constitutional prerogative of Congress that created problems for trade and SALT, any more than the principle of freedom of the press is responsible for the dogmatic anti-Sovietism prevailing in the American news media. The problem is that the pluralism existing in America is used most effectively by the well-established, entrenched, overreaching forces in the power elite, like the military-industrial complex, which is interested in undermining détente and subverting Soviet-American relations. Those who have different interests, even those who must represent the national interests as a whole, have failed to oppose these onslaughts effectively, and détente is now in trouble.

But how about the argument that, being less organized, the United States is less able to marshal its total resources for fierce competition with the Soviet Union?

Actually, this argument is the obverse of the notion that the Soviet Union must become a less organized society before the United States agrees to coexist with it. The liberals generally favor a "less organized" Soviet Union. The conservatives favor a "more organized" United States. The Far Right wants both. But although they have a right to organize the United States as they want, Americans must leave to us our own constitutional prerogatives and the organization of our own society. Besides, all these simplistic comparisons miss the crucial point I've already mentioned: the real competition is between social systems; that is, between their abilities to provide for a happy and meaningful life for modern mankind. It is important to emphasize this, for when Americans talk about "marshaling resources," they hardly mean more money for the poor or the elderly. They don't mean peaceful coexistence and peaceful competition. The military connotation of the word *marshal* is not without symbolism.

You would not deny that the USSR seems to be better prepared for a confrontation with the United States than Americans are ready for a confrontation with Russia?

I think that since there is more unity in our society, and a greater ability to rally around a national purpose, we are better prepared to pursue consistently any national policy—preferably a policy of détente, but, if necessary, measures that might become unavoidable in case of a confrontation. At the same time, one shouldn't underestimate the American ability to do the same, but regrettably with much more readiness when the issue concerns not détente but confrontation, when the drums of patriotism and even jingoism have begun to beat, and the battle cry sounds: "Give 'em hell, Harry!" The end of the seventies and the beginning of the eighties demonstrated this once again.

But in the final analysis, such ability to rally for confrontation might not be too important nowadays. If it doesn't come to the worst, and confrontation is sooner or later succeeded by a new period of relaxation, this ability won't play a substantial role. If it does come to the worst, who will care about the preceding preparedness, unity, or national emotions?

Reginald Bartholomew, formerly on Brzezinski's staff, was director of the State Department Bureau of Political and Military Affairs when he suggested to me that the White House sometimes gets the impression that the Soviet Union is testing American manhood.

I often wonder about the preoccupation of American politicians with their manhood—I mean political, not personal manhood, which of course is also important. They seem to like this macho style, this strutting about like matadors in the bullring. But grandstanding can have extremely dangerous results for public policy. The goal cannot and should not be to show off one's toughness at each occasion for the entire world to see. Such attitudes tend to inspire false and unrealistic approaches to public affairs. What really matters in policy making is wisdom and restraint, the ability to understand the other side, to find solutions that are possible and can be obtained, because policy making has always been and will always be the art of the possible. This ought to be fully understood and accepted as especially important in the nuclear age.

But maybe the public is not educated enough about these matters. And politicians trying to sell themselves and their policies to the public are tempted to arouse this yearning for oversized manhood, so visibly symbolized by ICBMs, bombers, aircraft carriers, and other military hardware, especially because it is much easier and requires much less brains and courage, and it is easy not to pay attention to how irrelevant it all becomes. The more so if you have in mind major problems like peace, economic well-being, energy, and other global problems.

Leslie Gelb suggested that it is high time for the United States "to have a clearer sense of our own interests, and the Russians must know them in advance." Referring to the failure of U.S. leaders to develop effective ways of influencing Soviet behavior, he added: ". . . the carrots were invariably paltry and the sticks inevitably inadequate. We had too little to offer and not enough with which to threaten."[9]

Frankly, with all due respect for Leslie Gelb, I find this carrot-and-stick symbolism a rather simplistic way to discuss contemporary problems. What Leslie Gelb must have had in mind is that the United States chose not to offer a carrot big and sweet enough. Soon there remained rather miserable crumbs, and finally the U.S. government, in an outburst of biblical wrath, snatched away even those. As to the big stick, to stay with Gelb's comparison, of course there was none, apart from war—that is, suicide. As to those smaller sticks the United States did have, they have been used up very quickly, demonstrating in the process that they are also double-ended, inflicting no less harm on the United States than on us. Take the grain embargo, trade cutoffs, and so forth. I think these are what Mr. Gelb had in mind, and up to this point I would not argue with him. I would only add in this connection that there is obvious confusion as to which category—carrot or stick—some issues belong. Take, for instance, the SALT II treaty. No matter how this question will finally be settled, the entire agreement seems to be falling victim to this vengeful eagerness to "punish" the Soviet Union. However, both our nations are going to suffer from this, and to the same degree.

But generally speaking, the very idea of reducing the core of a policy to the use of carrots and sticks can hardly work nowadays. I don't think any nation would like to become so pliable to bribes and threats that it would allow its policy to be directed from a foreign capital. Certainly, both the United States and the Soviet Union have avoided and will continue to avoid getting into such a situation. In other words, carrot and stick doesn't work because it's a form of behavior control that no sovereign nation would tolerate in our time.

But you would not deny that economic sanctions imposed by Carter and now by Reagan do work as a stick, given your stake in economic relations with the United States?

Our economic interest in trade with the United States is usually grossly exaggerated. In 1981, for instance, the U.S. share of our foreign trade was only 1.7 percent, and less than 0.5 percent with grain excluded. So these sanctions have only marginal impact on our economy, especially since we can always make up for these losses somewhere else. Nor are they harmless for the Americans themselves, as midwestern farmers and many companies involved can testify. But the real issue here goes beyond purely economic gains or losses. We have always viewed trade and economic relations as means to reinforce a foundation for détente. In the last years the United States increasingly has tried to use its trade with the socialist countries as a cold-war weapon aimed at "punishment" or as a means of blackmailing others into political concessions.

As Felix Rohatyn, a well-known American financier and public figure, recently said, "Capital can be as potent a weapon as an intercontinental ballistic missile."[10]

In response to this, let me first of all say that from the very beginning of our revolution we realized that the capitalists outside would use their economic influence as a weapon against us. Throughout many years we lived with the experience of economic blockades and pressures. That is why we have developed our economy and foreign trade in such a way as to prevent a situation of excessive economic dependence upon the West, realizing that until there is a drastic reconstruction of international relations we must have basically a self-sustained economy. For the same reason, we find the "helping the enemy" view of American-Soviet trade fashionable nowadays in the United States absolutely ridiculous, for it has never worked this way.

Second, it should not be forgotten that trade may also be a double-edged sword. The whole point is that this logic itself is a dangerous anachronism, a hangover of the old imperialist mentality. To step onto the path of all-out economic warfare in today's increasingly complex, fragile, and interdependent world is dangerous not only for us, but other countries as well, for it threatens to undermine the very foundations of international economic and political relations. We may argue about the value of international economic ties for consolidating détente—in my view it can be great —but there is no doubt that disrupting those ties inevitably results in increasing tensions between states. In this sense, Mr. Rohatyn has a point. But an approach designed to inflict maximum feasible damage on the other party makes sense only if you interpret your long-term goals in terms of a zero-sum game, in terms of hostility and confrontation.

Don't you agree that international behavior is becoming less controllable and more chaotic? The dangers of such a trend, if there is one, seem obvious.

External control of a nation's foreign policy is, indeed, becoming less and less feasible. Whether it's more or less dangerous is another question. Remember the time when the world was divided between several empires, which operated as tight control systems. There were endless wars. Each of them was bloodier than the previous one. We in the Soviet Union believe that national sovereignty and equality among nations are necessary preconditions for peace and international stability. It is on that bedrock of sovereignty and equality that a new international system of controls and checks can be based, a system that would preclude some policies and encourage others. But the control will not be in the hands of another nation or military bloc. This system can only be guaranteed by international law or by collective security institutions like the United Nations. Otherwise, we'll be back to imperial times with all the inevitable conflagrations.

What rewards and punishments can there be in such a system?

The rewards could include a guarantee of security, which allows one to allocate more resources for internal development. There could also be direct benefits from increased international cooperation. As to punishments, a country would be punishing itself if it behaved in such a way that it denied itself the benefits I mentioned and harmed the existing security system. Other forms of punishment would be the increased danger of war and denunciation by world public opinion. In extreme cases, some kinds of collective measures could be used, like those stipulated by the U.N. Charter. Stability of this new international system would also be guarded by a broad interdependence of nations.

What does the West understand and what does it not understand in Soviet foreign policy?

Your question tempts me to start complaining about all the injustices against us. Even though there are more than solid grounds for such complaints, I prefer to refrain from voicing them. I would rather try to outline the main problems.

The principal problem is not misunderstanding or lack of understanding, but general attitudes. For a long time the West refused to put up with our very existence, and there are people today who still refuse to accept it. Some have developed true paranoia about us. This obstinate rejection of reality is both the main root of the difficulties and the main cause of misunderstandings. One can be more eloquent than Cicero in disproving the arguments of people like Richard Pipes and Senator Henry Jackson. But they will refuse to be persuaded because their views are determined by their iron-cast anti-Sovietism. Of course, such people are in the minority nowadays. But their attitude is only an extremity, while many who are free of such outspoken extremism are still tainted with the same political attitudes, which, carried forth to their logical conclusions, obliterate the very idea of peaceful coexistence with the USSR and other socialist countries.

Of course, there are also other political leaders in the West, otherwise there would have been no détente at all. Those people think in broad civilizational terms. They can see farther ahead. They are reasonable enough to understand the ultimate necessity to coexist with the Soviet Union, whether they like our society or not.

Can you name a few?

De Gaulle and Brandt are, perhaps, two of the most prominent examples in terms of the influence they had on practical policy. It is very difficult, of course, to place those two figures in the same category, different as they are in their political beliefs, as well as in other respects. But what they had in common was their ability to overcome prejudices and stereotypes and to see things in more realistic terms than many of their Western contemporaries. They clearly observed the fundamental interests of their own nations and did not try to ignore those of the Soviet Union. Perhaps one reason for their grasp of reality was their wartime experience. Brandt was hounded out of Germany by the Nazis and took part in the fight against them. De Gaulle was a staunch fighter for the liberation of France from

Nazi occupation. Those experiences may have been of key importance because one of the most important things misunderstood in the West about the Soviet Union is our attitude toward war. It is often not realized by Westerners, particularly by Americans, just what World War II meant to the Soviet people. One sometimes hears talk like this in the West: well, the Russians lost twenty million in the last war, so they are hardened enough to take quite easily another twenty or even forty million casualties in a nuclear exchange.

What's behind such thinking?

Attempts to prove that the Soviet Union can start a nuclear war and will not be deterred by the prospect of great losses. It's like saying about a person who was severely injured in an auto accident: now he will drive carelessly because he's used to severe injuries. This has nothing to do with reality. World War II did bring us a glorious victory. But it has also made the Soviet people value peace even more than before. Peace is our highest priority, and the policy of peace and détente has solid and broad support among our people.

Is this peace policy identified with the personality of President Brezhnev?

President Brezhnev has made a great personal contribution to this policy, and he has stressed that it is the policy of the entire party. It's the mandate of several Party Congresses being carried out by the Central Committee of the CPSU.

There is another important thing I'd like to add. Our commitment to peace does not mean that we will buckle under pressure. Our people hate war, but they are proud and patriotic, and once they feel that somebody threatens their security they are ready to meet the threat. I consider it very important that this be understood in the United States, for it looks like there is again growing in the United States an illusion that involving us in another arms race would wear us down. We may have a smaller gross national product than the United States, but we can stand greater hardship.

Another fact that is often not understood properly is our sensitivity to foreign interference in our domestic affairs. Throughout our history since 1917 we have been subjected to endless attempts from outside to frustrate and hamper our development in one way or another. In order to prevent us from following the road we took in 1917, a massive arsenal has been used, from armed intervention to sophisticated propaganda. All that has made us much more sensitive to any meddling in our affairs than those who have never experienced a really hostile environment. It's not that we are afraid. No, we are strong and confident enough. But we are more inclined to see any meddling as motivated by hostility and subversive aims.

Are you talking about your leadership's attitude or about broad public opinion in the USSR?

Both. Actually, your question brings us to another area of misunderstanding of the Soviet policy: the role of public opinion in the USSR. The standard assumption in the West is that public opinion doesn't count in this country, or that the attitude of our leadership is necessarily contrary to what common people think. The truth is quite the opposite. Public opinion plays an important role in determining Soviet policy, even though that influence works in its own way, which may be different from what one sees in the United States. Certainly, it operates without the American penchant for showing off, but at the same time with great substance.

You see, some Americans seem to proceed from the premise that, no matter what they do, the Soviet public, if it were not influenced by official Soviet indoctrination, would always love them. They seem to believe that they can act like hoodlums today, but that if tomorrow they say a couple of nice things or open a couple of doors, everything will be okay, the bad things will be forgotten. That's a very chauvinistic attitude. We do reckon with public opinion, which must not only be persuaded that our foreign policy is correct, if that policy is to have substance, but which plays a major role in formulating the ideas and policies of the party and the government.

The United States has been sowing some very bad seeds of distrust in our public opinion. Some American actions in recent years have been truly outrageous.

One of the constant themes that has emerged in our conversations is your appeal to Americans to take the Soviets for what they are, to bring their perceptions of the Soviet Union closer to reality.

Yes, I think confusing images with reality has always created unnecessary difficulties in international relations. That brings us back to American egocentrism. America, in the eyes of many Americans, has a monopoly on the good, but if there is evil in America, the same evil is assumed to exist everywhere else. For example, if the United States has a problem with its military-industrial complex, it is automatically assumed that a similar problem exists in the Soviet Union. It is totally disregarded that our economic system operates by quite different laws, that the kind of freedom the military-industrial complex has in the United States as a special interest group is a unique characteristic of the American society and political system.

Standard Western treatment of the real problems we have is still another example of misunderstanding. There is endless denigration of the Soviet way of life as poor, shabby, backward, and so on.

But Soviet living standards are obviously lower than in most of the Western capitalist countries.

We ourselves know that we don't yet have in abundance some material goods that affluent Westerners are used to. I am not ashamed to admit it. But it makes me furious to hear some Americans talk glibly and condescendingly about Russians. I think our people are entitled to great respect for having achieved what they have achieved despite all the tremendous difficulties. And, by the way, our standard of living is improving.

In the West, a hard line is shaping up vis-à-vis the USSR on the grounds that only a united allied front can teach the Soviets that they should not repeat Afghanistan—in Poland, for instance.

The wording of your statement is based on false premises. I do see definite attempts to build up a united anti-Soviet front in the West, but I would seriously question not only the realism of such plans, but also the motives behind them. Those motives are offensive, not defensive. I have already pointed to the facts that, I think, prove that the intensified anti-Soviet trend in the policies of the United States and some American allies preceded the events in Afghanistan, and thus could not have been caused by them. As to events in Poland, the U.S. hard-liners were far from interested in any peaceful and early solution of the domestic conflict in that country. They treated the Polish events from the viewpoint of "the worse, the better," seeing a deterioration there as a rare opportunity to achieve all their goals: a full collapse of détente, the taming of the allies, and the rallying of Americans around the most militaristic and adventurist policy.

But wasn't the introduction of martial law in Poland in December 1981 a real deterioration of the situation there?

Martial law is never a pleasant thing, and I am sure that the Polish leadership would have preferred not to introduce it. But think of the options that General Jaruzelski had. What would have happened in Poland if martial law had not been introduced? Economic collapse, a civil war, chaos, and bloodshed. Compared to that, martial law is a lesser evil.

The U.S. policy toward Poland (and the USSR) after the introduction of martial law made a strange impression. The fact that the Polish leadership and Poland's allies succeeded in avoiding a major international crisis seemed to have enraged the American government and impelled it to revenge. What's more, the United States set about creating such a crisis by artificial means, clearly trying to internationalize the events in Poland.

Martial law in Poland was interpreted by some in the West as a violation of the Helsinki accords and a throwback to the Yalta agreement.

Now, this line is really astounding. Playing Helsinki against Yalta is like using the New Testament to disprove the Old. To begin with, both the Yalta and the Helsinki agreements have the same origin—they codify a certain political structure in Europe, which was born as a result of the war, Hitler's defeat, and the huge sacrifices paid by the peoples of Europe, including, of course, the people of the USSR. In this sense, those accords were written in blood. And they cannot be treated in a mindless and capricious way.

The accords also embody another trend in East-West relations, namely the trend of peaceful coexistence, of the recognition by the West of the Soviet Union, and later the other socialist states, as sovereign and equal participants in international politics, with security interests as legitimate as those of the Western states.

One of the reasons I am seriously concerned by the policies of the United States and other NATO countries in connection with the events in Poland is that I see in those sanctions, ultimatums, and threats a violation of some ground rules of peaceful coexistence. Sanctions were imposed on the government of a sovereign state as punishment for its steps to defend the country's social system, to prevent a violent overthrow of that system—in short, for actions always considered related to domestic affairs. Helsinki was clearly not designed for such meddling in internal affairs of other countries.

But I would remind you of one essential fact: martial law means a harsh regime based on military force. That is why it cannot be seen by the Western public other than in a very negative way.

Let me repeat. Everybody knows that martial law is not a pleasant thing. The Polish leadership openly admits this and stresses that the measure was taken only as a last resort and will soon be lifted.

But it is just as clear that that measure did not violate international law and did not present any threat to peace in Europe. On the contrary, it removed the threat of very dramatic events that could have led to a major international crisis.

I am not sure your assessment of the attitude of "the Western public" to the Polish events is accurate. I think that reaction was at least cautious, despite all the massive psychological pressures exerted by Western governments and media.

As to the attitude of Western governments, particularly the U.S. government, it was a case study of the most blatant double standards. It would take unusual gullibility to believe in the sincerity of the Reagan administration's loud denunciations of alleged "human rights violations" in Poland, while the same administration is actively supporting the bloody dictatorships in El Salvador and Guatemala, having classified them, along with the other pro-American juntas in Latin America, as only "moderately repressive" and thus deserving of American backing. And, of course, everybody knows the Reagan administration's real attitude toward labor unions.

Talking of double standard, I could mention Chile, South Korea, Turkey, and quite a few other places, but I would not draw parallels between the Polish situation and the coups in those countries. There was no coup d'état in Poland. Martial law was introduced by the legitimate government of Poland, in accordance with the national constitution. The Polish parliament was not disbanded. The number of people arrested was very small, the prosecution of those found guilty of violating the law was carried out with appropriate legal procedures, and the sentences were extremely mild. Can one possibly compare it, say, with the bloodbath in Chile in 1973?

Having said all this, I'd like to emphasize that no one expected the sympathies of the American and other Western ruling circles to be on the side of Polish communists, of those who have been defending socialism in Poland. The dividing line on these issues clearly reflects class interests, sympathies, and world views.

But at the same time, policy making, in a nuclear age especially, is influenced to a significant degree by other considerations. For instance, one has to think of how this or that local event will affect the international situation, whether one should let an event grow into an international crisis, into a political, to say nothing of a military, confrontation between the biggest powers. What would have happened in the years since World War II if major participants in international relations had not been guided by, or at least taken account of, such considerations? What if they had blindly followed their instincts, sympathies, and antipathies? I think the answer to this question is quite clear—the world would have been hopelessly mired in the most dangerous conflicts and would have almost certainly crossed the brink beyond which mankind faces nuclear holocaust. It was the understanding of this truth that has given an irrepressible vitality to the principles of peaceful coexistence between states belonging to different social systems.

I would like to stress that the Soviet Union formed its attitude to the events in Poland, just as to other situations, with due consideration to all aspects, including the impact on the international situation.

I would stress that, in general, even when confronted with the hostile actions of the United States and NATO, the Soviet Union does everything possible to avoid steps that would increase tensions and harm détente.

Perhaps this is one of the reasons why Soviets are often perceived as being more interested in détente than the West.

You know, that notion is double-edged. On the one hand, I regard it as a compliment when people say that we are tremendously interested in peace and détente. I'd rather be accused of peacemongering than warmongering. On the other hand, of course, that notion is not being spread for the sake of proving how peaceful the Soviets are. The aim is often sinister and cynical: if the Russians need détente more than the West does, the West can raise the price. It's called hard bargaining, tough Yankee trading. But we are not talking of selling patent medicine or peanuts when we discuss foreign policy basics. We are talking of human survival on this planet. A petty market mentality does not apply here.

So, in general, you believe that Soviet perceptions of the United States are more accurate than American perceptions of the Soviet Union?

I would rather say less inaccurate. It is always difficult to understand a foreign country. The accuracy of our perceptions of each other remains a tremendously important problem in Soviet-American relations, because it is closely connected with mutual understanding, and through this with mutual trust. Accurate perceptions are a very important additional safeguard against the final breakdown of relations—a nuclear war. I am not exaggerating, because such a breakdown cannot be a rational choice, but must inevitably be tied with bad mistakes in evaluating behavior, intentions, and the ultimate aims of the other side.

Has there been any progress in mutual understanding in recent years?

I think we have made substantial progress in this area. Détente played a major role in the seventies, of course, as it led to the development of political and scientific contacts, cultural ties, tourism, and people-to-people contacts. But those were only the very first steps. The problem remains acute. Actually, it may be growing more acute now, as a result of increasing tensions between our countries.

If perceptions are that important, what can be done in order to sharpen them?

There are no easy answers. I could put it this way: we must do just what we were doing during the years of détente, but do more of it and do it more consistently. We should aim at the creation of a normal political environment to facilitate rational, rather than emotional, perceptions of events. We should concentrate on hard work to root out prejudices and preconceptions. We should promote an objective attitude and a permanent interest in the other country—its people, culture, and political life. And, of course, we should encourage the development of contacts and a permanent dialogue at various levels. In other words, we must continue what we began when we chose the way of détente. And we must overcome those obstacles that stand in our way.

Chapter 2 | On the History of Soviet-American Relations

Let's continue discussing the possibilities of the coexistence of countries with basically differing social systems.

As I told you already, I do not think that differences between our two societies create insurmountable difficulties for maintaining normal and fruitful relations. Let us recall the history of Russian-American relations before 1917. The old Russia and United States were very different from each other in terms of social and political organization. Take the late eighteenth century. On the one side there was feudal, czarist Russia and on the other side there was the young American Republic, born out of one of the first bourgeois democratic revolutions in the world. And who maintained what may have been the best relations with the newly born United States of America? It was Russia. Those relations were based on properly understood mutual interest. Later, during the Civil War in the United States, the czar even sent the navy to demonstrate Russian support for President Abraham Lincoln. Russian warships showed up in New York and San Francisco. Obviously, the czar was not motivated by any sympathy with the plight of the American slaves. He had his own foreign policy objectives in mind, which led him to support the United States. But the fact is still there. Alas, I cannot say that Americans reciprocated when we had our Revolution in October 1917.

How would you describe American attitudes to the October Revolution?

Most Americans at the time were much more provincial than they are now and simply did not know what had happened here, or had only the vaguest idea. Among the more politically conscious intellectuals and workers, there was great interest and sympathy. An American newsman, John Reed, symbolized that attitude in his eyewitness account of the Revolution, called *Ten Days That Shook the World*, which remains one of the best-written books about those historic events. As to the United States government and the broader American political elite, including the media, the attitude was one of unmitigated hostility. To say nothing of the American Right. Even within the more "enlightened" factions of the political leadership in the United States, our new society was looked upon as a child born out of wedlock, bound to be treated as a bastard of history forever. Thus the basis was laid for a long-term American attitude toward socialism and Soviet Russia.

You mean it still prevails?

Yes, that traditional attitude still plays a part in present American behavior toward us. Ironically, it was the American Declaration of Independence that gave an early and very definite formulation to the thesis that each nation had an inherent right to revolution, a right to rise up in arms and carry out the necessary changes in its social and political system. But in 1917, the wisdom of the Founding Fathers was not drawn upon in formulating the United States' response to the Russian Revolution.

It would have hardly mattered to us just what the American government thought about our Revolution, had not their hostility almost immediately materialized into action. The United States took an active part in the coalition of nations that tried to strangle our Revolution. American troops participated in the invasion of the northern and eastern parts of our country. More important, during our civil war, they rendered significant assistance to our enemies, including supplying loans and delivery of arms. They openly supported counterrevolutionary leaders like Admiral Kolchak, Ataman Semyonov, and others. The United States spent some $4 billion trying to unseat the new Russian government.

But some Sovietologists claim that this new government virtually invited Western hostility by threatening worldwide revolution and breaking off many of Russia's relations with the outside world.

As for the notion of worldwide revolution, I have already dealt with Lenin's position on that point. As for the changes the Revolution brought about in Russia's foreign relations, it should be kept in mind that czarist Russia, while being a colonial power, was itself a semicolony of the West.

During World War I millions of Russians were used by the Entente as cannon fodder in its imperial rivalry with the German kaiser and his allies. The Russian people had a strong feeling that they were being used, exploited, and were dying for a cause that was wholly unjust and contrary to their vital needs and interests. That feeling was one of the main factors that caused the 1917 Revolution. Therefore, among the very first things the Lenin government did was to take Russia out of the war and abolish the forms of semicolonial dependence on France, Britain, and other countries. This did not mean that we turned away from the world or were refusing to deal with it until and unless it turned socialist. We wanted to deal with the world as it was. But we wanted to deal with it on equal terms, to secure our sovereignty over our own economy and our resources, and to have a foreign policy based on our national interests, rather than the interest rates of foreign banks. In other words, we strove for a democratization of our relations with the West. We changed our relations with Asian countries, too. Among other things, we renounced all the czarist government's colonial claims in Asia.

But did the revolutionary government of Russia express in clear terms its desire to establish relations with other countries?

Certainly. At the very beginning of the Revolution, to be precise, on its second day, we issued an appeal to all countries, including the United States, to end the war and start peace negotiations. Soon afterward, we offered to establish normal relations with the United States. That request was followed in May of 1918 with the proposal to establish economic ties on the basis of mutual benefit. Lenin sent a letter through the chairman of the American Red Cross mission in Russia, Colonel Robbins, outlining his plan for giving the United States trade concessions and establishing other commercial relations. But there was no reply.

Our trade representative to the United States, L. Martens, started active negotiations with American businessmen on economic relations between the two countries. By the end of 1919 he established contacts with about a thousand firms in thirty-two American states. Martens got the impression that a significant part of the American business community favored trade with Soviet Russia. A number of contracts were signed, but the United States government intervened, and Martens was expelled from America as "an undesirable alien."

Was that the time that Armand Hammer, chairman of the Occidental Petroleum Company, arrived in Russia?

Yes, he was among the first Americans to establish business relations with the new Russia. He came on his own initiative, and we welcomed him. Later we issued a broad invitation to other American businessmen to come and open up economic relations with us. The estimate was that business with foreign companies could reach the volume of some $3 billion.

That is more than the annual volume of business between the USSR and the United States in recent years!

Yes, even if you disregard the fact that the greenback is now worth but a fraction of what it was then. The potential for our trade with the West was big. From the early days of our Revolution, it was our official policy to develop economic relations with all countries, including the United States. Lenin even stressed at the time, "especially with the United States." There were several reasons why he put special emphasis on the United States. The size and efficiency of American industries was an important consideration. There was also the fact that our relations with Europe those days were more strained than with the United States. I think Lenin also had in mind the political importance of well-developed Soviet-American economic relations, expecting them to become an essential factor for world stability and peace.

What other American businessmen received concessions from the Soviet government in those early days?

There were quite a few, including the Harriman family.

Did W. Averell Harriman have financial interests in the Soviet Union?

His family firm operated a massive manganese mining concession.

But the U.S. government's attitude toward Moscow remained hostile.

Yes, indeed. The United States took part in all coalitions that tried to follow Winston Churchill's advice at the time: strangle the baby in its crib. When the military interventions failed to accomplish that aim, the West adopted a policy of economic boycott and diplomatic nonrecognition. That was just another, if more passive, form of the same nonacceptance of the Soviet state. The basic presumption remained the same: there can be no common ground between the West and the Soviet Union, whose very existence, as U.S. Secretary of State Bainbridge Colby alleged in 1920, was dependent on the overthrow of the governments in all other great civilized nations. He also said that there were no coinciding interests that could justify an establishment of normal relations with such an antagonist.

But did Soviet leaders not look upon the United States as an antagonist as well?

Clearly, we could have made a much stronger case out of the American hostility and aggressiveness against us, but the Soviet government did not stop its efforts to normalize relations between the two countries. Let me quote from the response to Secretary Colby's statements, by Georgi Chicherin, who was then our Commissar for Foreign Affairs: "Mr. Colby is very mistaken in his belief that our countries can only have normal relations if a capitalist system prevails in Russia. We hold, on the contrary, that it is essential to the interests of both Russia and North America to establish between them even now, despite the fact that their social and political systems are antithetical, completely proper, lawful, peaceful, and friendly relations, necessary for the development of commerce between them and for the satisfaction of the economic needs of both countries."[1] However, it was to take quite a few years before American political leaders reached similar conclusions.

It all hardly looked like the enthusiastic beginning of a new relationship.

I was speaking about official policy, but it was only part of a broader picture. We were aware that many Americans held different views. There were many examples of American goodwill, of a realistic approach, and of genuinely generous efforts. We even received some material help from the American people, and we have not forgotten it. In the early twenties, at a time of starvation and great economic strain in our country, about ten thousand Americans came here through the Society for Technical Aid to Soviet Russia. They came to help rebuild our country. American and Soviet workers and specialists working side by side helped build farms and other enterprises. Substantial funds were raised for that purpose in the United States.

Were those Americans also threatened with the loss of their passports?

Actually, they took great personal risks, considering the anticommunist hysteria in the United States at that time. But the feelings of solidarity and the great interest in the unique Russian revolutionary experiment were too strong. At the same time, more and more people from the American business community were finding it profitable to deal with Soviet Russia. We offered them contracts on good terms, and they came. The total number of American businessmen that dealt with us at that time reached two thousand. By the early thirties, some forty American companies were operating here, including such giants as the Ford Motor Company and General Electric. Several thousand American workers and specialists were working here. Among those who helped construct our first major automobile plant in the city of Gorky were Walter and Victor Reuther, who later became prominent in the American labor movement. Some Americans received high decorations of our state, like Mr. H. Cooper, who assisted us in building our first large-scale hydroelectric power station.

In 1931, no less than 40 percent of the total American export of industrial equipment went to the Soviet Union. That same year, we invited some four thousand specialists to come and work here, and received over one hundred thousand applications. It was a bright page indeed in the history of our cooperation. Common sense and concurrent economic interests proved stronger than any desire to inflict maximum damage on each other during difficult times. After all, we did help ease the strains of depression in the United States, while American businessmen and specialists did contribute to building up our economy.

There are millions of unemployed in the United States now. Why not place an ad in the New York Times *for manpower to work in Siberia?*

I can imagine the uproar such a move would cause, given the peculiar image of Siberia in the West. But speaking seriously, our proposals go further and deeper than that. We want to remove all obstacles that prevent due development of trade and economic relations between our two countries. This alone would provide for many thousands of new jobs in the United States. And, of course, in a demilitarized economy, which would be possible under real détente, there would also be much more employment than in the present one. The combined economic consequences of détente would considerably improve the overall employment situation in the United States and other Western countries.

But let me return to history. There was a good prelude to future détente in the twenties and the early thirties, but that prelude did not last very long. The year 1931 brought difficulties for trade relations. A campaign got under way in the United States about "freedom of religion" in the Soviet Union. It was quite similar to what we have seen in recent years. There was another campaign about "the threat of Soviet dumping," followed by the introduction of discriminatory trade measures against us. U.S.-Soviet trade plummeted.

But then at last came the establishment of diplomatic ties in 1933. That was a turning point, wasn't it?

Yes, in at least two respects. First, it laid the groundwork for normal relations in the future. Second, it meant a new departure in the attitude of the White House, which, after sixteen years of nonrecognition, finally ceased to behave as if the Soviet Union did not exist. There was an exchange of letters between President Franklin D. Roosevelt and Commissar for Foreign Affairs Maxim Maximovich Litvinov. At the insistence of Washington, both sides gave a solemn pledge not to interfere in each other's internal affairs. Moreover, both sides pledged to restrain any organizations controlled by or dependent on either of the two governments, from any direct or covert actions damaging the other nation's internal peace, welfare, or security. Among such forbidden practices were agitation and propaganda aimed at a forceful change of either country's political and social order.

It's worthwhile to remember that, for today Washington considers subversive activities against us quite normal, for instance, the activities of Radio Liberty and Radio Free Europe. The United States has been engaged in a whole range of covert or semicovert operations against the Soviet Union in violation of that bilateral agreement of recognition between our two states.

Are you implying that the Soviet Union undertakes nothing of the kind against the United States?

In full accordance with the provisions of the 1933 document I mentioned, we do not encourage any acts "overt or covert, liable in any way whatsoever to injure the tranquility, property, order, or security" of the United States. Nor do we engage in "agitation or propaganda having as an aim the violation of the territorial integrity of the United States, its territories or possessions, or the bringing about by force of a change in the political order of the whole, or any part of, the United States. . . ."[2]

The Second World War worked in favor of closer ties.

No doubt. The war itself was a truly remarkable period in Soviet-American relations. Those were years of close cooperation between our political leaders and military establishments, of an unprecedented upsurge of friendly and even fraternal feelings between our peoples. All this, I think, left its mark in national memories. Americans, at that time, especially those involved in combat, were most appreciative of the giant Soviet war effort. I remember an excerpt from an order of one of the American field commanders in Germany, quoted by C. L. Sulzberger in his memoirs: "Millions of Russian soldiers and civilians died to save our skins. Just remember that. If propaganda causes you to hate Russians, stop and think. They died for you, too."[3] It took years of cold war and intense anti-Soviet brainwashing to erase those feelings.

But there were shadows over the honeymoon.

Of course, there were some problems and difficulties. Despite the numerous promises, the opening of the second front in Western Europe had been delayed for two years at a great cost to Soviet lives. The delays naturally produced some bitter feelings among our people. There were also some behind-the-scenes negotiations between the United States and Nazi Germany. Allen Dulles was talking with the Nazis in Bern, Switzerland, and there were other contacts in Ankara, Turkey, as one of our historians documented recently. Looking back, it's also difficult to shrug off the fact that the development of the A-bomb had been kept secret from us. But the overall balance of our relations was definitely positive, and it could have served as a basis for improved relations after World War II.

Instead we moved almost immediately into the Cold War.

The Cold War has become the subject of numerous books, and many others are yet to appear. It remains a hot topic, and our perspective here is quite different from the dominant American view that blames the Soviet Union for the Cold War. We feel that the main responsibility lies squarely on the United States and Britain. Incidentally, that fact has been amply documented by the so-called "revisionist" historians in the United States in the last two decades.

Are you familiar with the neo-orthodox critique of that school?

Yes, all orthodoxies die hard. But I would not like to intrude into this family quarrel among American historians. I can only explain how the whole situation looked from our point of view.

Did not the Cold War really gain speed when the Soviet Union rejected the Marshall Plan?

As seen from Moscow, the Cold War started much earlier. By the spring of 1945, some weeks prior to the end of World War II, we noticed changes in American policies. President Harry S Truman took a different position from Roosevelt in many areas of Soviet-American relations. Lend-Lease supplies were abruptly terminated the very day the war ended, and some ships already on the way to the USSR were turned back. The promise of a massive reconstruction loan was broken. And, of course, there was the atomic bombing of Hiroshima and Nagasaki, which in our view was not the last salvo of World War II, but rather the first one heralding the Cold War. It was fired to intimidate both the enemy and the ally. Or, as Secretary of War Henry Stimson put it in his diary, "to persuade Russia to play ball."

Next, and also prior to the Marshall Plan, Winston Churchill delivered his notorious speech at Fulton, Missouri, which actually contained the formal declaration of the Cold War. It should be remembered that Churchill's "Iron Curtain" speech was publicly sanctioned by the president of the United States, Harry Truman, who was present at the occasion. Then, in February of 1947, the Truman Doctrine was announced, which called for a worldwide anticommunist crusade. Such was the political context in which the Marshall Plan was announced, and that context revealed the plan's true meaning. Later, a version was fabricated that we had rejected "a fair deal," choosing instead to intensify the Cold War. But when the recently declassified American documents on the Marshall Plan are examined, it will become clear that the offer was deliberately calculated to be rejected by the USSR. American officials were even fearful that the Soviet Union would agree to enter the plan. Privately, James Forrestal was saying at the time, ". . . the most disastrous thing would be if they did [come in]." Charles Bohlen confessed much later that they had taken "a hell of a big gamble" in not explicitly excluding Russia.[4]

In other words, you definitely felt hostility from the United States after 1945?

We realized the cards had completely changed. We actually even reckoned with a threat of war from Washington.

In Western Europe, after 1945, fear of a Soviet invasion was real. For this reason my family moved to South Africa and I came to Yale University in 1948 to take classes in international relations.

Fears of this kind were there, I imagine. Partially, they were rooted in the very unstable psychological climate of postwar Europe, which had gone through a terrible ordeal between 1939 and 1945. But the major reason for those fears was the "Soviet threat" campaign launched right after World War II to erase feelings of goodwill toward the USSR. Those feelings were genuine and widespread, for wasn't it the Soviet Union that played the decisive role in liberating Europe from the Nazis? There is a very disturbing parallel here with what is going on in the West today, when many irrational prejudices and fears are being exploited again for the same purpose and by the same means. And also like before, the purveyors of the scare, trying to mobilize the public and the elite around an anti-Soviet consensus, may end up succumbing to these false fears themselves. As far as postwar perceptions of the "Soviet threat" are concerned, I'd like to stress that, even allowing for Western fears, we had much more reason to feel threatened. And those feelings were proven quite well founded later, when the real American war plans became known.

War plans? Peace had just arrived.

Well, it makes revealing and painful reading even today when we can see in black and white that some of our worst suspicions about United States intentions were more than justified. By the end of 1945, top United States brass had begun preparing for a nuclear attack on the Soviet Union. Twenty of our largest cities, populated by thirteen million people, were selected as targets for the dropping of 196 A-bombs in a first strike.

We knew nothing about it in Western Europe, and most people there are unaware of these plans even today.

Still they were quite real, as shown by recently declassified U.S. government papers, such as Report No. 329 of the Joint Intelligence Committee of the Joint Chiefs of Staff, dated December 1945. This, and subsequent reports of this kind, served as a basis for elaborate war planning between 1946 and 1949 under the code names "Charioteer," "Double Star," "Fleetwood," "Trojan," and some others.

The war preparations climaxed in 1949 with "Dropshot," which was a plan for an all-out war against the Soviet Union by means of all NATO forces supported by some Middle Eastern and Asian countries. Actually, it was a blueprint for World War III. Not only was "Dropshot" a scheme for atomic destruction—"atomizing,". as it was routinely called—of our country by some three hundred bomb strikes, the plan also provided for the occupation of our country by American troops and the subsequent eradication of the Soviet system. Diligent Washington strategists even elaborated rules of behavior for future regimes on our territory.[5] A Carthaginian peace was in store for yesterday's ally, which had lost over twenty million lives to save the world from fascism.

It sounds insane, but, after all, it is a matter of record that the great war hero Winston Churchill suggested at the time to blast the USSR with nuclear bombs.

Yes, he did, on at least two occasions. The first time he made this suggestion was soon after the war, as recorded by Alan Brooke in his diary.

Henry Cabot Lodge speaks of a similar episode in his memoirs.

Back in those days, we received many such signals and had to take them very seriously. Those threats were not merely words.

Could it have been just wishful thinking on the part of the military drawing up these war plans?

Some of it was wishful thinking, no doubt. But there was also a real policy, which spoke louder than words. There was a gigantic arms race, the building up of NATO, and the encirclement of our nation with military bases and first-strike bomber forces. If those monstrous plans did remain on paper, we don't think it was so much because reason finally prevailed in Washington, as because our growing power, reflected, above all, the rapid termination of the American atomic monopoly. The U.S. government did consider a preventive nuclear war on the USSR as a serious option, but had to reject it when it became clear they could not win it. In 1949, a plan for a nuclear first strike by the U.S. Strategic Air Command, called "Trojan," was put aside as unrealistic. The National Security Council document NSC-68 described preventive war against the Soviet Union as impossible to win. "A powerful blow could be delivered upon the Soviet Union," it said, "but it is estimated that these operations alone would not force or induce the Kremlin to capitulate. . . ."[6] There were strong doubts about "Dropshot," as well.

Perhaps it was felt that they had not enough of such bombs.

Not only this. There was also deep apprehension that instead of a nuclear blitzkrieg the United States would have been in for an interminable and exhausting war destroying the whole world. So, by that time, it should have become evident that a military preponderance is of limited value in a nuclear age.

Apparently, this is still not clear.

Well, at that time Washington chose to modify somewhat the methods of cold-war policy; but the goals were left intact. Putting aside a preventive war for the time being, they adopted a doctrine of "containment" as the foundation of United States policy toward the USSR in the Cold War. In essence, that was a strategy aimed at the destruction of our political system by means of applying constant pressure to us at all points. Among other pressures, the arms race was regarded as a way to wear the Soviets down. Since I can hardly compete in the exposition of this doctrine with its architects, let me just quote some key passages from the official bible of containment, NSC-68, which was issued in 1950 and declassified in 1975.

The major instrument of this policy was to be an overwhelming military superiority. "Without superior aggregate military strength, in being and readily mobilizable," it flatly stated, "a policy of 'containment'—which is in effect a policy of calculated and gradual coercion—is no more than a policy bluff."[7] It also stated that, until such a superiority was achieved, any negotiations with the Soviet Union "could be only a tactic . . . desirable . . . to gain public support for the program [of a military buildup]."[8]

Among other means proposed and then actively used were "overt psychological warfare, calculated to encourage mass defections from Soviet allegiance," "intensification of affirmative and timely measures and operations by covert means in the fields of economic warfare and political and psychological warfare with a view to fomenting and supporting unrest and revolt in selected strategic satellite countries. . . ."[9]

But plans often remain plans. Not always are such wild ideas necessarily meant to be put to the test.

Oh, no. They certainly were not mere fantasies, but real working guidelines. We did go through this kind of treatment by the United States during the fifties. Another interesting aspect of NSC-68 was an obsession with preserving an innocent defensive look while carrying out this aggressive course. "In any announcement of policy and in the character of the measures adopted," NSC-68 calmly suggested, "emphasis should be given to the essentially defensive character and care should be taken to minimize, so far as possible, unfavorable domestic and foreign reactions." All those means were directed toward the ultimate goal: the retraction of Soviet influence and "a fundamental change in the nature of the Soviet system."[10]

Zbigniew Brzezinski seemed to center his diplomacy on trying to influence internal developments in the Soviet Union.

Brzezinski's reputation as a stubborn advocate of such a policy has been well established. He contributed to its formulation in the past, and, as can well be presumed, did not abandon such efforts when in government. This theme of "remaking" the Soviet state by means of interference in our domestic affairs, doctrinized in the NSC-68, ran through many words and deeds of the Carter administration and has been readily picked up by its successors.

Ambassador Anatoly Dobrynin indicated to Henry Kissinger that between 1959 and 1963 a number of opportunities were lost to improve relations between the superpowers.[11]

I would fully agree with the ambassador. It was in the late fifties, after Sputnik, that many Americans began to realize that a nuclear war would be unthinkable, a suicide. Some steps were taken to break the ice of the Cold War. I am thinking of Soviet Premier Khrushchev's visit to the United States in 1959, which was to be followed by a visit by President Dwight D. Eisenhower to the USSR in 1960. Unfortunately, those efforts did not succeed.

You mean following the U-2 incident and the shooting down of Gary Powers over the USSR? This incident has been described by some analysts as a deliberate effort by the Central Intelligence Agency to prevent Eisenhower from having a successful meeting with Khrushchev in Paris.

I am not aware of CIA schemes in this respect, except that, as recently reported, they were installing some reconnaissance devices aboard Air Force One, in case Eisenhower's visit to Moscow materialized. The U-2 flight was sanctioned by the president himself, who also tried to cover it up in a most clumsy way, which torpedoed the Paris summit conference. The whole episode, while it seemed somewhat foolish and almost accidental, was very revealing: the administration rated routine intelligence gathering higher than a chance to improve relations with the USSR. That opportunity was lost, though it might have led to significant progress.

Other opportunities were missed during the first two years of the Kennedy administration, which was largely immobilized by its "missile gap" start and the Bay of Pigs adventure in Cuba. It took the Kennedy administration the shock of the Cuban missile crisis to start reassessing its cold-war posture toward the Soviet Union. It resulted in the Test Ban Treaty and some other positive steps. But then this process was abruptly interrupted by the president's assassination.

In the final analysis, there is no reasonable alternative to peaceful coexistence. But each relapse in the realization of this cardinal fact of international relations can be tremendously costly. The experience of the sixties is clear proof of this. In the early seventies we did manage to achieve the kind of breakthrough in our relations that we had been seeking unsuccessfully in the late fifties and early sixties. But a whole decade was lost, and it was a very costly loss. It brought a tremendous military buildup. The Cuban missile crisis pushed humanity to the brink of war.

Dean Rusk said "eyeball to eyeball."

Yes. Then the war in Southeast Asia began, which not only caused a national crisis in the United States itself, but also disturbed the international situation for a long time to come. Then there was the Six Day war in the Middle East in 1967. We still live in the protracted aftermath of that conflict, continuing for some fifteen years now. The Middle East remains a hotbed of constant trouble and there is nothing in sight that would resemble a suitable settlement. There were some lesser crises, too. Much of these could have been avoided in a general climate of détente.

But after the tension of the sixties, things did improve in the early seventies.

They certainly did. I would not like to minimize the importance of those events. That was a real moment of truth for United States foreign policy. The entire framework of policies designed in the late forties and early fifties began to show serious weaknesses; it was too divorced from reality, too irrelevant to the real problems confronting the United States and the world. It began to dawn on many Americans in the late sixties and early seventies that United States foreign policy had too often been counterproductive.

After all these fluctuations in relations, it looks indeed in the 1980s as if we're right back to the Cold War days of the fifties.

Yes, it does look this way. After all the traumatic experiences that should have taught everyone some solid lessons, the government of the United States is trying to talk the same language and play the same games all over again. But certainly, times have changed. I am sure that history cannot and will not repeat itself. We cannot afford to act as if we had forgotten the experiences of the past, let alone ignore them.

Eugene Rostow, in an interview before he became director of the ACDA, pointed out to me that American power had indeed diminished, for instance, to the extent that, whereas President Eisenhower had been able to send the marines into Lebanon in 1958, Washington was unable to repeat such a performance now.

The United States has not lost this capacity through any weakening of its military power. American military power has been steadily growing since 1958. But the deep changes in the international and domestic American environment have made such operations very costly. The Vietnam war made it quite clear. But now, Rostow's complaints notwithstanding, we see a different trend. Intense efforts are being undertaken to "unlearn" the lessons of Vietnam and bring back military interventionism as an instrument of United States policy.

   The cold-war policy being resurrected now was shaped in the late forties and early fifties, ostensibly as a response to the alleged "threat" to American interests—then solemnly identified with those of "the free world"—coming from a single enemy, the Soviet Union. Washington proclaimed that the goal was to be reached by means of the arms race, military bases and alliances, an economic blockade against us, psychological warfare, and other subversive activities. All these presumptions were flawed from the very beginning, for the "Soviet threat" was a hoax. Eventually, many people in America came to understand that their real problems had very little to do with the Soviet Union.

   Today, while these problems have multiplied, there is reemerging the primitive view of the USSR as the headquarters of the devil and the ultimate source of all American troubles. But if the United States were to take the most hostile course toward us, would this prevent another Iran or another Nicaragua? Would it help decrease unemployment, solve the energy problem, strengthen the dollar, or stop inflation? And most important, would such a policy contribute to the security of the United States?

It is a fact of life that United States military superiority over the Soviet Union is gone forever and will never return. It is simply astounding to find this goal resurrected as official American policy. And what would military superiority bring anyway? The development of ever newer types of mass-destruction weapons has obliterated many traditional concepts, and in fact puts in question the very idea of using military force for rational political purposes.

There is also a long-term change in relationships between the United States and its allies. American allies have become much stronger economically and less dependent on Washington politically. They demand that their interests be taken into account. And some of the overseas adventures undertaken by the United States have caused serious apprehension among them.

Vietnam?

That was just one adventure, but it had very serious consequences. Recently, we have seen more complications in relations between the United States and its allies on what may be the most important problems of foreign policy.

Henry Kissinger stresses, however, that no West German leader can afford to conduct a policy of which Washington would strongly disapprove. [12]

I would not argue with Kissinger over this. Indeed, the United States still enjoys a sort of hegemony within NATO. But wasn't it Kissinger who wrote in the same memoirs how cautious Washington had to be in regard to Willy Brandt's Ostpolitik, even though Americans did not particularly like that policy? Of course, America's relations with her allies have undergone some important changes. Where at one time Americans could just command, they now have to use politics and diplomacy.

Undoubtedly, Richard Nixon and Henry Kissinger had their share of setbacks in relations with other Western nations.

Yes, and when Carter ran for president, he and his team even made it one of their important campaign issues that Republicans had failed in West-West relations. But it turned out that the Carter administration was not very successful either in this respect. The same may be said about its successors. It looks like the allies are far from eager to follow the United States into a second cold war. They are making many sounds calculated to please Washington, but generally are rather reluctant to follow through with actions.

There are many indications that the allies' confidence in the United States has been undermined. But certainly, it is still an asymmetrical relationship. If the United States really wants to or needs to, it can probably compel the allies into obedience on a given issue. Kissinger's probably got a point here, although such attempts may become more and more costly both to the United States and her allies.

Summarizing your analysis, what the United States has been trying to adapt to includes the loss of America's military superiority, the new role of the Third World, and changes in West-West relations.

I would like to add one more development: the changes that took place inside the United States. From the early forties to the mid-sixties, foreign policy had an unquestioned priority in American public affairs. It was logical in a way, for that period had begun with a qualitative expansion of the American world role. After the New Deal and World War II, the whole context of American public policy was largely determined by the process of building and maintaining the empire. This outward thrust had a temporary tranquilizing impact on the domestic scene, but not for long. Instead of stabilizing America, the Cold War crusade at a certain stage became the catalyst for a major domestic crisis. Domestic problems demanded urgent and serious attention and called for a reallocation of resources, a deemphasis on global involvement, and a more reasonable foreign policy. The domestic crisis of the late sixties and early seventies provided an important background for new thinking on foreign policy. No real consensus was formed in terms of concrete policy prescriptions, but the overall trend in thinking was unmistakable: American policy had to change.

And Nixon started changing it. But are you saying that it didn't really matter who occupied the White House in 1969, a Republican or a Democrat, since some adaptation to the new realities was unavoidable?

Well, any president would have had to try to adapt in one way or another. I do agree with the notion that it does not matter much in policy terms whether a U.S. president is a Republican or Democrat, though some Democrats, John Kenneth Galbraith for one, think that Republicans have a better reputation in handling relations with the Soviet Union. It seems that there are sometimes more important internal political differences among the Republicans and Democrats than between the two parties themselves.

The overall correlation of political forces is very important, and that correlation was favorable to détente at that time. It does not mean, of course, that one need not take into account the personality cast at the top of government, particularly the personal characteristics of the president: his political views, value system, moral qualities, psychology, even his temper. All those things may often be more important than his party affiliation, especially nowadays, when the traditional party distinctions are being blurred.

But do Marxists attach special importance to personality?

Certainly. According to Marxism, the tide of historical events is determined basically and in the long run by objective factors and conditions, economic, social, cultural, etc. But in the day-to-day decisions on the highest state level, when this or that option is chosen within the broad, objectively determined context, the personality of the policy maker can play a significant, sometimes even a crucial, role. I can imagine situations when it could mean a difference between war and peace.

Did it surprise you that Richard Nixon, who based his entire political career on anticommunism, would preside over the policy of détente?

Without trying to look more perceptive than I or my colleagues in Moscow were, I would say that to a certain degree we expected it. Let me remind you that we had just started work at this institute in 1968, when Nixon ran for president. I remember the first articles and analytical papers prepared by the staff of the institute. There was a clear consensus among scholars here, shared by specialists in our government, that some important changes in Soviet-American relations were imminent, regardless of who would be in power in Washington.

How did you reach that conclusion?

Well, we analyzed the major objective factors that I've already referred to—the changes in both international and domestic American situations. Among the more fluid developments, we found the way Republican politics had evolved in 1967–68 rather suggestive. Here was a party, that, by veering sharply to the Right in the early sixties, provided a backdrop and a pressure lever for Lyndon Johnson's policy of escalation of the war in Vietnam. However, when it had become clear that the war could not be won, many Republicans, including Nixon, who actually inherited the Goldwater movement, began looking for alternatives. In terms of public policy, they were beginning to realize that the way out of the crisis lay in revising the broad context of East-West relations, in trying to negotiate that context with the Soviet Union. That shift in Republican thinking was an indication that a broad consensus was emerging in the United States power elite in favor of an important change. In terms of partisan politics, the GOP understood very well that it could only hope to regain power as "a party of peace."

Still, it remains peculiar that the beginning of détente, the first visit of an American president to the USSR, the first SALT agreement, and similar developments are connected with Nixon's name.

Trying to estimate the precise contribution of a personality to a given historical event is one of the most difficult tasks for a historian. It fell on Nixon and Kissinger to lead the United States government when progress along the road of détente began. We give them their due. Of course, there has been a whole stream of commentary in America about how paradoxical it was that none other than Richard Nixon, the red-baiter and witch hunter, who practiced McCarthyism even before Joe McCarthy got into the business, started to shift from confrontation to negotiation in U.S.-Soviet relations. In a way, Nixon's reputation certainly facilitated the shift to détente, for no one in his right mind would suspect Dick Nixon, the instigator of the Alger Hiss case and the kitchen debater in Moscow in 1959, of trying to sell America down the river. Hubert Humphrey may not have been able, had he been elected in 1968, to appease the conservatives as effectively. But this does not mean that there was any "new Nixon." We never bought that. Nixon stayed the same; it was the situation that changed. I think Nixon has always been, first and foremost, after political success: to get elected and reelected and get himself a prominent place in twentieth-century history.

In the late forties and fifties, Nixon saw the road to success in rabid anticommunism and anti-Sovietism. In the late sixties and early seventies, however, he was enough of a realist to see that a different tactic was needed if he were to get to the White House. This time, it was "negotiation instead of confrontation," "a generation of peace," détente with the Soviet Union and other socialist nations.

Nixon was clever enough to recognize he had to shift gears. Was he more successful in coping with the big changes on the international chess board than his successors?

If you take the final results, he definitely was, if only because the political situation in the U.S. pushed him very strongly in that direction. But still, the process of adjustment even then was far from being any smooth and ready acceptance of the new limits on American power. There was quite a lot of bucking the tide, double-dealing, trying to win time. Nixon came to power on the promise to end the Vietnam war, but he prolonged that war for five more years and even broadened it by his invasion of Cambodia. It took a lot of Vietnamese, Cambodian, and American lives, and a lot of turmoil in American society, to compel Nixon to fulfill his pledge. Generally speaking, Nixon's policies in most of the Third World retained a basic cold-war pattern. Latin America, and particularly Chile, are clear examples.

Iran is another case in point.

Of course, active American interference in Iran's affairs started as early as 1953, when the CIA helped overthrow the constitutional government of Premier Mohammad Mossadegh in Tehran. But it was precisely during the Nixon-Kissinger years that the United States set about turning Iran into a major stronghold of American power in the Middle East by enormous arms sales and other means. Doing that, the United States was literally laying a time bomb under its own positions in the region, which was to go off sooner or later. The revolution in Iran was the inevitable result of this long-time pattern of abuse of force by the United States in Iran and in the Middle East as a whole. The amazing thing is that the defeat of the cold-war policy in Iran has been used as a pretext to revive the same bankrupt policy. To go back to the early seventies, there were many manifestations of cold-war inertia in American foreign policy at that time. But there was also an important shift in American perceptions of the world situation and, step by step, in practical policy.

And Vietnam played the decisive role in bringing that shift about?

The American failure in Vietnam played a very serious role. But I think the process was more complicated and prolonged. Indications of a new global situation, implying the end of American supremacy and the necessity of coming to terms with the new realities, were numerous long prior to the Vietnam fiasco. Take, for instance, the Cuban missile crisis of 1962. Although strategic parity between the United States and the Soviet Union did not exist at that time, the crisis clearly demonstrated that the United States could not simply dictate its terms and do whatever it wished. The situation in Europe also developed in such a way as to call for greater American restraint and flexibility. Had not the old United States policy been bound by so many traditions, prejudices, and, most important, by the powerful interests that so often prevented America from facing reality, the reappraisal could have taken place before the Vietnam war, thus making it altogether avoidable. But, alas, it took the tragedy of Vietnam to make certain truths evident to both the public and the policy makers.

Who, from the Soviet point of view, is considered the most impressive American president of the last half century?

Doubtlessly, Franklin D. Roosevelt.

Because he extended diplomatic recognition to the Soviet Union and became your ally in the antifascist coalition during World War II?

These are, naturally, very important reasons. Any nation, like any human being, tends to judge others by the way it is treated by them. It may be especially true in this particular case, since here we deal with an attitude toward the Soviet Union and its people during the most trying times of their history. Still, our estimate of Roosevelt as the most outstanding president of the past decades isn't explained solely by his impact on Soviet-American relations, which did reach a peak during his presidency. A lot has been written in our country about that period of American history, including a number of books on Roosevelt personally. A great number of our people are quite familiar with his life and actions. I think he is also appreciated for the New Deal, which significantly alleviated the hardships of the American people in the wake of the Great Depression. And, of course, he is greatly respected for his generally consistent antifascist policy during World War II.

But if Roosevelt had lived a bit longer the Cold War would have begun under his administration, and he might have been viewed in the Soviet Union differently. The Soviet attitude toward Winston Churchill did change after 1945.

Churchill was viewed differently from Roosevelt throughout World War II. He had a long anti-Soviet record behind him. Roosevelt always had a much more favorable image here. And I am not at all sure that, had Roosevelt lived, the situation would have developed the way it did. There is no doubt that after V-Day, when our common foe had been crushed, relations were bound to change. Many difficulties, contradictions, and tensions were inevitable, given our disagreements over the organization of the postwar world and different attitudes toward the process of revolutionary change stimulated by the destruction of fascism. Still, I personally think the Cold War was avoidable. And if there was a Western leader able to contribute to such a development, it was Franklin D. Roosevelt. However, this is an opinion that can never be verified. History does not recognize the subjunctive mood.

FDR apparently remains a controversial figure in America, judging by the way his centennial was observed there in February 1982.

Yes, the official attitude of the U.S. government to that event was rather peculiar. The Reagan administration even rejected such a modest proposal as putting up FDR photo exhibits in U.S. embassies around the world. If you compare Washington's apparent unwillingness to remind people of the Roosevelt legacy in 1982 to the lavish celebrations of, say, the Teddy Roosevelt or Woodrow Wilson anniversaries, FDR, indeed, begins to look like a controversial figure by today's Washington standards.

But Ronald Reagan does invoke Roosevelt's name from time to time in his speeches.

Yes, but usually in a profoundly anti-Rooseveltian context. Or he says that he voted for Roosevelt four times, but each time hoped Roosevelt would change his policies.

Do you think such an attitude has ideological reasons?

Of course. The brand of politics and ideology that gained an upper hand in Washington in 1980 is rooted in the anti–New Deal tradition dating back to the Alf Landon campaign and the Liberty League. The American Right in the last five decades has been obsessed with what it regarded as "the Roosevelt revolution," working hard to undo its legacy. The Right has certainly whittled down that legacy, but the Reagan administration is seen by the right wing as the first real chance to do away with it.

How about Harry Truman?

I would say he may have one of the worst images here of all the postwar U.S. presidents, which is understandable if you take into account the sharp reversal in U.S. policy over which he presided.

Jimmy Carter put on his White House desk the Truman sign "The buck stops here." Some Americans rank Truman among the greatest.

I received the same impression on my very first visit to the United States in 1969. It somewhat puzzled me then. First, I tended to think that "Give 'em hell, Harry!" was a popular American slogan because it expressed habitual American arrogance. But then I came to the opinion that this attitude toward Truman might have grown from American nostalgia for those unique early postwar years. Everything seemed to Americans to be so simple and clear, durable and attainable back in those days. Only a few sensed that such a situation was due to temporary and exceptional circumstances.

The second most popular American president in the Soviet Union in the last fifty years?

I would say John F. Kennedy.

In spite of the Bay of Pigs and the missile crisis?

Yes, and even in spite of a new mad round in the arms race launched under the phony pretext of a "missile gap." Yes, all those blunders were made, but Kennedy was statesman enough to realize that U.S.-Soviet relations had to be changed; that the Cold War was not a natural state of affairs. Hence, the remarkable speech delivered at the American University, postulating for the first time in many years a new approach to world politics, to relations with the Soviet Union. It was essentially the approach that almost a decade later we learned to call détente.

After that historic speech, there was the nuclear Test Ban Treaty of 1963, the first significant step on the way to arms control. We are talking about another hypothetical situation here, but many people in the USSR are convinced that the Kennedy assassination prevented a major positive shift in Soviet-American relations. This, as I have already mentioned, was not the only lost opportunity in American-Soviet relations. Even now I believe that we could have achieved much more under Dwight D. Eisenhower. Sometimes I wonder whether this president is being given his due, at least as far as his foreign policy is concerned. Of course, for most of his presidency, he stayed under the sinister shadow of John Foster Dulles, anticommunist crusader number one, a great moralizer and a great connoisseur of "brinkmanship." Part of the responsibility for disrupting efforts to improve the international situation, including the ill-timed U-2 adventure, lies with Eisenhower himself. Nevertheless, it was under his administration, and with his participation, that the first attempts were made to break the ice of the Cold War. It is very remarkable that Eisenhower, a professional soldier, whose whole life was devoted to military service, happened to be the first political leader in the United States to alert the country to the dangers of militarism. Actually, he turned his political testament into a warning to the nation about the military-industrial complex.

So you think what ultimately became known as détente might have started as early as Eisenhower's second term?

Here we are faced with another unverifiable historical situation. But your suggestion seems quite plausible to me. And if it had occurred, the 1960s would have been different.

President Nixon must be rated rather highly by the Russians.

Yes, because it was under Nixon, with his personal participation, that the turnabout from confrontation to negotiation, from the Cold War to what we call détente, took place. But it may be too early to pass a final judgment on Nixon, if only because a statesman's reputation is often established not so much on the basis of his own accomplishments as by comparing them with those of his successors. A successor may turn out to be so miserable that even a mediocre politician can grow into an impressive historical figure. And vice versa: quite a big-time statesman may be overshadowed by a successor with even greater accomplishments.

The latter perspective doesn't endanger Nixon as yet?

No, he seems to be safe, at least through 1984. You know I keep wondering about Nixon. From my personal experience of dealing with many American political and public figures, I have the impression that on leaving public office they tend to become or at least look wiser, more balanced and farsighted, more statesmanlike. Perhaps it is sheer hindsight. Perhaps government office imposes some strict limits on people's natural capacities. But Nixon and many leading figures of his administration provide a striking exception to this rule. In their case we witness just the opposite.

As far as Nixon is concerned, I think it's more than the psychological trauma of Watergate and compulsory retirement. Nixon happened to occupy the presidency at an historical juncture that had a strong compelling logic about it. That logic led him to make some important and realistic decisions. In other words, it may well be that history lifted Nixon beyond his own personality and background. But then, removed from the White House, he again decoupled himself from history and returned, so to say, to his initial dimensions—intellectual, political, and personal. Détente had been the peak of his political career, but he started deriding it, as if trying to apologize for what he had done. Sometimes he seemed to be revising his own record to make himself acceptable for some political role in the future.

You don't think Nixon will go down in history as a great president?

History sometimes plays very strange tricks with reputations. So let us abstain from this type of guesswork. But it would be fair, I think, if history records that, as president, he led his country through a very difficult period and made a rather significant contribution to defining a new, more realistic American role in the world. I am speaking, of course, only about foreign policy, although even there Nixon's record is contradictory. As for Nixon's domestic policy, it was quite a different story, crowned by Watergate, though the trend toward an imperial presidency was not started by Nixon, but has been a long tradition in American history.

Nixon toured Europe in the spring of 1980 to promote his book The Real War. *He observed, for instance, that during the entire length of his presidency "we were at war with the Soviet Union."*

If that was so, where was his "generation of peace," which he proclaimed after the 1972 summit in Moscow? He was so proud of his achievements then that he was even criticized by Kissinger for his "euphoria." All this is just another clear manifestation of the matters we have already discussed. I recall Nixon in 1974, during his last summit with our leaders, when he stressed at all public occasions his friendly attitude toward the USSR and his personal "friendship" with our president.

To a certain degree I deplore the statements he is making now. In a way, I feel sorry for Nixon, because he is now undermining, degrading, the one big achievement of his lifetime, the transition to détente. What else will remain of his political achievements in history? His Alger Hiss affair? Or the Checkers speech?

In May 1980, Nixon declared in West Germany that Afghanistan was just a phase in World War III.

I ask myself how people who once occupied such high positions in their society can throw words around so easily. If you label each international development you don't like as another start of World War III, you gradually lose all sense of reality, while to perceive the world as it really is remains a sine qua non for a sensible foreign policy.

How was President Ford's role assessed in the Soviet Union?

We give President Ford his due for his serious political achievements, such as the Vladivostok agreement on SALT II in 1974. But as soon as the Right put pressure on him, he began falling back onto a hard-line policy. I have in mind such actions as freezing the SALT talks, adopting rearmament programs, even trying to banish the word *détente* from American political vocabulary. Later, having lost the election, he was said to believe that panicking in the face of the right-wing pressure had been a mistake and was possibly a reason why he lost. Sorry to say, Ford's election-time behavior was not exceptional in American political practice.

How would you size up the impact of the Carter administration on U.S.-Soviet relations?

In the light of what took place in Soviet-American relations in 1979–80, one is tempted to isolate his administration as the major source of all troubles in this field. But, the more you listen nowadays to Nixon, Kissinger, or Reagan, the easier it is to resist this temptation. And I want to be fair. The negative trends in our relations started well before Carter.

The first counterattacks against détente were felt as early as in 1972. Later, in the last months of the Nixon administration, the Pentagon significantly curbed the president's freedom of diplomatic action, the result being that he came to Moscow in 1974 with very few substantive subjects to talk about in connection with SALT II. At the end of 1974, Congress wrecked the Soviet-American trade agreement. Later, President Ford froze the American position at the SALT talks and introduced a major rearmament program. Far from reversing the trend, Carter gave it a strong boost. But at the beginning of the Carter presidency, developments were not so one dimensional.

What was the initial attitude toward Carter in the USSR?

If Mr. Carter was practically unknown in his own country, what would you expect from us? We did know something about him, of course, and, as usual in such cases, there were some facts that could give cause for concern, just as other facts could be interpreted as hopeful signs. After Carter became president, the Soviet government felt it appropriate to make it absolutely clear that it remained ready to improve relations with the United States and to work together in spheres of common interests. But our attitude was not reciprocated.

Again, I would not like to simplify the situation. There were intense struggles in the American power elite at that time over foreign policy. Carter gave some hopes to the hard-liners, but his emerging administration as a whole was not committed to wrecking arms control and détente. So, the Right began portraying Carter as a liberal and creating new groups to put pressure on the administration, trying to block any positive move in Soviet-American relations and, at the same time, to create incentives for Carter to move rightward. The Committee on the Present Danger was set up almost like a shadow government, with its strong elitist credentials, intimate connections with the power centers, and its overall "respectable" facade. The older hawkish groups became more active.

What do you think made Carter yield to those pressures?

If the Carter administration had been unequivocally committed to détente, it would have been able to withstand those pressures and provide constructive leadership both in the Congress and in the realm of public opinion. But the problem was, first, that Carter himself did not have either an indubitable position or clear-cut commitments. Second, the antidétente camp had rather prominent representatives within the administration, like Zbigniew Brzezinski and James Schlesinger. Third, Carter overestimated his ability to forge a broad consensus that would have satisfied all groups. As a result, Carter's approach to foreign policy was initially characterized by attempts to include in his policy important elements of both the pro-détente and the antidétente positions. This ambivalence not only damaged Soviet-American relations, but created a justified impression that Carter indeed did not have a coherent foreign policy. Once you do create such an impression, you shouldn't wonder why you cannot mobilize support for your actions.

You mentioned Soviet signals to Mr. Carter.

Even before the inauguration, Mr. Carter had established contacts with the Soviet government. Apparently, he had been led to suspect that we would try to "test" him in the course of the lame-duck period or in the first weeks of his presidency. He seemed very apprehensive: one could see that he had heard a lot of bad things about us. Well, he got very positive answers here, like "Don't worry, we do not intend to 'test' the new president; we are ready to work for improved relations with the United States." Really, the Soviet Union took care not to create any difficulties during the process of transition from one administration to the other in the important field of Soviet-American relations.

Then came President Leonid Brezhnev's speech at Tula in January 1977, just on the eve of the inauguration.

Yes, President Brezhnev spoke of the tremendous effort that had gone into making détente a reality, of the necessity not to waste the assets of détente that had been accumulated. He said, "We are ready to make, together with the new U.S. administration, a major new stride in relations between our two countries." He called for a speedy conclusion of the SALT II treaty, to be followed quickly with SALT III talks, for new measures against nuclear proliferation, for reaching an agreement at the Vienna talks on mutual reduction of armaments and armed forces in Central Europe. He also clarified some important points connected with Soviet military doctrine and concepts that had become subjects of heated discussions in the United States. The Soviet government was saying that the road to better relations was open, that we were ready to continue détente. But the response from Washington that followed in a few weeks was of a different sort.

You mean the human rights campaign. But steps like sending the personal letter on White House stationery to dissident Sakharov were widely criticized in the United States by Time *magazine, James Reston, and many others.*

But the letter was there, and subsequent events showed that it couldn't be regarded as an isolated step. The sudden "human rights" campaign started out hand in hand with an abrupt change in the political position of the United States on some of the most important issues of its relations with the USSR. Secretary of State Cyrus Vance visited Moscow in March 1977, and the proposals on SALT II he presented here constituted a very sharp break with the Vladivostok agreement of 1974.

Did it come as a shock to you?

Well, we had indications that things were developing in this direction. But it did not make things much easier. I remember those days very well. My impression at the time was that our representatives at the talks with Vance and his team were expecting even up to the last moment of his stay in Moscow that Vance would put something more realistic on the table in the end, at least as a reserve for the next stage of negotiations. It was hard for them to believe that his original package was all he could offer, that he could have traveled all the way to Moscow to present us with proposals that were so blatantly one-sided and so openly aimed at getting unilateral advantages for the United States. Soon it became clear that Secretary Vance's first mission to Moscow was doomed.

Would you have considered Kissinger capable of embarking upon such an abortive mission?

I didn't expect it of Vance either—he personally deserves respect as a statesman and a diplomat. Frankly, even today I don't quite understand how all that happened. As for Kissinger, if you had asked me several years ago, I might have said no, he would not have done it. But now, in the light of his recent speeches and writings, I begin to have some serious doubts.

Henry Kissinger emerged from the huge financial womb of the Rockefellers, like Vance, Brzezinski, and more than half of the top of the Carter government.

I do not know a single American administration in recent decades that did not have someone in one way or another connected with the Rockefellers, or organizations in which they took an active part, like the Council on Foreign Relations or the Trilateral Commission. This goes beyond the Rockefellers, however, since they are only the most visible and publicized part of the American corporate elite, which, we believe, is served by the American foreign policy establishment.

So, the very first talks arranged by the Carter administration turned out to be a flop.

Yes, they were a failure. The talks made a very disappointing impression here. Most important, they made us more apprehensive of the whole approach of the new administration and its future policies. The very first months of the Carter presidency raised the question of continuity of the U.S. policy. The previous administration had concluded a number of agreements with the Soviet Union. But would Carter consider those agreements binding for himself? Or did the new administration want to start it all over from square one? Those were the questions we had to ask ourselves. Soon it became clear that a cycle pattern was emerging in our relations.

But frankly, in the West it is felt, on the contrary, that these perpetual hot-cold tactics are typical for the way foreign policy is conducted by the USSR.

The Soviet foreign policy has been highly consistent over the years. I think that at least in this respect even the West cannot deny us a good reputation. As to the American policy, especially under Carter, just look at the record. The year 1977 was off to a bad start, but late spring and summer improved things a little bit, and by October we were able to reach an understanding on SALT II and the Middle East. In a few days the latter was in fact cancelled, and in 1978 things were going downhill again. This time the events took an even more serious turn with Brzezinski's visit to China and the NATO meeting in Washington in May. By summer the relations were probably worse than at any time in the seventies.

So, during the Carter administration détente went down the drain?

I don't think you have used correct words. In my opinion, détente is not dead. But it is true that from 1977, Soviet-American relations progressively lost stability. Each cycle turned out to be more detrimental to détente than the previous one. What was also very damaging to our relations was the increasingly hysterical anti-Soviet tone, not only in the mass media, but in official pronouncements and propaganda as well. Instigating this campaign, the Carter and Reagan administrations ignored another vital link in our relations—between substance and atmosphere. That link was well described by Kissinger, who warned in 1974 that "we cannot have the atmosphere of détente without the substance. It is equally clear that the substance of détente will disappear in an atmosphere of suspicion and hostility." As a result, we have ended up with neither the atmosphere nor the substance of détente. Of course, as I have already mentioned, this deterioration of relations proceeded unevenly, especially during the Carter administration. There were moments of hope that things would change for the better.

You have in mind Vienna?

Yes, the SALT II treaty was finally signed in June 1979 in the Austrian capital. It was a very important event, indeed. It was not only a step forward in arms control, but also an achievement, against great odds, that could have a positive impact on other arms-control talks, and on the general political atmosphere. But the treaty had to be ratified, and it was clear that there would be a bitter struggle in Washington over the ratification process. The subsequent events hardly need to be recounted. All in all, I would say that if there is a historical example of how an important treaty can be wasted, here it is.

Does SALT II still have a chance?

I hope so. But I think we should now be concerned about the fate of the whole SALT process. Each month of further delay in the talks, especially when accompanied by a constant growth of the military budget and the launching of new weapons systems, brings grave new dangers. But to return to Carter, I don't think the president was lying in 1976 when he pledged his adherence to the ideas of arms control and military spending cuts and even proclaimed as his ultimate goal the exclusion of reliance on nuclear weapons altogether. Nor do I doubt his sincerity in including some strong proponents of arms control in his administration. But, obviously, he was no less sincere expressing quite the opposite views at other times. And what may have counted even more than his sincerity was the desire to consolidate his political support and secure his own reelection as president. Comparing Carter of 1976 and Carter of 1980, I can't help recalling a well-known saying about the road to hell being paved with good intentions.

Summing up, I would say that there was an erosion of the entire framework of Soviet-American relations, which, by the beginning of 1980, climaxed in an open turnaround from détente to cold war.

But this process of erosion, as you yourself said earlier, had started before Carter became president.

Right. The narrowing of possibilities for positive development of Soviet-American relations started earlier. The first link to be lost was trade, not in the sense that trade has stopped altogether, or that there is no hope that the situation could be improved eventually, but in 1972–73 trade was regarded as a very promising field of mutual cooperation, as well as a matter of major political importance. Then the Jackson-Vanik amendment was passed by the U.S. Congress, which killed the trade agreement, and the situation deteriorated.

Kissinger claims that the Jackson-Vanik amendment was a clear reaction to the sudden exit tax required by your government for Jewish emigration. This decision apparently "dumbfounded" both Nixon and Kissinger.

As far as I remember, by the time the Jackson-Vanik amendment was passed, the question of the exit tax no longer existed, and therefore did not have any direct connection with the congressional decision. As for the exit tax itself, it was an attempt to solve one of the problems that arose in conjunction with a new development—the increase in emigration. The problem had to do with the state spending huge sums of money on educating people who then left the country. This subject was thoroughly discussed, and finally the decision was made not to recover those sums.

Well, after the trade link was seriously weakened, there came the turn of the European link. Before 1975, Americans had been constructive, although not very active, in their attitude toward enhancing security and cooperation in Europe. But after 1975, their position underwent a drastic change. One could even say that they actually started trying to sabotage the process of rapprochement in Europe. This approach manifested itself so vividly in Belgrade and then in Madrid that it produced a certain resentment even among some of the Western European allies of the United States. The concentration of the American delegation on the issues of human rights was a convenient smoke screen for the lack of a constructive U.S. position on other important issues. After Europe it came the turn of the Middle East. In October 1977, Andrei Gromyko and Cyrus Vance published a joint document on the principles of a mutual approach to Middle East problems. This was a very important achievement, which came as a result of a long process of overcoming difficulties and continuous efforts to bring our points of view closer. But a few days later the United States broke its pledge to work together with the Soviet Union toward finding a solution to the problem.

Why do you think the United States abandoned the joint approach?

One of the reasons was apprehension voiced by some of the president's assistants that such an approach would complicate the administration's relations with influential segments of the Jewish community. So, the Carter administration took one more link out of Soviet-American relations—joint efforts to settle one of the most dangerous regional conflicts. With that link gone, hopes for a successful resolution of the conflicts in this most unstable region of the world faded away. Thus, gradually, we arrived at where only one major link still remained: arms control, a joint effort to contain the arms race. This, of course, is also the most important link, directly connected with the main issue of Soviet-American relations: prevention of a nuclear war. But because of negative developments in other fields, this link was also seriously weakened, and when everything came to be, so to say, hanging on one hook, Soviet-American relations became almost entirely dependent on SALT, with almost no other arrangements to take the pressure off SALT and arms control in general.

You mean that the now politically isolated matter of arms control, including SALT, became much more vulnerable?

Yes. I hoped, and I am sure such hopes were shared by many, that if things had taken the due course, with the treaty ratified and both sides fulfilling their obligations, a gradual restoration of the damaged links would have become possible. But, unfortunately, those hopes have been dashed. If and when we again begin to put Soviet-American relations in order, and I hope it will be in the not-too-distant future, we should keep these lessons in mind. Curbing the arms race will naturally remain the most important task. But other relations shouldn't be downgraded either, both for their own sake and because otherwise any progress in arms control itself will be more difficult to attain. On the other hand, an acceleration of the arms control process, so needlessly and incredibly delayed over the last few years, will be a major precondition for strengthening détente as a whole.

In other words, you believe in linkage?

Not at all.

But how is your viewpoint different from the old Kissinger concept of linkage, or from Reagan's insistence that there can be progress in arms limitation talks only if the Soviet Union withdraws its troops from Afghanistan, changes its African policy, and so on?

Well, no one can deny that all spheres of our relations with the United States are interconnected in one way or another, and that their improvement in one sphere creates greater mutual trust, a better overall climate, which is helpful for improvement in other spheres. Conversely, deterioration in one sphere can affect the situation in others.

The big question, however, is not whether these interconnections exist, but what we do about them. Here one must have a clear set of priorities. None of the spheres of Soviet-American relations is more important than arms control. Thus, if you really care about preventing war and stopping the arms race, how can you possibly put a brake on arms control on the grounds that the two sides are at odds over some local problem? How can you put forward as a precondition of solving one difficult problem the solution of other problems, sometimes even more difficult? This is a sure way of pushing oneself into a dead end. So, what linkage does is stimulate the interconnections to work for a deterioration of relations in all spheres, including the most vital.

What's the alternative?

As an absolute minimum, to work for the improvement of relations in whatever sphere is possible, to try to isolate arms control and disarmament as an area where progress must continue despite all the difficulties in other areas.

Incidentally, SALT I did not take place in an ideal atmosphere. And it is not only the United States that grumbles about some aspects of the other side's policy. The Soviet Union has more than enough reasons to be displeased with American policy. Following the logic of linkage, both sides should cease the dialogue, or rather restrict it to an exchange of enraged accusations and wait for the problems causing their discontent to settle themselves. But it will never happen.

On the other hand, as we have witnessed in the last three years, arms control will be up against great obstacles if the overall political atmosphere between the Soviet Union and the United States deteriorates. Therefore, we must strive to improve the overall atmosphere and increase mutual understanding, which would strengthen peace and facilitate progress in the main area of relations—arms control and disarmament.

President Nixon launched a system of yearly summit meetings with Soviet leaders. That development has been abrogated.

Yes, the already established practice of meetings between leaders of our two countries has been almost discontinued. And this does not help, of course. At the same time, I would say that although they are tremendously important, we should not wait for a summit meeting to improve the political climate.

Following the 1961 nonaligned conference in Belgrade, Nehru, Sukarno, Nkrumah, and Keita were sent as emissaries to Moscow and Washington, urging such regular pourparlers between the superpowers.

Summits are important, yes. But the more powerful an instrument of international politics, the greater the care and precision it should be used with. Otherwise, results may be different from those intended. A summit handled clumsily or unskillfully can have dangerous consequences. Summit meetings turned into empty routine can jeopardize the whole structure of existing relations. We are for summits with definite substance.

Both Nixon and Kissinger express the same view in their memoirs. What was your impression of the Kissinger memoirs?

My impression is somewhat ambivalent. For a student of the United States, reading this book is a must. The author is often impressive and sometimes brilliant. At the same time he is so famous and well established that he could have afforded to avoid some of the distortions, especially concerning Soviet foreign policy. Attempts to revise the historical record are always disappointing. Could they have been inspired by a desire to update his record according to the latest political fashions? I wonder. But too often it looks like a projection of the present hard anti-Soviet posture back onto recent history.

Kissinger presents himself as an absolute success story in his memoirs.

Well, no memoirs are written for the purpose of downgrading their authors. The question is how you define success in this particular case. I cannot get rid of an impression that Kissinger almost apologizes for détente, and by doing so presents his success story in terms of deceiving and manipulating the Russians, getting unilateral gains for the American side, etc. I am sure that he would not have achieved anything of real value in Soviet-American relations had this been his principal method of work. No doubt, Henry Kissinger does have significant achievements to his credit. But they were due to his realistic inclinations and to his ability to perceive and locate spheres of mutual interests and then to search for mutually acceptable solutions within the framework of those interests. Personally, I'm more impressed with Kissinger the statesman, who said in 1974, "There can be no peaceful international order without a constructive relationship between the United States and the Soviet Union," than with Kissinger the politician, who several years later tried in his memoirs to downgrade the importance of what was done in our relations in the first half of the seventies. And of course, I find more attractive, both as a political figure and a scholar, Henry Kissinger proving that military power doesn't translate itself into political influence anymore, and that "the prospect of a decisive military advantage, even if theoretically possible, is politically intolerable since neither side will passively permit a massive shift in the nuclear balance," than the Kissinger who was instrumental in defining as a precondition for the ratification of the SALT II treaty a new round of the arms race, or the Kissinger accusing Messrs. Reagan and Haig of being soft on the Russians.

What particular inaccuracies have you found in his memoirs concerning Soviet-American relations?

It was my impression during the first summits that Kissinger was sincerely jubilant about the success of those summits, and I strongly doubt the authenticity of the description of those events in his memoirs. In my recollection of the 1972 summit, the mood of the American delegation was quite different from the rather cynical, self-confident attitude described by Kissinger. They came very nervous about our response to the bombing of Hanoi and the mining of the Haiphong harbor, committed a couple of weeks before, and about a possible breakdown of the summit, which would have been a very painful blow for the Nixon administration in that year of domestic turmoil and the presidential election. And when it became clear that, while condemning those American actions, our leadership was responsible and courageous enough to realize that it was not the time to claim an eye for an eye, but the time for a major breakthrough in our relations, the Americans were greatly impressed. I remember one of them musing privately about the steps of history being heard in the Granovitaya Chamber of the Kremlin during the first official reception. Even those hard-boiled people of the Nixon administration felt that a major historical turnaround was happening and had great hopes for the future. That was a very remarkable and symptomatic feeling, but it is almost completely absent from the memoirs.

How did the Carter foreign policy look to you compared to the Kissinger approach?

Kissinger, in effect, attempted to transcend the cold-war pattern, even though the attempts might have been at times inadequate and limited by the traditional balance-of-power perception. Of course, some people from the Carter team did all they could to differentiate between their policy and the Kissinger policy, but ultimately they failed to come up with a realistic alternative. It was nearly impossible to define any comprehensive design in Carter's foreign policy. In the beginning there were some conceptual innovations concerning North-South relations, arms control, new priorities for American foreign policy; then, after many fluctuations and zigzags, it all came down to a repatched cold-war pattern, completely disregarding all the lessons of recent history. This brings us again to the real challenge American foreign policy faces today—that of an accommodation to the new realities of the international situation, to the changing foreign and domestic conditions under which United States policy is shaped. Sometimes this process of accommodation can be delayed or checked, as is happening now, but the basic trend is irreversible, and it will reassert itself again.

Comparing Kissinger and Brzezinski, what in your view is the main difference between them as diplomatic managers?

Even putting aside their very different intellectual and political potentials, there still remain, I think, some important distinctions of style. The major point is that Kissinger is above all a true disciple of the Realpolitik school, a realist in the sense of recognizing only the more tangible factors of policy, while Brzezinski is an ideologue, whose views are colored to a very large extent by ideas and approaches springing from a priori ideological schemes. You can see many such people in the Reagan administration, though perhaps Brzezinski was better educated.

And what are the implications of this difference for Soviet-American relations?

One is that, in Kissinger's view, the Soviet Union is but another actor on the international scene, and, depending on circumstances, may be regarded as being anything from an irreconcilable foe to a more traditional rival, or even a partner. According to Brzezinski, the USSR is above all an "illegitimate" kind of society with which normal durable relations are impossible unless basic internal changes take place in it. I think it goes beyond the personal differences between the two men, because actually what we have here are reflections of the two influential schools of American political thinking.

Kissinger seemed more preoccupied with East-West relations, while some feel that Brzezinski concentrated on West-West and North-South problems.

True, the shifting focus of attention toward West-West and North-South relations was one of Brzezinski's favorite ideas in the framework of trilateralism. It was all covered up by sophisticated rhetoric, but the real essence was unmistakable—to rationalize a freeze on further progress toward détente in East-West relations, and a retreat from solving the most acute problems in this area. As a result, neither West-West nor North-South, to say nothing of East-West, gained from such a design.

Under the Carter administration, there was no substantial progress in North-South relations. The initial flirtation with the developing countries gradually gave way to more traditional military-interventionist concepts. At the same time, after futile attempts to downgrade the priority of East-West relations, they were brought back to the top of the U.S. foreign policy agenda; but unfortunately the administration was not able to do it in the context of détente and did it, rather, in the context of confrontation. This, in its turn, distorted the whole structure of U.S. foreign policy. It was like tampering with a compass instead of letting it show what it has to according to the laws of magnetism. The predictable result was a loss of orientation in foreign policy.

In saying this, I have no intention at all to downgrade in any way the importance of United States relations with Western Europe and Japan, or other parts of the world. Nor do I deny anyone's right, including that of the United States, to build up a system of relations that best fits its interests. But what I do want to stress is that, however important other factors might be, one cannot push East-West relations to the bottom of one's list of priorities without committing a tremendously grave mistake. Very serious and pressing problems have to be solved in East-West relations. This is not a matter of a free choice or preference. We are simply bound on both sides to take very special care of relations with each other, whether we like it or not. The major problems of contemporary international affairs are revolving around this East-West axis, including the problems of West-West and North-South relations. They are still greatly dependent on relationships between socialist and capitalist countries, including, of course, the big two—the Soviet Union and the United States.

Speculating on the prospects for Soviet-American relations under the Reagan administration, some observers have referred to "the Nixon model."

Nixon, like Reagan, was a tough anticommunist, but it was his administration that carried out the turnaround to détente. Would you expect a similar shift from the Reagan administration?

If a presidential term lasted longer than four years I would, perhaps, consider such a scenario plausible, if only because I am strongly convinced that there are no sensible alternatives to peaceful coexistence and détente, that the current platform of America's leaders lacks realism, and that objective conditions will simply not allow anyone to play irresponsible games for too long. Long-term trends are all in favor of a sober return to earth. But it is difficult to say how long it will take them to change their minds, and then their policies. In Nixon's case it took fifteen to twenty years, and I am not sure that the time left before 1984 would be enough.

To go back to the parallel with Nixon, it does not look very persuasive. The current situation, however fast it may change, is still very different from that of the late sixties and early seventies. Nixon came to power when the bankruptcy of cold-war policy was exposed in the starkest way. The country understood it, just as it understood the necessity of changing budgetary priorities—in particular, increasing social spending and reducing to some extent spending on the military. In recent years, strong attempts have been made to try and make Americans forget all that, to sell them once again on cold war and arms racing as the only way to security. These attempts will inevitably fail, and what's more, America's interests and well-being will be substantially damaged by them. But it is really difficult to expect that all this will become clear before the administration's policies have received a number of bruises and setbacks. In fact, that process may already have started.

Then there are differences between the two presidential personalities— admittedly a delicate subject. Let me just say one thing: Nixon became president already having substantial policy experience, including in foreign affairs. Reagan did not have such a background. Nixon was an active president, anxious to do big things in foreign policy. I don't know how active Reagan's nature is. Nixon, like Reagan, came from California, but Nixon's political views were hardly provincial. I would not like to go deeper into this subject.

There are differences between the entourages of the two presidents. Nixon was surrounded by all kinds of people—mediocre and talented, provincials and establishmentarians, novices and old hands, conservatives and moderates. And most of them were pragmatists. Reagan's entourage is very homogeneous. With rare exceptions, they are people who came to Washington without experience in national policy making, provincial novices in government, very conservative. I would even say they are extremist in their views, particularly people on the subcabinet level. And most of them are ideologues rather than pragmatists. I would add that this administration seems to contain a higher than usual number of people better equipped to create problems than to solve them.

What do you perceive as the main goal of Reagan's foreign policy?

The main goal, judging from all the evidence, is to bring back the old times of America's extremely exceptional position in the world. This illusory goal is to be realized primarily through the buildup of military power, making it more usable in foreign policy; in other words, by taking the course toward achieving military superiority and declaring a policy of cold war against the Soviet Union and other socialist countries. The Reagan administration seems to believe that an aggravation of its relations with the USSR and the launching of a global anti-Soviet crusade will help to consolidate the U.S. position in the world.

Do you think this design is doomed for failure?

It's too early to pass a final judgment on that, but by all accounts such a policy would hardly contribute to U.S. influence and prestige in the world.

The military parity that exists between the Soviet Union and the United States, between the Warsaw Treaty Organization and NATO, is pretty stable. Given the present numbers and the qualitative characteristics of the weapons, it would be extremely hard to change the balance of forces significantly in one's favor. In the long run, the goal becomes absolutely unattainable, because when one side threatens that stability, the other side takes the necessary countermeasures. Such is reality, and all the fuss the Reagan administration started about these military questions has failed to produce the least proof that it has succeeded in inventing something new capable of shaking this reality. Equally, this refers to other indisputable truths of the day: that to begin a nuclear war would be tantamount to suicide, that to count on a victory in such a war is madness, and that the very idea of a limited nuclear war is a dangerous illusion.

In an attempt to refute these truths one can spend thousands of billions of dollars more on the military buildup, but this will be of no avail. The dream of a safe and unopposed expansion of America's opportunities regarding the usability of armed forces, including nuclear weapons, will remain a pipe dream.

It was precisely the disregard of these realities that, in my view, led to the discrepancy between the goals and practical consequences of Reagan's policy and caused such a powerful resistance to it.

The antinuclear movement, you mean?

Yes. Reagan's course has forced enormous masses of people to think seriously about the problems of war and peace. The public in Western Europe and now in the United States itself has sensed the existence and growth of the nuclear threat more sharply than ever before. The changed political and psychological climate on both sides of the Atlantic has led to an increased opposition to the policy of intensified military buildup and confrontation.

The Reagan administration has ascribed this movement to Soviet propaganda.

Indeed, Washington has tried to beat this movement by means of that primitive libel, though it could have been taken as a compliment to the Soviet Union. It is no laughing matter—to organize such an enormous movement in dozens of countries all over the world. But this compliment is undeserved, and as a communist and Soviet citizen I may even regret it. If all it took were some intrigues and more dollars and conspiratorial activity, then the United States would have been far more competitive in this field. But somehow the situation has evolved not to Washington's liking, and the only reason is that movements of this kind are impossible without extremely broad public support, which cannot be bought or obtained by fraud. People are endowed with intelligence and also with an instinct for self-preservation. That is why this campaign about "the hand of Moscow" has failed to produce any substantial impression.

It has become more and more obvious that the Reagan administration itself has made the greatest impression on the public this time, with its policies, rhetoric, and words and deeds that terrify millions and millions of people. It has not done so by invoking the mythical "Soviet threat." People now have their eyes open to the real prospect of a nuclear catastrophe stemming from the arms race and the exacerbation of international tension, both of which are results of the policies of the U.S. government.

This government came into office fully confident that the American voters had given it a mandate for an unrestrained arms race, for the revival of the Cold War, for military adventures abroad. But the course of events has demonstrated that most Americans gave the government no such mandate. It is becoming increasingly clear that the administration's foreign policy is running against a rising tide of protest and discontent. While the antiwar movement of the 1960s was based primarily upon students, intellectuals, and liberals, today's antinuclear movement is strikingly broad-based in its composition. It includes Democrats and Republicans, liberals and conservatives, labor leaders and businessmen, physicians, lawyers, clergymen, and many others.

It has also proved wrong to calculate that the course toward destruction of détente and a return to the Cold War, toward a crusade against the

USSR and the other socialist countries, will enable Washington to rally its allies together and make them follow blindly in the wake of American policy. It has turned out that questions of détente, of disarmament, of relations with the USSR, including trade, have provided an additional source of friction between America and its allies.

By the beginning of 1982, some people in the Reagan administration had begun to realize that American foreign policy was faltering. There were certain attempts to correct it; Allen and Haig have stepped down, and the rhetoric has been changed.

No doubt, political setbacks have had their impact on Washington policy. On our part, we would welcome any reasonable step by the administration, as we did, for instance, with respect to its long-delayed decision to come back to the strategic arms limitation and reduction talks. Yet, overall, it does not seem to go further than political maneuvers designed to calm and mislead the public. Moreover, each peaceful move is followed by a series of militaristic actions that seem to confirm the invariability of the Reagan administration's aggressively anti-Soviet policy.

For example, after his May 9, 1982, speech at Eureka College in Illinois, where President Reagan agreed to resume negotiations on the limitation and reduction of strategic armaments, he addressed the British Parliament and the U.N. General Assembly in the spirit of the Cold War. The contents of the National Security Council's memorandum, signed by the president, and the Pentagon's Defense Guidance for Fiscal Years 1984–88 were deliberately made public. They are extremely bellicose documents—blueprints, actually, for total confrontation with the Soviet Union and other socialist countries by all means, from economic and technological war with unlimited subversive activities, to a war fought with conventional and even nuclear weapons.

What is your impression of the Pentagon directive?

This document is typical of many members of the present U.S. administration: it is impudent and rude, and at the same time light-minded and thoughtless. It contains a lot of obvious humbug, which forced even General David Jones, when he was retiring as chairman of the Joint Chiefs of Staff, to warn that an attempt to carry out some of the plans outlined in the directive would be tantamount to throwing money into a bottomless pit. The authors of the document obviously have become victims of their own propaganda, misjudging the potentialities of their own country and the problems that face others.

It may well be that these directives reflect mainly the position of the Pentagon, which does not necessarily speak for the administration as a whole.

I do not think so. This attitude can hardly be ascribed to the Pentagon's independence of mind—it does reflect some gut instincts of the leaders of the present administration. No wonder that, at the end of the 1982 NATO session in Bonn, President Reagan, having first assured his colleagues that he would negotiate arms limitations with the Soviet Union, immediately urged them to remember that, politically, the West continued to be in a state of war with the Soviet Union.

Here we witness another gaping discrepancy between U.S. policy and today's realities. The men in Washington have forgotten, or simply do not want to remember, that successful talks on arms limitation and the very prevention of nuclear war call for normal relations, relations of peaceful coexistence and détente between countries with different social systems, in the first place between the largest among them—the USSR and the United States. One cannot count on the preservation of peace, or on the success of the negotiations, while at the same time unleashing a wholesale political war against the socialist countries, spurring on the arms race, and fanning hatred and mistrust of the Soviet Union.

Professor George Kennan, a veteran of American diplomacy, has emphasized in a number of his recent speeches and articles that he finds the views of the Soviet Union prevailing today in the U.S. government and mass media to be extremist, subjective, and far removed from what any sensible study of existing realities would indicate, adding that as the basis for political action these views are not only ineffective, but dangerous.

Few people will, of course, be surprised by right-wing extremists in the United States hating the Soviet Union and wishing to make short shrift of it. But the directives to this end look ridiculous. Their authors forget that attempts of that kind have been made in the past both by the Entente and the Axis powers, and, in the years of the Cold War, by the United States itself. Invariably, these attempts have ended in fiascos, and they have even fewer chances of success today.

I am not belittling the dangers with which present U.S. policy is fraught. These are dangers for the cause of peace, for all nations, including the United States. Those whom the U.S. administration sees as its adversaries, and now even America's allies and the public at large, are by no means blind to these dangers.

What does the future hold for this policy, in your view?

As far as the near future is concerned, I would venture to say this:

The U.S. policy will be as good as it will not be allowed to be bad, and it will be as safe—not just for the USSR, but also for the United States itself and its allies—as it will not be allowed to be dangerous; as it will not be allowed by economic and political realities, by the policies of other countries, by the common sense of the American people, by humanity's desire for survival. I hope those factors will be strong enough to bring U.S. policy back to the understanding of the crucial fact that, besides the obvious contradictions between the two countries, there also exist very important and vital common interests—interests of peace, interests of survival, which demand not only negotiations but also agreements and general improvement of U.S.-Soviet relations.

Now, what if it will not happen? Then we can only hope that the time will come when we will be able to say: History did not begin with this administration, and history did not end with it.

Hegel once wrote that people never learn from history. Is this dictum applicable to Soviet-American relations?

Hegel left a great wealth of ideas, while my memory in the realm of philosophy, alas, is often imperfect. I recall some other thoughts of his, emphasizing the opposite: the ability of reason to understand history and learn from it. I have no doubt, though, that the great dialectician also had some ideas along the lines you suggested. I think both points can be argued, for each of them reflects one of the sides of the complex relationship between mankind and history. If human beings had been totally unable to learn, there would hardly be any history at all. But if they had been capable and diligent apprentices, thoroughly mastering the lessons of history, it would have been quite a different history. Mankind would have long been living in a kingdom of perpetual peace, complete security, and absolute justice.

But both history and mankind move somewhere between these extremes. Obviously, the same is true of Soviet-American relations. Our two countries have survived, which is already proof that reason can prevail. But the danger of war is still great, which means, among other things, that the lessons of history haven't been fully assimilated. The seventies brought many positive changes in Soviet-American relations—but still, reflecting on it now, I think we can call it by and large a decade of lost opportunities. As for the recent developments in our relations, they really make you wonder whether history is remembered at all.

Will the new American administration draw proper lessons from history?

Please ask me that question in 1984. But important as history is, it is not enough to learn from past experience. Each generation has to face new challenges for which the past gives no clue, challenges that are the responsibility of each generation alone to overcome. Some of the tasks facing our contemporaries are historically unique, and we have no margin for error in trying to fulfill them. The first in importance is, of course, the problem of preventing war.

The generation of our parents, which witnessed and fought in World War I, made a tragic mistake, failing to derive proper lessons from history, and thus allowing World War II to come. I repeat, it was a real tragedy. But mankind as a biological species, and even those individual nations that suffered most, managed to survive it. Should this tragic mistake be repeated, there most probably will be no one to learn any lessons. In this sense, our generation truly has a rendezvous with destiny.

Chapter 3 | On Peace and War, the Arms Race and Arms Control

"For the first time in nearly two decades, war with the Soviet Union has turned from seeming theoretically possible to seeming actually possible—and not just cold war but hot war, a shooting war— even a nuclear war." This is a quote from a recent statement by Stephen Rosenfeld, chief editorial writer for the Washington Post.

A statement like this is a very dangerous indication. It points to the fact that we are approaching a stage where the unthinkable is beginning to seem thinkable. It looks like the terms of the debate in the United States on matters of war and peace have changed in a way that sane ideas have been pushed off to the sidelines while the debate is centered on various degrees of insanity. In history, more than one nation has been able to talk itself into a catastrophic war.

In the first days of 1980 the hands of the symbolic clock on the cover of the *Bulletin of Atomic Scientists* were moved from nine minutes to twelve to seven minutes to twelve. This is the time that clock showed at very dangerous moments of the Cold War. A year later, the clock showed four minutes to twelve. I am afraid those clock hands may have to be moved even closer to midnight.

Would you explain it primarily as a result of the recent increase in world tensions?

Yes, but not only by that. Concern over a threat of war has been growing among scientists and experts for some time now. The primary reasons are the continuing arms race and a standstill at the arms limitation talks, and the failures of most attempts to settle crisis situations and conflicts.

Now that the tension has increased, and military competition has speeded up, the situation is naturally becoming even more alarming.

It follows from what you say that the crucial issue in Soviet-American relations—the prevention of nuclear war—has become even more acute.

Yes, it has. And it is important to remember that prevention of nuclear war is the main issue in Soviet-American relations and the principal theme of détente. This fact has been recognized and officially proclaimed by both powers on the top political level. Among common positions agreed upon by the leaders of the USSR and the United States at the first summit meeting in Moscow in 1972, nothing is more important than the statement that "in the nuclear age there is no alternative to conducting their mutual relations on the basis of peaceful coexistence." In 1973 the two countries signed a special agreement, "On Prevention of Nuclear War," which, at least from the Soviet viewpoint, is one of the most important joint Soviet-American documents to date.

I am not at all sure that the U.S. government adheres to this principle now. What is certain is that Washington no longer considers détente as *the* way to prevent a nuclear war. There is a massive campaign to persuade Americans that the only way to peace is through rearmament and confrontation.

Anyway, the anxiety is growing about the fatal clash to occur someday. Recently, I have come across a very dramatic statement to this effect by one of the world's leading authorities on nuclear weapons, George Kistiakowsky. He emphasized that, given the present military, technological, and political trends, "it would be a miracle if no nuclear warheads exploded by the end of this century and only a bit smaller miracle if that did not lead to a nuclear holocaust."[1] Though I find this pessimism excessive, I fully share in such a great concern.

Yes, we also believe that this danger is increasing. Especially because, as I see it, the danger of war is associated not only with someone deliberately planning it and being ready to push the button at some zero hour, but with a more anonymous yet very real danger. Situations arise that can lead to war; in a world saturated with weapons, their use is quite possible as a result of aggravation of international tensions or flareups of latent conflicts in various regions.

Even accidental war is a possibility. That is why, to create reliable guarantees of peace, it is not enough to realize the futility of starting a war, and not even enough to undertake appropriate formal commitments. Much remains to be done to remove the very possibility of war. This requires continued efforts to improve radically the whole international situation.

What do you mean by "radical improvement of the whole international situation"?

Not a worldwide socialist revolution, of course. I am talking of changes that are acceptable to both systems, of the consolidation of peaceful coexistence, of détente, to be more specific, progress toward arms control, toward stopping the arms race, toward negotiated settlement of existing crises and prevention of future international conflicts, toward the development of mutually beneficial cooperation in various spheres.

I am aware that it all may sound like a rather dull catalogue—particularly since everything has long been on the agenda for discussions and talks. But one major point must be kept in mind: success of these efforts requires a serious understanding of the realities of the nuclear age and a proper respect for those realities in practical policies. It is said that generals always prepare for the previous war. One often has the impression that politicians behave similarly as they ignore the new realities and canonize the experiences of yesteryear.

What realities are you referring to?

The nuclear age makes new demands on policy making and requires important policy changes. War has become so destructive that it can no longer be regarded as a rational instrument of policy.

Could you outline some of those new demands and requirements?

One requirement I've already mentioned is the necessity of revising drastically the attitude toward the role of force, particularly military force, in foreign policy. Generally speaking, this necessity has been recognized.

But now we are witnessing attempts to reject this necessity. I mean not only some militant statements, but the dominant American political mood in general. Persistent attempts are being made to get out of the dead end in which the policy of force has found itself.

You mean the impossibility of using force without inviting a destructive retaliatory blow?

Yes. The Pentagon hasn't been able to get over this fact of life. Thus there has emerged a very misguided and extremely dangerous trend— a search for new ways to use force; ways that supposedly would not endanger the United States itself. This trend is multifaceted. One process that merits special note is the search for new weapons systems, military doctrines, and methods of application of military force, all designed to make nuclear war thinkable.

Like the neutron bomb?

The neutron bomb, or, in official Pentagonese, the enhanced-radiation weapon, which is supposed to be much less destructive of property than ordinary nuclear weapons, is one of the results of the search for "usable" military force. But there's a lot more. There is the miniaturization of nuclear weapons and the increase in their accuracy, the increase in power of conventional weapons. There is the counterforce doctrine, the idea of "selective" or "surgical" strikes. There are attempts to introduce certain "rules of the game" into military conflicts, so as to make them more thinkable. There are rapid-deployment forces.

All this amounts to a mindless repudiation of the new realities. It is an easier road to take, admittedly—for there is a tremendous impetus, accumulated over the centuries, to continue to believe in war as an instrument of policy and, for some, even as an apex, a crucial test of policy. But this road does not lead away from the Damoclean sword of nuclear suicide. The real issue today is not one of finding ways to improve and refine the methods of using force, but of excluding the use and threat of force from international relations.

You speak of excluding the use and threat of force from international relations. But isn't it a far cry from what the USSR is doing? You pay close attention to your own defense problems. Several times the USSR has not refrained from using military force where it was deemed necessary.

I am talking about the process and its final purpose. In this imperfect world we can't afford to become perfect alone. Imagine a self-disarmed Soviet Union and the kind of policies other great powers would conduct under the pressure from people like Caspar Weinberger, Josef Luns, Richard Pipes, Richard Perle, Jesse Helms, and a number of generals and admirals.

Paul Nitze stressed to me that he is convinced the Soviet Union does not want nuclear war. But he also believes that the USSR reckons with the possibility of nuclear conflict and that you have prepared for winning it too.

Perhaps I should thank Nitze for the statement that we do not want a nuclear war, although made in a private conversation. This sounds like something new coming from him. But the rest sounds like more of the same old song.

Well, I'm sure you're aware that this position is not held by Nitze alone. There are others who maintain that, since the USSR considers it possible to fight and win a nuclear war, it does not exclude such a war from its political arsenal.

Yes, I'm familiar with this reasoning. You encounter it quite often, but this does not make it truthful.

But the allegations that the Soviet Union believes in fighting and winning a nuclear war are usually supported by quotes from articles, speeches, and books by Soviet military writers.

Yes, but those quotes are ten to twenty years old. And political and military thinking changes, reflecting changes in objective reality, including the development of weapons of mass destruction. Awareness of the consequences of nuclear war has increased in this time span.

As for today, most authoritative expressions of the present Soviet attitude to this problem leave no room for misunderstanding or misinterpretation. President L. I. Brezhnev repeatedly branded the idea of winning a nuclear war as "dangerous madness." The same attitude has been expressed by Soviet Defense Minister Dmitri Ustinov, Chief of General Staff of the Soviet Armed Forces Nikolai Ogarkov, and by other military and political leaders of the USSR.

Having said all this, I'd like to say a few words in defense of the often quoted—and still more often misquoted—Soviet military writers. Those people do discuss in their professional way how to fight a war, and I don't find anything unusual or alarming in that. It is the job of the military to consider what they should do in case a war is started by an adversary of the Soviet Union. It does not follow from this that they consider nuclear war an acceptable instrument of foreign policy.

I was visiting London in the early sixties, during another international crisis, and I saw a poster in a cafe. It read: "In case of atomic attack keep calm, pay your bill, and run like hell to the next cemetery." I'm afraid if the military in any country confined themselves just to this kind of advice no one would appreciate their sense of humor, and they would have to resign without any hope for a pension.

And again—let those who blame the Soviet Union look at what is being said in the United States, and not by obscure military writers, but by highly placed military leaders. General Curtis LeMay, for instance, who headed the U.S. Strategic Air Command, urged Americans to obtain an ability "to fight and win any war—including a general war" (and by general war he didn't mean simply a war led by generals). Former U.S. Secretary of Defense Melvin Laird wrote that American "strategy must aim at fighting, winning, and recovering," that the United States must develop "the willingness to wage total nuclear war," and that it must make it "credible to the enemy that we will take the initiative and strike first." I assure you, you will not find anything of this kind written or said by Soviet military leaders, or by anyone in the Soviet Union.

When they discuss these matters in the West, they refer not only to separate quotations, but to the overall Soviet military doctrine.

Yes, I know. But in reality, conclusions about the doctrine are made on the basis of the same quotations. Without going into details, I'd like to emphasize the main things. The Soviet military doctrine is strictly defensive in character. It is fully manifested in the Soviet position on the use of nuclear weapons. Let me cite such a source as the late commander-in-chief of the USSR Armed Forces, Marshal Leonid Brezhnev: "We are against the use of nuclear weapons; only extraordinary circumstances, an act of aggression against our country or its allies by another nuclear power, could compel us to resort to this extreme means of self-defense."[2]

Let me quote from the same source on the question of a possible first use of nuclear weapons. Speaking in the city of Tula in early 1977, President Brezhnev said: "Our efforts are directed precisely at averting the first strike and the second strike, indeed at averting nuclear war in general."[3]

"Preventive expansionist wars of any type and scale and the concepts of preemptive nuclear strikes are alien to the Soviet military doctrine," wrote Soviet Defense Minister Dmitri Ustinov in July 1981.[4]

I could quote other similar statements by Leonid Brezhnev, Yuri Andropov, and other Soviet leaders. The essence of those statements is that we see the mission of our strategic forces as deterring war. The Soviet Union considers it senseless to strive for military superiority. "Its very notion," as President Brezhnev emphasized, "loses any meaning in a situation where tremendous arsenals of nuclear weapons and their delivery means have already been stockpiled."[5]

The Soviet military doctrine, explained many times over by Soviet leaders, makes it quite clear that we consider nuclear war the most terrible disaster that could happen to mankind; that our strategy has a defensive character; that we oppose first-strike concepts; and that our strategic forces play the role of deterring a possible aggressor and are designed for a retaliatory strike. The Soviet Union has repeatedly proposed to negotiate agreements renouncing the first use of nuclear weapons and of military force in general. This is also part of our military doctrine, and you won't be able to find any other "secret" doctrine behind it, simply because none exists. All these things do contrast with some American official statements.

What American statements do you have in mind?

One example was Mr. Brzezinski's 1980 interview with British journalist Jonathan Power. Brzezinski stated that nuclear war should not be seen as such a terrible catastrophe, after all, for mankind would lose "only" 10 percent of its lives. "Only" 10 percent, by the way, means four hundred million people.

Having made his soothing assessment, Brzezinski went on to say that "in case of need" he would not hesitate to press the button and send the rockets flying. Another example: George Bush stated in a 1980 interview that he believes nuclear war can be won. When the surprised *Los Angeles Times* correspondent asked him to explain how it would be possible, he said, "You have survivability of command and control, survivability of industrial potential, protection of a percentage of your citizens, and you have a capability that inflicts more damage on the opposition than it can inflict upon you. That's the way you can have a winner. . . ." Then Mr. Bush gave his estimate of the number of survivors. He assured his interviewer that their number would be more than 2 to 5 percent of the population.[6] I wonder how big the headlines would be on the front pages of the *New York Times* and the *Washington Post* if a high-ranking spokesman of the Soviet government made such statements.

And these are not just words. The undisputed fact is that all the theoretical and technological innovations designed to make nuclear war thinkable or winnable are originating in the United States.

You do not mean that.

Surely, I do mean it. Carter's PD 59 is only one of the products of a whole school of strategic thought propagating limited nuclear war, "surgical strikes" against military targets, and other means of waging nuclear war "flexibly." President Reagan readily subscribed to that school, giving it his official blessing by his statement that a nuclear war can be limited to Europe. Far from being a purely intellectual exercise, all this is embodied in certain weapon technologies, in miniaturization and in higher accuracy of nuclear warheads, in increasing their yields, in devising special delivery systems, in placing some of them close to Soviet borders, and so on. Even if it were done only for the purpose of increasing the weight of American political threats, there would remain the dire risk that things would get out of hand and lead directly to a hot war, whatever the original intentions might have been. The continuous attempts to erase the dividing line between conventional and nuclear war are extremely dangerous, because they tend to obliterate what might have served as a main deterrent against a nuclear war, namely the prevailing abhorrence of such war, a view of it as of something loathsome, far too catastrophic to resort to. Once this attitude is lost, a nuclear confrontation becomes much more thinkable and then probable.

You seem to think that the possibility of nuclear war cannot be excluded, and that such a danger is even growing. Doesn't it follow that we should try to reduce its possible effects to the minimum?

Common logic would suggest that it does. But the realities of the nuclear age dictate a different approach. I have said already that the very idea of having a nice, little, clean and tidy nuclear war can undermine resistance to nuclear conflagration. But this is not all. If the price of such a war should seem more or less "acceptable," it can only foster the adventurism of those in charge of the buttons. One can assume they would be much less prudent in their policies, much more reckless, for they would believe that even if a miscalculation did occur, the war would be limited to an acceptable scale. And in a really acute situation that belief would make it much easier for a hand to grope for the button.

But one could argue that all this is outweighed by the prospect of sharply reduced losses and destruction.

No, there would hardly be any such reduction. As a matter of fact, I doubt very much that one would ever succeed even in creating the appearance that a tidy little nuclear war is possible. Look, every attempt to limit one's own possible losses, be it through antiballistic defense or civil defense, leads to the other side's response—to increased number of warheads, greater penetrating capacity, and greater destructive force.

What was the Soviet reaction to the new U.S. doctrine of limited nuclear war, promulgated by President Carter and then supported by President Reagan?

Actually, it had long been suspected that the United States would adopt the concept of limited nuclear war. Even now, Washington prefers to remain deliberately vague about the specific circumstances in which it would start such a war and about some other key aspects of the problem. The vagueness is probably intended to boost the psychological impact of the new doctrine, to preserve maximum freedom of action for the United States.

You asked about the Soviet opinion of that doctrine. I have already mentioned the most important point concerning limited nuclear war—namely, that it is, in our opinion, simply impossible. Such a war would require that both sides adopt some rules of conduct. But who can hope that the war would be like a courteous aristocratic duel, where all the rules are faithfully honored? If we did reach such a level of civility, not only prevention of nuclear war, but even general and complete disarmament would cease to be a problem.

No, we can't expect any gentlemanly duel. Nor any limited war, nor "surgical strikes." A nuclear war, if initiated, would be an all-out massacre. And it can never remain limited. Escalation is virtually inevitable, if only due to a natural reluctance on either side to concede defeat in such a situation.

Besides, who would be able to preserve his cool, registering nuclear strikes and evaluating what response they deserved so as not to violate the "rules of the game," while nuclear bombs were being dropped all over the place? The urge for escalation would simply be overwhelming.

The USSR has honestly stated that it has no intention to take part in such games. Let me quote from an article by Soviet Defense Minister Dmitri Ustinov published in *Pravda* in July 1981. He wrote, "Can one seriously talk of any limited nuclear war whatsoever? For it is clear to everybody that the aggressor's action would inevitably and instantly invite a devastating retaliation from the side attacked. None but utterly irresponsible individuals can claim that nuclear war can be fought under some rules established in advance whereby nuclear missiles will have to go off under a 'gentleman's agreement': only over specific targets without hitting the population in the process."[7]

I think the best description of the concept of limited nuclear war was given by former U.S. Senator John C. Culver. He compared it to "limiting the mission of a match thrown into a keg of gunpowder."[8]

But if such a war is impossible, why do you consider the doctrine dangerous?

Although this so-called "countervailing strategy" is often described by its authors as a mere continuation of the deterrence concept, actually it goes further than that. It sets out to lower the nuclear threshold, to widen the range of situations in which the United States considers it legitimate to use nuclear weapons. It provides a rationale for a new round of the arms race to the extent of virtually justifying an all-out race. Finally, it gives a boost to highly destabilizing trends in weapons technology and strategic thinking. While fanning fears of vulnerability to a first strike, it actually gears U.S. strategic forces to a first-strike posture.

But since the only guarantee for peace seems to be fear, the proverbial "balance of terror," maybe there isn't that much difference anyway.

Yes, there is a lot of difference. The concept of limited nuclear war is not aimed at reducing the mutual fear on which deterrence is based. Rather, it seeks to intensify the opponent's fear while at the same time emboldening the American side. Nuclear weapons will stay in the stockpile only so long as both sides feel equally threatened, so long as both are equally capable of destroying each other. One should be extremely wary of fooling around with this balance of terror, which so far has played a role in preventing numerous conflicts from escalating into nuclear war.

On the other hand, of course, it must be seen that a peace based on deterrence is far from ideal and, in the final analysis, not too stable or durable. Deterrence, the principle of mutual fear, generates threats by itself. First, for the sake of maintaining your deterrent, you have to keep an arsenal that can inspire awe on the other side, and the arms race continues. What's more, you have to maintain your credibility, which in this case means showing and proving your readiness to stage a holocaust, to burn half a planet down, to commit national suicide. And this means not only threats, saber rattling, and blackmail, but from time to time also practical actions designed to prove one's capacity for irresponsible action (like in a game of chicken), adventure, unpredictable behavior. The inherent dangers are obvious.

Let's put the moral aspect aside, however. We have here an example of that monstrously perverse logic imposed by the balance of terror. One has to constantly reaffirm the capacity for mass supermurder or megamurder, if you will. The dilemma can't be solved within this framework. On the one hand, it has to be admitted that war has become meaningless. On the other hand, you have to prepare for war around the clock and emphasize your readiness to start it. No matter what the original intentions are, this logic, if you cling to it tenaciously, inevitably leads to brinkmanship.

Where's the way out?

Well, when all is said and done, we are still better off with deterrence than we would be under the conditions of preparing for a "thinkable nuclear war." Deterrence is not too good, but nothing better exists so far, so you can regard it as a lesser evil. Of course, one thing must be understood: you cannot live with deterrence forever; sooner or later it will fail. So we have to move away from deterrence. The problem is—in what direction? To move in the direction of a "thinkable nuclear war" would be a disaster. There is only one reasonable way: to move toward a peace built on arms control and disarmament, on trust and cooperation. It is a difficult way, I admit. It requires tremendous efforts, a lot of wisdom, patience, and political courage. But there's hardly any other road to a durable and stable peace.

Kissinger once said that absolute security for one superpower is unachievable and undesirable, because it would mean absolute insecurity for the other. Is this not another of the new realities of the nuclear age?

It is. And indeed, this was one of Kissinger's bright ideas. I doubt that he or anybody else in U.S. government could rise so high above conventional wisdom as to consider his own absolute security undesirable. But for all practical reasons, it's enough if it is understood that absolute security is unachievable. This alone could have stopped the arms race. The Independent Commission on Disarmament and Security Issues, an international body chaired by Swedish Prime Minister Olof Palme and including in its ranks former U.S. Secretary of State Cyrus Vance and former British Foreign Secretary David Owen, among others, has developed and advanced this concept. Let me quote from one of the commission's documents: "Security cannot be achieved at the expense of a potential adversary, but only jointly with him and with due account of the security interests of both sides."

This reality of our time is closely tied with another—the existing means of destruction have made it impossible to "buy" national security with more and more arms, no matter how many or how good. Quite the opposite: the more arms, the less security. Some farsighted Americans began to understand it long ago. Jerome Wiesner and Herbert York, for instance, wrote: "Both sides in the arms race are thus confronted by the dilemma of steadily increasing military power and steadily decreasing national security. It is our considered professional judgement that this dilemma has no technical solution. . . . The clearly predictable course of the arms race is a steady open spiral downward into oblivion."[9]

When was it written?

In 1964. And I must emphasize that from the point of view of professional expertise, experience, and knowledge, it would be harder to find another two Americans whose opinions would be worth more attention. Mr. Wiesner was scientific adviser to President Kennedy. Mr. York is another well-known scientist who took a direct part in the production of weapons and at one time headed the Pentagon's department of research and development.

I repeat, it was said in 1964. What if these words had been heeded back then! How many billions of dollars and rubles could have been saved! How much safer our world might have been!

I caught a similar thought during a conversation with Lord Chalfont, a former British cabinet minister and military expert: "Ever more arms and less security."

Welcome aboard, Lord Chalfont. Meanwhile, another old principle is no longer valid: "If you want peace, prepare for war." Preparing for war industriously enough, you will only make war inevitable. And, despite the great difficulty of parting with such notions, a process of the realization of the world's new realities did begin in the 1960s, including the realization that there can be no security without arms control and arms reduction. Of course, the idea itself isn't new. But while in the past it sounded highly idealistic, it has now become the only realistic option, even though, for a number of reasons, its implementation is still hampered by many obstacles.

To some extent history is repeated, since all wars are preceded by a mad arms race.

You're right, but in the past the arms were created in order to fight and win a war. The paradox of the present situation is that, even as sane people can no longer regard nuclear war as an acceptable means to reach political ends, the arms race is continuing.

"End the arms race, not the human race!" is a sticker frequently seen in America in recent years. Yet, the arms race is gaining momentum.

There isn't a story of greater woe. I think we should take into account yet another important change brought about by the nuclear age. For ages, arms races were produced by bad political relations. Today, an arms race turns more and more into a major source of bad relations, for the buildup and qualitative refining of arms generate fears and suspicions, increasing distrust and poisoning the political atmosphere.

Take Soviet-American relations. If it became possible to remove fears and suspicions connected with the arms race, particularly with arms possessing a monstrous destructive force unequaled in history, we would see a disappearance of the major source of tension.

So the arms race represents the principal headache in Soviet-American relations?

Yes. To put it more precisely, the main problem is the problem of war and peace, with which the arms race is so closely connected.

But today's conventional wisdom is that it is precisely the destructive potential of nuclear weapons that helps prevent war, for otherwise a big war would have already occurred.

Conventional wisdom tends to mislead when we deal with such an unconventional thing as nuclear war. As we have discussed already, at this point we have to rely on the balance of terror inspired by nuclear weapons, but it's not a very durable guarantee of peace. The fact that it's worked for thirty years doesn't allow us to make optimistic conclusions about the future.

Not so long ago you said in a speech: "We have been lucky so far, but let us not press our luck beyond reason."

Indeed. The world has been on the brink of catastrophe several times by now. And statesmanship has hardly been the only thing saving mankind from nuclear holocaust so far. We have been lucky, and in the future we will have to base our hope for survival on something more solid than good luck. Especially because the new round of the arms race—and it has already started—will be more dangerous than anything we have seen so far.

What are the main features of this new round?

The latest technological advances in armaments make it possible to produce weapons systems with an increased counterforce capability, meaning more accurate and powerful warheads that would be used to destroy the adversary's strategic weapons. The MX missile and new warheads like the MK-12A are examples. All this in itself is sufficient to increase the worries of the other side, which, it can be assumed, will consider these programs threatening, detrimental to the balance and strategic stability, and will therefore take appropriate measures in response.

If, in addition to the worries over these programs, an impression forms that some breakthroughs are possible in antiballistic defense and/or antisubmarine warfare, this may lead to new anxieties about the adversary achieving a first-strike capability. Even if such anxieties are based on illusions, they are very dangerous because they tend to connect security, survival, with a hair-trigger readiness to strike, or even with the possibility of a preemptive strike, let alone their impact on the political atmosphere.

Other new systems threaten to pull the rug from under the arms-control negotiations, making verification tremendously difficult, if not impossible. Cruise missiles, especially land- and sea-based, can serve as an example.

Finally, continuation of the arms race between the United States and the Soviet Union will encourage nuclear proliferation elsewhere.

Do you consider these prospects of doom coming closer?

Yes, at least many of them. You see, I personally may not believe in the technical feasibility of acquiring a first-strike potential, at least in the observable future. Many experts would agree with me on this. But the arms race has been moving into the sphere of creating invulnerable counterforce capabilities, which will inevitably generate illusions and fears about a first-strike capability. This is very dangerous, and it tends to draw the whole arms race even farther away from reality, from the real problems, toward dangerously abstract games and daydream scenarios.

Who is responsible for the arms race?

The initiator of the arms race and its main moving force is the United States.

That is one side of the story. I am sure you are aware of the existence of quite a different view, of the increasing fears in the United States, in Western Europe, in the West in general, of the Soviet military buildup. Let me quote, for example, the statement made by Henry Kissinger at the conference commemorating the thirtieth anniversary of NATO in Brussels in September 1979:

"*Since the middle 1960's the growth of the Soviet strategic force has been massive. It grew from 220 intercontinental ballistic missiles in 1965 to 1,600 around 1972–1973. Soviet submarine-launched missiles grew from negligible numbers to over 900 in the 1970's. And the amazing phenomenon which historians will ponder is that all of this happened without the United States attempting to make a significant effort to rectify that state of affairs. One reason was the growth of a school of thought to which I myself contributed, and many around this conference table also contributed, which considered that strategic stability was a military asset, and in which the historically amazing theory developed that vulnerability contributed to peace and invulnerability contributed to risks of war.*"[10]

Whenever I read such statements, particularly those made by a well-known and authoritative figure like Mr. Kissinger, I feel a little awkward.

I consider it quite normal to have differences of opinion with these people, different interpretations of events, different sympathies, and so on. But I feel really awkward when what they say turns out to be blatant untruth, and one can hardly imagine that they do not know very well, maybe even better than anyone else, what the truth is. And it is not only Kissinger, of course. In the last few years we have witnessed an unprecedentedly massive and well-organized campaign about the nonexistent "Soviet strategic superiority," which poisons the political atmosphere in the United States. I am sure it fully deserves to be named the hoax of the century.

But how about the figures?

Remember the famous saying of Disraeli that there are three kinds of lies: lies, damned lies, and statistics. That's also true for the numbers cited by Kissinger.

Look at the figure of 220 for the number of Soviet intercontinental ballistic missiles in 1965. How many missiles did the Americans have at that time? According to official American sources, 901—four times more. Why did Kissinger not mention that?

Take the SLBMs. Kissinger says the USSR had very few of them in 1965. Well, the United States had as many as 464 at that point.

But what about the trend?

The American numbers I've cited were the result of the massive buildup the Kennedy administration started in 1962 under the false pretext of a "missile gap." It brought the United States very substantial superiority and put us in a position where we had no other way to respond in order to obtain parity with America. Here is the reason for the "massive growth" of which we are accused by Kissinger. And the numbers we had reached in the seventies—sixteen hundred ICBMs and over seven hundred SLBMs—were regarded by Americans as meaning parity. These numbers were codified by the SALT I agreement, whose main architect on the American side, by the way, was Mr. Kissinger. According to the SALT II treaty, the number of our missiles was to be reduced, and the total number of launchers made equal for both sides. It was not our fault that the treaty did not become law.

Even more misleading is his statement that this "massive" Soviet buildup "happened without the United States attempting to make a significant effort to rectify that state of affairs." Quite to the contrary, the United States undertook some very strong efforts. It started MIRVing its missiles, that is, putting several independently targetable warheads on each missile, thus doubling the number of American warheads every two years and securing at the moment of SALT I a fourfold American superiority in the number of warheads.

In other words, the new American buildup, in the form of the MIRVing of their missiles, was already recognized by SALT I?

Of course it was. The United States was by no means sitting on its hands in the face of the Soviet attempt to catch up. It is hard to believe that Kissinger has forgotten that in the early seventies, when he was President Nixon's national security advisor, the United States was starting a new Big Leap Forward in the arms race. The result was that the number of warheads on American ICBMs grew from 1,054 in the late sixties to 2,154 in the late seventies, and the number of SLBM warheads increased during the same period from 656 to about 7000.

In the early seventies the United States also began work on the cruise missile, the new Trident submarine, the B-1 bomber, and a number of other things.

By the way, just a few years ago, Kissinger's memory worked a little better. In 1978, for example, he said: "We speeded up our programs after the SALT agreement in 1972. I think if you look at the record, you will find that the White House always chose the highest defense option that came over from the Pentagon. There was no illusion, on our part, that we could deal with the Soviet Union from a position of weakness."[11]

But all those American programs were explained as "bargaining chips" to make the U.S. position at the talks stronger.

If they were bargaining chips, why was not a single program stopped, despite progress at the SALT talks? Take for instance MIRVs, which were at the time justified as bargaining chips. The United States took special care not to let them be banned or even delayed by the SALT I talks. I recollect that later even Kissinger deplored it.

But let us go back to the Kissinger statement that you asked me to comment on. It turns out to be a very misleading assessment, if one looks at it in light of the facts pertinent to the U.S.-Soviet military balance.

What is particularly sinister is his questioning of the idea that "strategic stability is a military asset," and of those views of mutual vulnerability that allowed both sides at least to begin some progress in arms control. If such thinking is gaining ground in Washington, if these ideas develop and reach their logical conclusion, their implementation can only mean a very grim and dangerous period for international relations.

Do you think the Reagan administration is seriously committed to the goal of achieving military superiority over the USSR?

This massive U.S. rearmament program is not aimed at making the United States equal to the USSR in military power. The goal is military superiority. I think they seriously believe in it and are trying to achieve it. The GOP 1980 election platform proclaimed as one of its chief goals the restoration of the United States to a position of number one in the world militarily. Administration spokesmen have talked of it openly. For instance, Defense Secretary Weinberger, when interviewed by the *New York Times* in the fall of 1981, referred to the 1950s as "a very safe era," when the United States had "a degree of superiority." "Now we've got to regain it," he said.[12] Other members of the administration, though, usually avoid the use of the word *superiority,* and the surrogate term *margin of safety* has been coined.

In the real world, of course, military superiority is meaningless, and what is more, it just can't be achieved. It is simply a blank check for an endless arms race devoid of any strategic or political sense whatsoever. And yet they still proclaim it.

The central idea behind all this talk of superiority is to give the United States greater ability to intimidate those countries whose foreign policies Washington may object to. That intimidation capacity has certainly declined since the 1950s, which may have been "a very safe era" for people like Mr. Weinberger, but a highly dangerous time for many countries that became victims of U.S. intervention or pressure. At that time the United States had what some Americans referred to as an "unbroken chain of deterrence," stretching from the individual marine wading ashore in some faraway land all the way to the nuclear arsenal. The American leaders felt that if they escalated a conflict, they could control the escalation process. Many times they threatened to use nuclear weapons. And, having many more of these weapons than their adversary had, they felt more secure and free to start dangerous capers overseas. Now the "margin of safety" is gone, and American hawks consider that to be the major reason for the U.S. decline of power.

One can understand the U.S. nostalgia for better times, but nostalgia is too deceptive to be used as a policy guide. If you go into a library and read what American hawks said in the fifties and early sixties, you won't get the impression that that was "a very safe era." Ironically, the same right-wing movement that was Mr. Reagan's home base in his long quest for the White House started out in the late fifties to a large extent in protest against the Eisenhower foreign policy, which the Right bitterly castigated as too soft, defeatist, and so forth. The rightists were in a panic over the scope and direction of the changes that were taking place in the world at the time. The United States could do nothing about those changes. The "margin of safety" gave only marginal benefits. The limits to the use of military power as a tool of foreign policy were perfectly clear.

In other words, you think that even if the United States did gain a superiority over the USSR, it would not bring substantial benefits to American foreign policy?

It should be clear that the United States will not be able to get any substantial military advantage over us. We shall never let the United States gain superiority, because it would endanger our security, our vital interests.

I would say more. The United States should not expect to achieve even the marginal benefits it was able to enjoy in the past. We are living in a world that will not let any one nation play the role of a controlling force, a guardian of world order.

A most important motive of this drive for military superiority is the push of the U.S. military-industrial complex for profits, political power, and influence. I would also mention such a motive as an attempt to impose on the Soviet Union and other socialist countries such defense expenditures that would undermine their economies.

Some American analysts are pointing to some other, less tangible motives behind the arms race. Indeed, the current U.S. remilitarization effort may have to do not so much with reality as with certain shifts in the American national mood and the leadership's attempts to manipulate those shifts. James Fallows, a former White House staffer, wrote recently that when the Reagan administration was making its decision to produce and deploy the MX missiles, "the missiles themselves never mattered as much as the 'will' of the country to replace the Minuteman with the MX. . . . We have again entered a period in which words like 'will' and 'nerve' are used to define our policy—rather than words like 'national interest.' "[13]

Whatever the motives, the dangers emanating from the new American military buildup are difficult to overestimate.

But there are a lot of charges that the USSR compels the West to arm and prepare for war. Surely not all these charges are false?

Why not? There is a saying that people never lie so much as during wars and elections, and I would add, during and because of the arms race. How can you make citizens, year in year out, pay billions for arms unless you have a "mortal threat" to point to? This is the true function of the "Soviet threat." It's been carrying out this function for a long time, ever since the 1917 Revolution. We were used as a bugaboo even when we were very weak. What can be expected now that we are really strong? I'm certainly not going to deny that we are strong today, that we have a firm defense to which we have been paying good attention.

Isn't it precisely this strength that arouses fears?

Well, first, it is strength but not superiority, i.e., the other side is just as strong. Second, the fears were blown out of all proportion even when there was no such strength. Let us recall the situation just after World War II, for example. Here we were, the Soviet Union that had suffered terrible losses in the war. America had become stronger, acquired nuclear weapons, and was trying to retain a monopoly on them, so as to dictate her will to the world.

Granted, that as a result of Hitler's scorched-earth policy, the Soviet Union had more urgent priorities in 1945 than to start building nuclear bombs.

Of course we would have preferred to spend our resources on different and very urgent projects. But there was no other way because the United States made use of its position of strength. We have discussed this in our talk about the history of the Cold War. Challenged by the United States as we were after World War II, we had to regard defense as our highest priority. Here lies the true origin of the arms race. It was, and still is, imposed on us.

The Americans say exactly the opposite.

Those who say it seem to forget that all those years we actually were constantly running behind the United States. The United States had nuclear weapons; we had to acquire them. They had the means to deliver nuclear weapons. We did not possess such means; we had to develop them.

The same is true of practically all major strategic weapons systems—SLBMs, MIRVs, cruise missiles, etc. The Americans were the first to introduce them, involving us in another competition, forcing us to follow suit

—and at the same time making loud noises about the terrible military dangers emanating from the USSR, about alleged Soviet military superiority. In fact, we were five to ten years behind the United States with each of those weapons systems.

How would you account for the remarkable durability of the "Soviet threat" issue?

Fear is a very strong emotion. Politicians know it, particularly American politicians. It would suffice to recollect the famous advice of Senator Vandenberg to President Truman: "to scare the hell out of the country" in order to push the Truman Doctrine through the Congress. And you really have to produce such an emotion if you intend to impose a dangerous and costly arms race on your nation. Only when you scare people to death will you get your hundreds of billions of dollars for "defense." And nothing will scare the public more effectively than "the Russians are coming!"

Grouped around this fear are powerful vested interests: the defense industries and the Pentagon, the groups serving them within the government bureaucracy, the academic community, and the media.

For all of them, militarism has become a way of life. They are ready to defend it by all means available. They thrive and prosper on the phantom of the "Soviet threat." They always take good care to nurture it when it gets too worn out through heavy use.

But don't the Americans, as well as the Western Europeans, have grounds to be scared? Hasn't the Soviet Union amassed enough weapons to turn their cities into piles of radioactive rubble and ashes?

I can fully agree with you that awesome means of destruction have been created and that they inspire fear. But not just among Americans and Western Europeans. We in the Soviet Union have been living with this fear for an even longer time. Look at the perverted world we all, people in the West and in the East, are finding ourselves in: our cities, landmarks of culture and the arts, all that the human civilization prides itself on, all that we hold as dear to us as life itself—tens of millions of people, ourselves, our children—all have been reduced to just targets. And we've been living with it; we're becoming used to it to the extent that we've begun to forget just what the situation is. It is this situation that must inspire real fear, and not the Soviet Union. Our cities, too, can be turned into piles of radioactive rubble.

Still, loud shouts are heard all the time that it isn't enough, that more arms and more military spending are necessary. What is really astonishing is that these methods continue to work—although it cannot be so difficult to understand the absurdity of this situation and to see that such shouting has been heard many times over and amounted to nothing, to see that there exist influential circles and groups that profit by deceiving and scaring the public over and over again in total disregard of the dangers that have arisen.

The defense establishment is now the biggest conglomerate in the United States, with over $200 billion a year in sales, employing millions of people, dominating whole areas of the country, well represented in the administration and the Congress. Of course, Americans know it all very well; they've been told the story many times.

But the military business still enjoys the reputation of being a patriotic business. Its commodity is American security; its profit is American honor and dignity. As to the pecuniary interest involved in the arms race, it's not considered good manners to discuss it. This side is hidden, passed over in silence. For, as John K. Galbraith put it, people "do not like to think that, as a nation, we risk potential suicide for present economic advantage."[14] Thus, the song stays largely unsung, despite all the proverbial American love for investigations.

What makes you think there is something to investigate here?

There's too much money at stake. Besides, there's been enough direct evidence, like the Lockheed scandals. They involved foreign countries, but why should those people operate differently at home? Look how the armaments prices are growing; according to *Time* magazine, even the prices of old weapons outstrip inflation several times.

And we know how unscrupulous the military business is about the means. Using the cloak of "national security" and its connections in the government and the media, it can cook up a "threat" out of nothing. Remember how "the missile gap" was born?

What's the story?

In 1957, after the first Soviet Sputnik scared America so much, a special group of experts called the Gaither Panel reported that in a few years the threat created by Soviet missiles would "become critical" and proposed a huge increase in military expenditures and programs. President Eisenhower did not fully agree with the recommendation. But the Democrats took up the issue, and in the 1960 election campaign Senator John F. Kennedy did not miss a chance to accuse the Republicans of neglecting national defense. He made so many promises to correct the situation that even when he learned the truth on his arrival at the White House, he still went ahead with a rapid buildup of the American missile forces.

You mean there was no missile gap at all?

There was a gap, all right, but of a different kind. George Kistiakowsky, who was President Eisenhower's adviser on science and technology at the time, later testified: "The real missile gap, in point of fact, had been in our favor."[15]

Could the missile gap story be an exception to the rule?

As far as I can see, it is the rule. To deceive and scare the Americans by the fake "Soviet threat" there is a fine-tuned machine at work capable of manipulating any government body. Take the recent book by Richard Helms in which he describes how the CIA, under insistent prodding by the Pentagon, committed a direct forgery, producing the estimate according to which, in the late sixties, the Soviet missiles identified in the United States as SS-9 were equipped with MIRVs. The estimate soon turned out to be completely wrong. There have been lots of leaks aimed at frustrating progress toward agreements in SALT talks, and many other episodes that show how integral a part of the military appropriations process the phantom of the "Soviet threat" has become.

And all of it is compounded by vested interests and political calculations.

Yes, of course. Plus outright deception. For some reason or other, none of those who deceived Americans about the events abroad, who made them spend billions of dollars on arms, who needlessly drew the country into crises and conflicts with other nations—none of them has been called to account. What's more, some of those very people who regularly misled the public in the critical situations when important long-term decisions were made on military matters—in the late fifties, in the sixties, and the seventies—are still very much in circulation, regarded as top authorities, as "those who know" and whose opinions ought to be heeded both by the public and by the policy makers. And many of them got high posts in the government under President Reagan.

Now, I don't believe in the conspiracy theory of history. I am not one of those who see conspiracies as the ultimate sources of all large-scale disasters. But in this particular case, in this mythology about the "Soviet threat" and the arms race, I am deeply convinced that we are dealing with a conspiracy or even a whole network of conspiracies.

From living some thirty years in the United States, I came to realize that the interests involved in the American war machine are certainly colossal. But isn't there the Soviet military-industrial complex, too, which also plays a decisive role in the arms race?

You should not try to create a symmetry where the situation is very different. Besides, to have a good arms race, you really need just one military-industrial complex. And it was the American one that started every round of the arms race since the end of World War II.

Why is it not right to search for parallels between the American military-industrial complex and the arms industry in the Soviet Union?

Of course, we have generals and a defense industry. But our defense industry does not operate for profit and thus lacks the expansionist drive that characterizes the arms industry in the West. Besides, our economy does not need the booster of military spending that has been turned on more than once in the West to tackle the problem of insufficient demand in the economy.

Then who makes money when a Soviet tank or missile is produced?

Workers, engineers, plant managers, designers, and so on; all those who have designed and produced a tank or a missile will undoubtedly get their salaries. If they work well, they may even get a bonus. But the thing is, they would get the same if they produced a tractor or a harvester or a combine, or any sophisticated hardware for energy production or peaceful exploration of outer space. And we have no unemployment. On the contrary, we constantly experience labor shortages. There is no idle production capacity at our plants—we experience shortages here as well. That is why we have to build more and more in order to satisfy the country's needs. Hence, if we undertake a conversion and turn to civil production, not only could our country as a whole benefit, but in principle no one would sustain damage. As a matter of fact, even today our defense branches of industry produce a fair amount of civilian goods. In 1971, L. I. Brezhnev stated that 42 percent of the entire defense-industry output went for civilian purposes. In the fall of 1980, he called on the managers of the defense industry to increase production of consumer goods and devote a greater portion of their research and development facilities to the development of new technology for the civilian sectors of the economy.

Do you have any comparative figures for the current military expenditures of East and West?

Of course. The official U.S. figures for American military expenditures have risen from $127.8 billion in fiscal year 1978/79 to $200 billion for 1981/82. The Reagan administration has requested $260 billion for fiscal year 1982/83. The Soviet military expenditures were 17.2 billion rubles ($24.6 billion) in 1978, and the budget allocation for 1982 is 17.05 billion rubles ($24.3 billion).

This difference looks absolutely improbable. You must be aware that far different figures on the Soviet military budget circulate in the West.

Details of our budget are not made public, so I can give only a rather general explanation for the difference. The United States has a professional army, whereas ours is based on conscription. To attract qualified personnel to the army, the U.S. government has to pay rather substantial salaries to the GIs. About half of the American military budget goes for salaries and rents. A GI gets something like $300 to $500 a month. A Soviet soldier can only buy cigarettes with the money he gets. The life style in a conscript army where citizens serve out of duty rather than for material considerations is far more modest than in a professional army.

I could mention another factor having to do with our defense industry. Our price system does not allow that industry to arbitrarily raise the prices on its products.

The CIA estimates current Soviet military spending to be in the range of $180 billion.

All right, let's take, for instance, the data on military spending published by the International Institute of Strategic Studies in London. According to the 1981/82 edition of their biannual *Military Balance,* which uses data based on vastly overrated estimates of Soviet defense spending, NATO spent $241 billion on military purposes in 1980, while the Warsaw Pact spent $164.7 billion. Thus, the spending ratio is nearly 1.5 to 1 in favor of NATO. And we have many fewer people in the armed forces than our potential adversaries. According to official Soviet figures, NATO, including the United States, has 4,933,000 in regular armed forces, while the Warsaw Pact, including the USSR, has 4,788,000.[16] If we take the nuclear balance, according to the London institute's statistics, NATO has 2.2 times as many nuclear warheads as the Warsaw Pact.

There is a striking difference between the two sides in policy postures, as well. The United States and NATO plan a steady and massive increase in military preparations for years to come. The Soviet Union has so far not followed that example.

This is what the balance is really like, even if you use Western figures, which are extremely biased against us in many cases. We think we have a rough parity, despite the disadvantages to us made evident by the figures I have cited. By the way, the fact of parity is officially recognized by the Pentagon, even though the Pentagon does not advertise it. According to the U.S. Defense Department Annual Report to Congress concerning the 1981/82 military budget, "... While the era of U.S. superiority is long past, parity—not U.S. inferiority—has replaced it, and the United States and the Soviet Union are roughly equal in strategic nuclear power."[17]

You have said that the capitalist economy needs military spending to keep going. How does that square with the view that there should be a mutual interest in cutting the military expenditures?

I have said that military spending is used as a way to generate additional demand in the economy, but the fact that it is used does not necessarily mean it's good for the economy. A military boom is "helpful" in the sense that it can increase activity for a time in one sector of the economy, namely the military industry. A short-term "ripple" effect for the whole economy may also result. If there is a real benefit in all this, it goes to the arms manufacturers. But the economy as a whole has suffered as a result of this quick fix. Its basic problems have been exacerbated; its long-term prospects have dimmed further.

Our specialists think that the recognition of the evils of a militarized economy began in the United States during the war in Southeast Asia. Public debates in the late sixties helped to clarify the fact that the huge appropriations for armaments were becoming ruinous for the American economy. The war budget drove up inflation. It undermined the competitive posture of the United States in world markets. Many American businessmen concluded that one of the reasons the Japanese and West German industries were so successful in competing with the United States was the abnormal budgetary appropriations for the war in Vietnam. Soviet specialists note that some Americans have become aware of other adverse effects of big military spending as well.

Which effects in particular?

In recent years Americans have complained that the United States is beginning to lag behind some other countries in the numbers of inventions and scientific innovations. Some see one of the reasons for it in the fact that America's very best brains are being tapped and used up for the military economy. One-third to 40 percent of American engineers work in the arms industry, which is quite a brain drain. More and more people in the United States are beginning to understand that inflation is connected with arms spending and that the arms race plays a significant role there.

Economic analyses of the Reagan remilitarization program have only strengthened the view that the arms buildup could further aggravate American economic problems. For instance, George F. Brown, Jr., vice president of Data Resources, Inc., testifying before the Joint Economic Committee of the U.S. Congress in October 1981, pointed out that, according to his firm's estimates, the Reagan military buildup would put a severe strain not only on the U.S. financial system, but on the productive capacity of American industries as well. According to M. Kathryn Eickhoff, president of the National Association of Business Economists, the American economy will be able to cope with the growing foreign competition only if there is a huge investment in the expansion and modernization of the civilian sector of the economy—a task that the military buildup effectively frustrates.[18]

The attitudes toward military-generated jobs are also changing in the American labor movement. Growing numbers in the labor circles are realizing that money spent on civilian production opens up more jobs than the same money going into military production, because the arms industry is getting less labor-intensive.

Which reminds me that when, in Amsterdam, a gigantic rally was taking place against the production of neutron weapons, in Livermore, California, kids were buying T-shirts with slogans supporting the production of these horrors because their fathers owed their jobs to these factories.

I think it's tragic when people are faced with the dilemma of making death or going hungry. Yes, whole areas in the United States are dependent on the Pentagon orders to provide them with jobs. But the fact that military spending creates fewer jobs than the same money would if it were spent in civilian sectors of the economy has become better known. This is one of the reasons why some labor unions representing the workers employed by the arms industry are now actively working together with church and business groups on practical plans for converting the military economy to peaceful needs.

I think there exist substantial grass-roots sentiments for an alternative to militarism. In the early 1980s, those sentiments became less visible. Talking of peaceful conversion of the war economy can be portrayed as unpatriotic when the nation is back on a warpath. But more recently, there has been a new resurgence of antimilitarism.

Nobody would argue that U.S. military expenditures are not enormous. But I'm sure you're aware that they amount to a smaller share of the gross national product (GNP) and of the budget than, say, fifteen years ago. Nonmilitary spending now takes a bigger share than military spending, while in the late sixties it was the other way around. Even with the current sharp rise in military expenditures, the 1981 military budget commits the same amount of real resources to the Pentagon as prior to the war in Indochina.

Yes, I'm familiar with this line of argument.

Then please comment.

All right, let's start with the share of the GNP. Of course, 5 or 6 percent of the GNP, which has been the level of U.S. military spending in recent years, is less than 9 or 13 percent, as it was at times in the past. But it does not mean that 6 percent is peanuts. When you assess the growth of the GNP, each single percentage point makes a tremendous difference, to say nothing of 6 percent. And each year this percent is simply cut out and thrown away.

The budget picture is even starker. The budget—and not even the whole of it—reflects the amount of resources the society allocates to the solution of national problems. Those problems include not only military security but also social security, health, education, urban problems, environmental protection, energy, basic research. If almost a third of those resources goes for military purposes, it is a great damage to the society and its ability to solve its most pressing problems.

But is not a long-term change of priorities in the budget a fact?

Well, right now we are witnessing the change of priorities back in favor of greater military spending. But even if the correlation established in the 1970s were preserved, that still wouldn't mean that social spending is big, while the military goes hungry. To say nothing of the fact that comparison of the current level with the pre–Indochina war level can be very misleading. The pre–Indochina war period in this respect was certainly not a period of "normalcy." We have to remember that at that time, which was at the peak of the Cold War, the United States was carrying out a massive program of strategic buildup adopted in the atmosphere of the "missile-gap" hysteria, as well as a rapid increase in its conventional forces in accordance with the doctrine of "flexible response," that is, preparedness for waging simultaneously two and a half wars—two big ones plus a small war.

It is also very important when making such comparisons to take note of the fact that the level of military spending is under constant downward pressure from the growing societal demands, which the government can't ignore if it wants any stability at all. I mean development of energy resources, environmental protection, and social spending to compensate for growing economic difficulties faced by a majority of citizens. You have to take all these factors and pressures into account when you try to answer the question of whether the current share of the GNP eaten up by military appropriations is big or small. If you look at America's domestic problems, you won't get the impression that they are swimming in money to solve them.

But social spending did increase.

Yes, it did. A very significant role was played here by the serious domestic disturbances in the United States during the 1960s. People went into the streets. There were riots. The entire decade was full of social unrest. People refused to put up with what they had to endure. The rise in social spending was initiated by President Johnson. Certainly, there was a lot of rhetoric in the concept of the Great Society. No doubt, L.B.J. also had his personal and political interests in mind when he called for this major effort to ameliorate pressing social problems in America. But there was also a deeper motive involved here, I think.

As a keen politician, Johnson must have realized that much greater attention ought to be paid to social problems, or domestic instability would reach explosive proportions.

But the same Johnson sent hundreds of thousands of young men into the quagmire of Vietnam.

Yes, and the Vietnam war torpedoed the Great Society and the Johnson reign resulted in a complete mess.

All of this has to be remembered if we want to have an accurate assessment of changing priorities. When the seventies arrived, the Vietnam war and militarism in general were running into stiff and often violent opposition throughout America, while demands for social spending were steadily growing.

Nixon did not have much of a choice. The whole situation required an increase of domestic spending and a decrease of military spending.

But now the whole mood in the country seems to have changed.

Yes, we observe active attempts to reverse the proportion between military and social spending once more. And the government has succeeded —at least for a few years—in weakening the popular resistance to massive increases in military expenditures. But, as the Carter-Reagan rearmament program began to unfold, public opinion began to turn against the "guns instead of butter" policy. There are growing worries that the exorbitant military buildup may seriously undermine the American economy. Pressures for more serious governmental attention to domestic problems have not abated because the old problems have not been solved. Many of these have grown even more urgent, and new problems have appeared. The United States government cannot close its eyes to the domestic scene. It cannot run away from it. After all, the United States remains one of the most backward among Western nations in terms of social policy.

But the current theme in Washington is that people don't trust the government to solve their problems. Isn't this one of the reasons Reagan was elected president?

I think American conservatives really commit a serious mistake if they assume that an anti-inflationary mood among the public presents a firm basis for an about-face in social policy; that their mandate calls for a return to nineteenth-century capitalism, or pre–New Deal capitalism. Americans are angry indeed about inflation and taxes, but at the same time support for most specific social programs initiated by the government has grown throughout the seventies.

I do not see a contradiction here. People are simply saying, "Yes, the government can be helpful in alleviating difficulties and injustices created by the market, but at the same time, the government should bring order to its own finances and spread the tax burden more fairly." This sums it up, in my opinion. Americans are now expecting more rather than less from their government. And then, if you have already given something to the people, it is tremendously difficult simply to take it away.

You have said that the arms race undermines rather than strengthens national security.

Yes. We have already discussed the purely military side of the problem. The same goes for the economic impact of the arms race. Siphoning off increasingly large sums from the economy—the social and cultural spheres —the arms race is gnawing at the nation's welfare. The emerging dilemma is whether it's worth strengthening the protection of a household if the cost of such strengthening completely ruins it. As I have said, increases in the numbers of weapons and the creation of new weapons can upset military and political stability and thus create additional threats to national security.

Can you give an example?

Well, I guess the MIRV story is as good as any. We have talked already about the problem of counterforce capabilities. If a nation acquires a capability for knocking out all or a significant part of her adversary's strategic forces by means of a preemptive strike, this increases fears and insecurity on the other side, encourages it to create similar capabilities to threaten the adversary, to create new systems that would be safe from such a strike, and to put its own rockets on the hair trigger. So, the result, as you see, is more instability. Such a counterforce capability might become possible, however, only given a large increase in the numbers of warheads, since to knock out one of your adversary's rockets you need more than one warhead of your own, because you can't guarantee 100 percent accuracy and reliability. This fact had stabilized the situation before the appearance of multiple independently targetable reentry vehicles. It was so easy to outstrip any attempt to gain counterforce capability just by adding as many or even a bit fewer missiles than the adversary.

The United States changed the situation by introducing MIRVs. Since we didn't have any at that time, Americans were not concerned about the consequences. Then the Soviet MIRVs appeared, and the United States became very much concerned, and then even hysterical about the "vulnerability" of its Minuteman force. It became the main theme of the anti-SALT campaign. It was this "vulnerability" that became the pretext—if not the reason—for introducing a new, very dangerous and destabilizing strategic system, the MX, with all its exotic modes of deployment, and also the pretext for a new attitude toward the limitation of ABMs. In other words, the MIRV served as the fuse that lit up a whole chain of events that undermined stability.

Indeed, many U.S. experts seem to be greatly worried about the vulnerability of their ICBMs, citing the fact that, having a greater throw weight, the Russian missiles will be able to carry more warheads if the USSR continues MIRVing them in the 1980s. This, they say, gives you a substantial superiority—at least until the MX is deployed.

As I mentioned, the vulnerability of land-based missiles has become the subject of a heated discussion touching upon the problems of the "Soviet threat," the strategic balance, and the SALT II treaty. Whether this question deserves such emotions is open to doubt. I don't think it does—but this is the opinion of a layman, not of a professional.

Why do you downplay the problems of ICBM vulnerability?

Let us look at the substance of the problem. Are the ICBMs becoming technically more vulnerable with the appearance of MIRVs and the increased accuracy and power of warheads? Of course they are. If the Americans are concerned about it, let them remember that it was the United States that initiated the MIRV race, the counterforce concept, and the programs to increase the accuracy of warheads.

But I would not agree with the proposition that the growing ICBM vulnerability gives advantages to the Soviet Union. This proposition is false. The American Minuteman III missile equipped with the new Mark 12A warhead is a powerful counterforce weapon making the Soviet strategic forces now—not in the future—more vulnerable than the American forces. As to the future, we know that the early eighties is considered in the United States as an especially dangerous period. At the SALT II hearings in the Foreign Relations Committee of the U.S. Senate, estimates were made concerning comparative vulnerability of American and Soviet missiles. According to these estimates, the United States would be able to destroy 60 percent of our ICBMs, while we would be able to knock out 90 percent of theirs. But it was emphasized in the same testimony that the ICBMs are only one "leg" of the triad, and that this leg is of far less significance for the United States because it accounts for only 24 percent of the total number of American warheads, while the Soviet Union has 70 percent of its warheads on ICBMs. Accordingly, the comparative capabilities for a disarming strike were estimated this way: the USSR in the early eighties will be able to destroy 22 percent of the American strategic potential by such a strike while the United States will be able to destroy 42 percent of ours.[19]

This is how the situation looks with present weapons. The introduction of the MX will hardly reduce the vulnerability of U.S. ICBMs, but—and you don't hear this very often from this system's supporters—increase the vulnerability of Soviet ICBMs. Other weapons systems scheduled by the United States, like Trident II or Pershing II (the latter, by the way, cuts the warning time to five or six minutes with regard to targets in the European part of the USSR), will also have significant counterforce capabilities.

In other words, you consider the talk about the "Soviet threat" to American ICBMs groundless?

There is no doubt that, in case of an attack on the USSR or its allies, the Soviet strategic forces will be able to inflict what is called "unacceptable damage" on the United States. It is just as certain that the USSR possesses the physical capability to destroy a certain number of American ICBMs. But the United States has at least the same capabilities. In this sense the threats are mutual. And with regard to ICBM kill capability, the American plans are aimed at gaining a substantial superiority here. It will be only logical to assume that the Soviet Union will try to prevent this from happening, which, in turn, will not be liked by Americans and will cause a new fit of paranoia about the "Soviet threat."

But you have put in doubt the crucial importance of the very problem of ICBM vulnerability.

Yes, with a qualifier that I'm not a professional expert in the field. I have noted, however, that quite a few experts have also pointed to the flaws of the idea of vulnerability and think that this should hardly be regarded as a crucial problem. For instance, there is the extreme technical complexity of firing a salvo aimed at hitting well over a thousand targets simultaneously. And this is something no one has ever, or is ever likely to, experiment with. There is then the problem of "fratricide effect"—after the first warheads hit the targets, the impact of their explosions would inevitably create great difficulties for the flight of the rest of the warheads to their targets, damaging or deflecting them.

What is even more important, experts point out that even if it were possible to destroy all the adversary ICBMs on the ground, this would not be a really disarming strike. There are the SLBMs—the ballistic missiles on submarines, which are for all practical purposes invulnerable to modern weapons—and the strategic bombers, which can very quickly take off and strike back. These two "legs" of the U.S. strategic triad—the SLBMs and the bombers—account for almost 70 percent of the American strategic potential. If one is worried about a Soviet first strike, one should keep in mind that those two legs would remain almost intact for a response. I could add to all this a couple of other thoughts.

Please.

All the scare stories, all the scenarios of a disarming strike against ICBMs, are based on an assumption that the adversary will wait for this strike to happen, and only after it will he be immersed in a Hamlesian situation—torn by the question of what to do, if anything, and to be or not to be, of course.

But I can't imagine that the government and the military command of a country receiving the news that several thousand warheads are flying in its direction would sit idly by and wait for them to explode, so that they can determine whether it's a counterforce or a countervalue strike, and then start to indulge in these painful reflections and intellectual exercises.

By the way, what is the difference between a counterforce strike and a countervalue one?

A counterforce strike aims at military targets, primarily at strategic forces, while a countervalue strike is aimed at the cities and the economic potential. Well, instead of waiting to see just what kind of strike it is, the country under attack would, I think, promptly launch a retaliatory strike. Naturally, its targets would not be limited to the enemy's ICBM silos, empty, or at least half empty, by that time, but would certainly include the cities. Thus, instead of a limited exchange of "counterforce strikes," we'd have an all-out thermonuclear war that would bring an end to human history. So anyone planning for a preemptive strike on the other side's ICBMs must consider such a prospect not only possible, but highly probable.

This goes to the heart of the miscalculations by the authors of such scenarios. Making a decision to strike at the adversary's ICBMs is, in my opinion, absolutely tantamount to a decision to start an all-out nuclear war. If deterrence works and you count on your adversary's common sense, he won't start such a war, and the concern about ICBM vulnerability loses ground. If, however, you expect the adversary to be capable of easily starting a general nuclear war—of committing national suicide—then it means that deterrence has failed, and in this case the problem of ICBM vulnerability becomes even less relevant. In the latter case, one should pray to his own God and be quick to push his own button.

Having come to this conclusion, I don't have the slightest doubt that it will produce skeptical smiles among many experts, at least in the United States. But I, for my part, would like to say that these armchair strategists themselves are becoming a real threat. Drawing the most incredible scenarios, they only manage to find new excuses for pushing on the arms race and for increasing fears, uncertainties, and tensions in the world. They don't understand a damn thing about real policy. And by this I mean not only Realpolitik; they also disregard elementary human psychology. Most of them have never seen action and do not know what real war is all about.

You seem rather annoyed by them. But if what you said is correct, their version of vulnerability is wrong and therefore harmless.

You know, when baptism almost became a state religion in the United States I started to study the Bible. Remember the line from Ecclesiastes? "Wisdom is better than weapons of war, but one sinner destroyeth much good" (Eccles. 9:18). These scenarios are begetting new fears, undermining mutual trust, and giving additional impulses to the new thrust in the arms race.

But I've interrupted your discussion of strategy.

You see, I think in general that deterrence looks quite different to politicians and sensible military leaders than to these armchair strategists. From the leaders' viewpoint, the very prospect of the destruction of the capital city is already a very serious deterrence. I think it was McGeorge Bundy who once pointed to this fact. And what about the prospect of losing ten of the biggest cities? What would the United States be like without New York and Washington, Boston and Chicago, San Francisco and Los Angeles, New Orleans and Houston, Minneapolis and St. Louis? Or, for that matter, the Soviet Union without Moscow, Leningrad, Kiev, Sverdlovsk, Baku, Tashkent, Minsk, Dnepropetrovsk, Gorki, and Riga? What war aims could possibly justify such monstrous losses?

Now imagine our two countries without a hundred of their biggest cities each. Theoretically, just one submarine can inflict such damage to our respective countries, and the number of nuclear warheads accumulated today amounts to thousands. But it turns out that some people still want many more and are thinking up even more fantastic scenarios for Armageddon.

But the Soviet programs and arsenals also grew, following predesigned goals and scenarios.

Yes, I've already discussed this interaction. The United States makes a push ahead, and we move to catch up with it. It is the mad inertia of the arms race. The accumulation of weapons goes far beyond any rational requirements. If we don't put an end to it, this will go on and on. And the threat of war will grow. It is all most deplorable, but the U.S. approach does not leave us any options.

Some strange things happen nowadays indeed: new weapons are being developed and accumulated, new wars are being prepared for and made even more probable under quite different pretexts and often with quite different purposes in mind.

What do you have in mind?

You know, I often have a feeling that these periodic attempts by the United States to get a military edge over the USSR have become for her a kind of Freudian compensation for . . . well, the lack of omnipotence that that country has been feeling in her dealings with the world in recent years.

Professor Edward Teller, the so-called father of the H-bomb, told me in 1980 that the Soviet Union would be the absolute victor if a nuclear war were to erupt. "With what does Mr. Carter intend to stop the Soviets?" he asked. The same goes for Ronald Reagan, I suppose.

I can understand Dr. Teller's parental feelings. He seems upset that his baby hasn't been used. He seems upset about so many facts of life in this world—like the existence of a Soviet Union that will not be bullied, or the fact that a nuclear war cannot be won. I'm afraid his case is hopeless. There is just one sane attitude toward such a war—prevent it at all costs. I think the American physicians who are concerned about nuclear war put it very well, stating that it is beyond medicine's capacity to cope with the consequences of nuclear war. They stress that, as with incurable diseases, the only possible solution is preventive medicine—prevention of the war itself. The United States, which introduced the nuclear weapon as a tool of foreign policy, has periodically tried to get around this maxim of the nuclear age. Right now it is in another such period.

According to the U.S. government, Soviet military preparations go beyond the requirements of defense. This is what bothers Americans.

I just wonder how the Americans would have estimated their defense requirements had they been in our position, having to consider at least three potential adversaries—the United States, with both its strategic and conventional arms; the NATO allies of the United States in Europe, and Japan, another American ally.

On the other hand, we can respond with our own assessment of American military preparations, and it would be a much better-founded calculation. We in the Soviet Union do have a strong impression that the size and direction of the American military programs cannot be explained by defensive considerations. The United States outnumbers the Soviet Union in nuclear warheads and now develops its strategic forces with a great stress on counterforce capabilities. It has many strike aircraft carriers and large amphibious forces in the proximity of Soviet borders. Generally speaking, about half of America's troops are stationed overseas, and with the special Rapid Deployment Force being organized, the U.S. military doctrine openly presumes that it can intervene abroad, even with a first use of nuclear weapons. That does not look very defensive, particularly if you consider the relatively safe geographical position of the United States—with oceans to the east and the west, with friendly and militarily weak neighbors to the north and the south.

Thus, one's defense requirements always look different from the outside. After all, each of us can be strongly convinced of being a good guy and not wishing to do harm to anyone. I'd add that, in a broader sense, if you don't single out any particular power, there is really too much military hardware accumulated in the world in recent decades. It goes far beyond requirements of defense and security. That's why we have been advocating disarmament. And there's tremendous overkill capability, which the biggest powers could easily part with, provided there is the political will on all sides. At the very least, there is a full possibility not to build more.

But the Soviet Union does have more troops, tanks, guns, and God knows what.

Wait a minute. We have fewer troops than our potential adversaries in NATO. We may have, let us say, more tanks than NATO, but, then, NATO has more advanced antitank weapons. If you assume we have more guns, there's even by the Western assessment a NATO superiority in self-propelled guns and in tactical nuclear weapons. Of course there are asymmetries, but if you take them all together, there's an overall rough balance, parity, equality—whatever you may wish to call it. This has been confirmed time and again not only by us, but by many Western analysts and political leaders as well.

Are you speaking of an overall military balance or of a balance in Europe?

I'm speaking of both. Of course, there are different assessments of both balances in the West, but I refer to the more authoritative ones made by former U.S. Defense Secretary Brown, former Bundeskanzler of the Federal Republic of Germany Helmut Schmidt, the International Institute for Strategic Studies in London, etc.

Do they include the SS-20 and other nuclear weapons deployed in Europe?

Yes, of course. For instance, the International Institute for Strategic Studies has confirmed the existence of a nuclear balance in Europe.[20] Such well-known American specialists as Paul Doty and Robert Metzger speak of a rough parity in "Eurostrategic" weapons systems with a six-hundred-kilometer-plus range.

You must be aware of the uproar caused by the deployment of the SS-20 missiles in the Western part of the USSR. Why did the Soviet Union insist on doing this, especially during an era of blossoming détente?

Yes, we are very much aware of the uproar you're talking about, and we think the reasons for it are very similar to the other uproars over this or that variety of "Soviet threat." Namely, such an uproar is usually caused by the desire to justify new NATO military programs, in this particular case the Pershing II and the land-based cruise missiles.

As for the SS-20, it is a rocket that replaces old Soviet medium-range ballistic missiles referred to in the West as SS-4 and SS-5, which were introduced twenty years ago and have become obsolete. Mind you, as Leonid Brezhnev stated with all seriousness, the overall number of Soviet MRBMs in Europe, far from increasing, became somewhat smaller. For each deployed SS-20 we remove one or two older missiles.

But NATO experts maintain, and many in the West are convinced, that the introduction of the SS-20 cannot be seen as a simple modernization. These are supposed to be new missiles of a superior class.

Well, what would the West think of the USSR if we replaced twenty-year-old missiles with something other than new and better missiles? The crux of the matter is that the mission of these rockets hasn't changed. Just like the SS-4 and the SS-5, the SS-20 doesn't reach the United States; it remains really a theater weapon, not a strategic weapon. It is our response to the forward-based systems the United States has in Western Europe—about sixteen hundred delivery systems along with U.S. submarines carrying long-range missiles, nuclear-armed planes on aircraft carriers in the Mediterranean Sea and the northern Atlantic, which are capable of striking Soviet territory, as well as the numerous missiles and planes of America's nuclear allies in Europe: Britain and France. The Soviet MRBMs are called upon to perform the role of our deterrent against all these weapons.

The NATO version of the reasons for their deployment of cruise and Pershing II missiles is similar: they also talk of modernization and of restoring a balance.

It looks similar only until you take a closer look. The new NATO missiles will perform new roles, new functions, for they'll be able to reach deep into Soviet territory. It means, according to the existing criteria, that these American weapons are not just theater weapons, ones used in the theaters of war outside the territories of either the USSR or the United States, but strategic weapons as well. At the same time, they are not covered by the SALT agreements. Doesn't this alone create new problems?

You mean that the NATO modernization program affects the SALT process?

Yes, it does. According to the SALT II treaty, we are to cut our strategic weapons by 250 launchers and have an equal number of launchers as the United States has. The Americans have strongly insisted on such equality ever since 1972, and the two sides have been arguing over every dozen missiles, if not over every single one. We finally agreed, although we had earlier insisted on including the American forward-based systems. Well, now the United States is planning to add to their strategic force about six hundred new launchers not covered by the SALT II treaty. Why should we care where a missile aimed at our territory takes off from, be it Montana or North Dakota, West Germany or Holland? Actually, the latter situation would be worse because of the forbiddingly short warning time of Pershing II.

And how about the next agreement on strategic arms? As already agreed, we would be talking of further cuts, even significant cuts, in strategic weapons. But how should we approach these talks, if the USSR is to decrease the numbers of weapons, but the United States, while agreeing to limit its Minutemen, SLBMs, and cruise missiles on strategic bombers, goes ahead with deploying Pershing II and ground-launched cruise missiles in Europe?

So these are the primary Soviet objections against production and deployment of new American missiles in Europe?

Yes. And I would add a few more. The deployment of these missiles will mean a new round of the nuclear arms race. They also can play a very destabilizing role, creating an illusion that the United States can acquire the capability to wage a nuclear war against USSR on a regional level, leaving safe U.S. territory. All in all, it weakens the nuclear deterrence in Europe. And, this is not a kind of a weapon capable of strengthening West European security. Just the opposite—it undermines it. The true rationale for this weapon, as Marshal D. F. Ustinov pointed out, "is not the concern for Europe but the reduction of the strength of the retaliatory blow at the U.S. territory in case of an aggression against the USSR."

It is obvious that a new round in the arms race is hardly likely to create greater stability either in Europe or in the world at large. But what can be done about it? What does the USSR do to prevent this round?

We have done a lot not only to prevent this new round, but to achieve real disarmament in Europe. Our readiness to solve the INF problem through negotiations was repeatedly stated before and after NATO's December 1979 decision. The Soviet position was specified at the Twenty-sixth Party

Congress of the CPSU, in a number of President Brezhnev's subsequent statements, and in the Soviet Union's official proposals at the INF talks in Geneva in 1982.

Most of all, we would like to see a nuclear-free Europe, and therefore we have proposed to get rid of not only medium-range but also tactical nuclear weapons in Europe. In case the West is not ready for such a radical solution, we have made other far-reaching proposals. According to them, both sides would agree to reduce their numbers of intermediate-range nuclear weapons from the current level of about one thousand to three hundred by 1990. Most of the weapons would be destroyed, and those not destroyed on our side would be put far enough behind the Urals not to be able to reach Western Europe. Adequate verification procedures would be worked out.

To facilitate progress at the INF talks, we have stopped the deployment of SS-20 missiles and begun to remove some of our IRBMs in advance of the limits to be agreed upon. Unfortunately, the United States insists on the so-called "zero option" proposal put forth by President Reagan in November 1981. It is a curious kind of proposal—we get zero, while NATO gets new options. According to the Reagan plan, the Soviet Union would dismantle both the new and the old intermediate-range ballistic missiles in its forces, while NATO would only refrain from deploying its new missiles, keeping all the forces it already has, including the quite substantial number of British and French nuclear forces—both planes and missiles. And it is far from clear whether the United States will be ready to refrain from deploying its sea-based cruise missiles, particularly in the vicinity of Europe. What's more, the Reagan plan stipulates that such unilateral reductions be imposed on the Soviet Union not only in Europe, but in the Far East as well.

Meanwhile, time is running out. The deadline for the deployment of U.S. missiles is getting nearer every day. The Geneva talks are clearly being used by Washington to defuse the growing political power of the antinuclear movement in Western Europe, rather than to work out an agreement that would stop the impending dangerous round in the arms race.

NATO didn't make any sense, either, when it rejected our moratorium proposal of early 1981. NATO said it was afraid of the new SS-20 missiles the Soviet Union was already deploying, so they decided to deploy new American missiles in response, starting in 1983. In early 1981 we suggested that both sides refrain from any new deployment while we negotiated the problem. We virtually proposed a measure of unilateral restraint, affecting only ourselves. Why then did NATO reject the moratorium idea? I have only one explanation: the United States viewed, and still views, the moratorium as an obstacle, fearing that its introduction would reduce tensions in Europe and thus impede the NATO rearmament.

So, you are blaming the Americans.

Yes, but not only them. Those Europeans who belong to the so-called "NATO community" were very active. Fred Kaplan, an expert on military and political issues on the staff of the U.S. House of Representatives, traced the origins of the Euromissile decision to a small group of influential experts called the European-American Workshop, chaired by a well-known American hawk, Albert Wohlstetter, and tied in with the London-based International Institute for Strategic Studies. It included consultants and analysts from Germany, Britain, Norway, and other NATO countries. This group first persuaded Helmut Schmidt, who raised the issue in October 1977. Carter was not slow to pick it up.[21]

What was the rationale for that? An important argument in favor of the Euromissile decision was the open or hidden doubt about the credibility of the American nuclear "umbrella" over Western Europe—the doubt that in the case of a war in Europe the United States would use its strategic forces against the Soviet Union in the light of Soviet-American strategic parity. Was this doubt wholly unfounded?

First, the deployment of new American medium-range missiles won't have any impact on the situation regarding the U.S. umbrella. If these missiles —I repeat, American missiles—hit the Soviet territory, the retaliatory strike would be aimed not only at the countries where they took off, but at the United States, too, just as it would be if the rockets came from Wyoming.

Second, these doubts are based on a totally preposterous idea that one can wage a war in Europe, even a nuclear one, which would not grow into a general holocaust. Here again we run into the sphere of American armchair strategists' creative thinking, of this strategic hairsplitting divorced from reality and devoid of common sense. The trouble is that this hairsplitting is not just a mental exercise. It serves to justify the enormous expenditures and efforts to build up nuclear and conventional arms in Europe.

Meanwhile, it's quite evident that anyone who decides to start a war in Europe will have to accept that it will be a world war with the use of modern weapons of mass destruction. Probably the most absurd notion in this regard is that it will be possible to limit the use of nuclear weapons in such a war to medium-range or tactical weapons, keeping the war in the framework of a "local conflict."

Most Europeans are well aware that such expectations are nonsense.

Certainly, because for them such a conflict would be total, absolutely strategic, if I may say so. Even if the war were limited to the use of tactical weapons. As early as in the 1960s, it was calculated that even "a very limited" use of such weapons in Europe would cost up to twenty million lives. If, as is much more likely, the war transcended such limits, the number of casualties would reach, according to some experts, at least a hundred million.[22]

Neutron weapons have been a subject of heated discussion in Europe in recent years. What effect would they have on the overall situation?

Aside from the moral aspect of a weapon designed to kill people but save property, the ERW—enhanced radiation weapon—encountered opposition on two major grounds. For one thing, a new type of weapon means a new round in the arms race. For another, there appears the threat of lowering the nuclear threshold. After all, the whole idea behind the ERW was to convince Europeans that, in case of war, nuclear weapons could be used in the European theater without excessive danger to the countries and peoples of Europe.

One argument in favor of the neutron bomb is that it's only effective for defensive purposes.

In my view, this notion should have become too shameful to repeat after all the discussions held on the subject. By the very nature of its major functions the neutron weapon is more offensive than any other nuclear weapon. Behind President Reagan's decision to start its mass production there is a clear design to make nuclear war more thinkable and more feasible, even in the tightly built and overcrowded conditions of Europe— and, more than that, to demonstrate to the Soviet Union and the whole world that Washington would not hesitate to start such a war.

Aside from this political aspect, in a narrower, technical sense, the neutron weapon is still far from being defensive in character. It is effective against tanks, but it is no less usable against defensive fortifications. It can annihilate the defenders of a town, as well as its residents, while keeping its streets free of debris. It can preserve bridges, highways, or airfields, while killing all their defenders. Finally, since this weapon produces only half the radioactive fallout that an ordinary atomic bomb does, it can be a very tempting weapon for an attacking side to use when it wants to occupy an area.

Let's go back to what the USSR calls the "alleged Soviet threat." Recently, much has been written and spoken in the United States about Soviet civil-defense programs. It is asserted that those programs are so massive and elaborate that they will enable the Soviet Union to wage a nuclear war and yet avoid "unacceptable damage."

Yes, we have the civil-defense service in the Soviet Union, just like the

Americans, the Dutch, or any other nation. Yet nobody in the USSR believes that civil defense could make nuclear war painless or acceptable, or could lower the inevitable casualties and losses to some tolerable level. Do you think we would have agreed to limiting ABMs if we had hoped for civil defense? All this, by the way, was carefully explained by a deputy chief of our general staff to the American senators who visited Moscow in 1979. I took part in those discussions and remember very well that the senators were told the Soviet Union spends on its civil defense about the same share of its military expenditures as the United States does—about one-tenth of one percent. As a matter of fact, it is the United States that from time to time becomes overenthusiastic about civil defense. It happened in the early sixties, and it is happening again now. When I travel in the United States, I often encounter the sign "Fallout Shelter." I have never come across one in the Soviet Union. It's conceivable that another civil-defense hysteria in the United States might not be so bad from the Soviet military point of view: these programs would siphon off a lot of Pentagon money for useless things.

In the meantime, scare stories of the Soviet civil defense continue to spread. Major General George Keegan is among the most active in this field. Before retirement, he was chief of intelligence of the U.S. Air Force, using that post to dress up his fantasies and concoctions as intelligence data.

General Keegan told me that you were the most dangerous propagandist the Kremlin ever let loose on Americans.

Since Keegan is one of the main mouthpieces of an anti-Soviet campaign as deceitful as it is dangerous, I would consider such an assessment flattering.

We have finally arrived at the subject of American generals. What is your opinion about the role they play in American politics?

American generals are, undoubtedly, a separate matter. To begin with, you may find different personalities among them. Some of them are still remembered by us since the times we were allies. Even after the war quite a few American generals and admirals were putting forward sane political ideas. All through the seventies I had a chance to participate in discussions and seminars with such American officers as Generals James Gavin, Brent Scowcroft, and Royal Allison; Admirals George Miller, Gene LaRoque, and Noel Gayler. I have nothing but deep respect for these people, although, naturally, we disagree on a lot of things. I have come across, for instance, this statement by General Richard M. Ellis (commander-in-chief of Strategic Air Command): "I suggest to you that the best hope for the future is through SALT negotiated arms limitation agreement and a subsequent mutual reduction of forces. The alternatives to a SALT agreement are unacceptable. . . ."[23] I can only applaud such a statement. Worthy of attention in my view are some ideas of Generals Maxwell Taylor and Mathew Ridgway, and of some others. But if we are to talk about American generals as a group and to evaluate the political role of the entire "top brass," then we have to state that they comprise an important component of the American military-industrial complex. To my mind, there is hardly another country in the world, aside from military dictatorships, where the generals, and the admirals for that matter, play as important a role as they do in the United States and bear such a considerable influence over the public opinion, the Congress, and the administration. This tradition is even more amazing if we recall that the United States has not really fought too many major wars in its history.

One of the reasons for such a situation is to be found, in my view, in the overwhelming militarization of U.S. foreign policy so typical of the period of the Cold War. No wonder that, with the Cold War subsiding since the late sixties, confidence in the Pentagon and the generals has been decreasing. It seems that Vietnam in particular made the public increasingly doubtful of the generals' judgment on matters of war, peace, and national security. Americans came to recollect the popular wisdom that war is too serious a matter to be entrusted to the generals. But, of course, the United States has recently entered a new period of militarization, and the situation may change again.

What about Soviet generals?

I have a great respect for them. They do know what a really bad war means.

It looks as if, in your opinion, a dangerous role is being played not only by the American generals, but by the civilian specialists on military matters, by those whom you call the "armchair strategists."

I am not alone in such an opinion. They have undoubtedly made a considerable contribution to the arms race, to the fact that U.S. military thought has been developing in such a dangerous direction. That contribution was quite vividly characterized by one such strategist, Herman Kahn, who said, "We want to make . . . nuclear war more rational. . . ."[24]

Could you name the most prominent of these specialists?

I could, but I would not. Many of them are now in government. What if they repent, change their minds, and would like to make up for it by good deeds? Such things have happened in the past. Besides, I don't want to give them publicity.

But this would be criticism, not publicity.

Never mind. In America, I heard, any publicity is considered positive, with the single exception of an obituary. And if it comes to the military experts, I would like to mention another group. Some time after the end of the sixties there appeared in the United States an influential group of specialists on military affairs and armaments that began to speak publicly in favor of curtailing the arms race and preventing the war threat. Mind you, they did so in their capacity as professionals. That was particularly important, since previously a similar standpoint had been supported by the people who, although quite often respected, had practically no credentials in the spheres of military technology, strategy, or policy and who were opposed by those who had the most reliable credentials in these matters. It is only natural that the arguments of common sense assumed additional credibility when put forward by the people whom you could not suspect of ignorance: former presidential advisors on science and technology George Kistiakowsky and Jerome Wiesner, the Pentagon's Herbert York and Jan Lodal, the CIA's Herbert Scoville and Arthur Cox, ACDA's George Rathjens, as well as such prominent scientists as Wolfgang Panofsky, Richard Garwin, Bernard Feld, Paul Doty, et al.

One of the most prominent American naval officers, Admiral Elmo R. Zumwalt, Jr., chief of naval operations during the Nixon years, impressed upon me that Admiral Gorshkov built up your naval forces in a miraculously short time. Take submarines. Gorshkov built so many of them that the Soviet navy has three times more submarines than the U.S. Navy.

Recently I read an assessment of this asymmetry made by a well-known American specialist, William W. Kaufmann. He points out that these submarines, many of them old and diesel powered, are divided between four fleets, two of them—the Black Sea and the Baltic fleets—due to their geographical location, are unable to threaten the American lines of communications. And the two other fleets, in order to reach those lines, would have to pass through narrow and dangerous waters where they could be expected by the enemy. And he comes to the conclusion that to make a comparison on the basis of numbers alone means not only "a high probability of error, it would not even have provided an adequate data base for any such calculations."[25] I would add that I know for sure that, even if we do not take into account the naval forces of American allies, the U.S. Navy has been and remains the strongest navy in the world.

But many in the West are convinced that the USSR has exerted a strenuous effort to build up its navy.

Unquestionably, our navy has been strengthened. But is there any particular reason why it should have remained unchanged since, let us say, the end of the last war? Besides, I would not look for any evil, let alone aggressive designs, behind the strengthening of our navy. We have extensive sea borders that have to be guarded. It is even more imperative to do so since the naval forces confronting us, the American forces in the first place, are clearly offensive in nature, comprising large aircraft-carrier formations, numerous marine units, landing craft, etc. In all of these categories, the United States has considerable superiority over the Soviet Union, while in some of them this superiority is overwhelming. And the bulk of these forces is deployed close to our shores.

But the Soviet navy and its submarines have offensive capabilities as well. In particular, the Soviet navy can cut off communication lines that are of vital importance to the West.

As to the capability of cutting off communication lines, that is not always connected with offensive intentions. It may also be part of defense. As far as I understand, NATO considers the Atlantic a route for American supplies to Europe in case of war. Is it not logical for the USSR, for the Warsaw Pact, to foresee a counteraction to such plans? Such a reaction, in our view, is purely defensive, since the war may be unleashed only by the West.

And what about the Indian Ocean?

You have to understand that, in terms of communications, this ocean is as important for us as the Panama Canal is for the United States, since it provides the only reliable route connecting the western and eastern parts of our country. It is our vital communication line and we are naturally keen on ensuring its security.

But does that not create dangers for the vital communication line of the West, since the larger part of the Persian Gulf oil imported to Western Europe, the United States, and Japan goes through the Indian Ocean?

I have heard concern expressed in this regard more than once, but I still fail to visualize what they are afraid of in real terms. If they are worried about this communication line in case of an all-out nuclear war, then such worries are purely academic. A war of this kind will make this problem irrelevant, like an uncomfortable shoe on an amputated foot. And I cannot understand their concerns if we discuss a situation of peace. Are they afraid that we will start sinking Western tankers? Once you have decided to start the Big War, you can also do it in this way. But then again, what are the reasons for the West to be concerned about these communication lines in such a case?

Why don't you accept that a beefing up of the American navy will improve the security of Western communication lines, while insisting that it is necessary to provide for a Soviet naval presence in the Indian Ocean, since the Soviet Union too has important routes there?

As far as the first part of your question is concerned, I do not think, in general, that the problem of oil supply can be resolved by military means. Something, undeniably, can be done with the help of military force—oil fields and pipelines may be bombed, set on fire, and destroyed. The recent war between Iran and Iraq has proven it. But will this produce oil? No, the task of ensuring a continuous supply of oil from the Middle East, from the Persian Gulf countries, can be accomplished only through establishing peace in the region, through rejecting interference in the internal affairs of these countries, and by building up just and equal relations with them.

As far as the second part of your question goes, I would not like you to construe the aforesaid as a justification for any foreign (including Soviet) military presence in the Indian Ocean. The USSR is for the strictest restraints on any such presence. We conducted appropriate negotiations with the United States on this subject, negotiations that were subsequently frozen on the initiative of the American side. In December 1980, Leonid Brezhnev put forward new specific proposals for a demilitarization of the area around the Persian Gulf, including the abolition of foreign military bases, nondeployment of nuclear weapons, and noninterference in the normal operation of trade and other communications routes in the area. Had the security of oil supply and sea communications really been at the heart of the Western concept, it would have been more responsive to these proposals.

The Soviet Union has been putting forward more general proposals on restricting the arms race at sea. Among them was a proposal to do away with the permanent presence of foreign navies outside their own territorial waters. If the West doubts that the Soviet Union will be a reliable partner in any such efforts, as in any efforts to stop the arms race, let it test the Soviet intentions instead of whipping up the campaign about the "Soviet threat."

What is your evaluation of the various arms control negotiations at this point?

Almost all of the bilateral Soviet-American talks started before 1979 were practically frozen, which is an unavoidable consequence and even a constituent part of the recent shift in policy effectuated by the United States.

Again you seem to blame the United States. Without trying to exonerate Washington, why does the Soviet Union not share in the blame? There might be certain difficulties inherent in the complex nature of the problems discussed.

No doubt such difficulties do exist. At times they hamper negotiations and may even lead to additional friction. I have in mind the difficulties emanating from the complexity of modern technology, the difficulties of verification and so on, as well as of the asymmetries in geographical and political situations, and last but not least, suspicion, caused by a long period of tensions. To this I should add that in negotiations no one is immune from making certain mistakes in evaluating the other side's position. Here I am ready to allow that we might have done better and more effectively in some instances. All these difficulties should not be underestimated, but they are not the main point. The main point is that the United States and NATO, as far as we can see, are still after military superiority, and, seeking such superiority, have recently accelerated the arms race. This kind of policy does not leave much room for successful negotiations and agreements on arms limitation. Is the Soviet Union to blame for all this? Certainly it is to blame. It is blamed for the sheer fact of its existence, and for its desire to go on living as an independent nation. It is blamed for not putting up with American superiority and for insisting on a parity, on an equality with the United States. It is blamed for being unwilling to be left at the mercy of the superior military might of the United States and other Western powers, and for an unwillingness to make unilateral concessions. In Western opinion these attitudes may be serious faults, but I doubt that we could be persuaded to change them.

Such a view seems excessively categorical and self-righteous. Perhaps we should analyze in specific terms at least the most important negotiations.

Why not? Let us start with the SALT negotiations. The last agreement was signed in June 1979 but has not been ratified so far by the United States. Some may certainly put the blame on Moscow, in particular on the events in Afghanistan. But let us recollect that, according to the predominant opinion in the United States, the ratification had to be completed in 1979, before the election campaign came into full swing. But it didn't happen, and the blame lies squarely on the U.S. government. First the United States started the Cuban pseudocrisis with the so-called Soviet brigade; then it simply forgot about SALT because of the crisis in U.S.-Iranian relations. So I have grave doubts that the treaty would have been ratified in 1980 even if nothing had happened in Afghanistan. But this is only part of the story. The United States is responsible for seven years of delays in the SALT II negotiations. Had it not been for those delays, we might have been discussing SALT III now, or even SALT IV.

It is my firm belief that, had the Carter administration's policy not been so inconsistent and ambiguous, the ratification in the Congress would not have been accompanied by so many complications. As late as 1977 no one would have foreseen them.

And now you have to deal with a new administration, which during the election campaign promised to scrap SALT II, or at least to return it for renegotiations.

Yes, we are again in a new situation, which raises the problem of continuity in U.S. policy. As far as the Soviet Union is concerned, we negotiated this agreement in good faith with two Republican and one Democratic administration, and we consider it a good document even now. But, of course, time has passed and some new negotiations are needed. The protocol has expired and there must be a new decision on the issues covered by it. So far, both sides have stuck to the SALT I and SALT II treaties, although the first has expired and the second has not been ratified. But such a situation cannot last forever, and there should be valid formal agreements.

It is a widespread opinion in the United States that they have made more concessions in SALT II than the Soviet Union.

It is widespread only among opponents of SALT II.

How would you describe the actual situation?

We think that the treaty is based on a balance of concessions from both sides. We could imagine a better treaty from the point of view of our own interests. The same is true of the United States. This is only natural, since the principle of mutual concessions is the basis of such a treaty. Security is better insured with the treaty than without it. It's true for us, it's true for the United States—even the Pentagon has agreed with that—and it's true for the whole world. It is often forgotten what the SALT process is all about. A possibility of cutting and limiting strategic forces and programs without endangering one's own security is essentially not a concession, but a gain—a win, not a loss.

In April 1982, the Reagan administration proposed to resume the talks on strategic armaments, this time aiming at their reduction and not simply limitation. The Soviet side sharply criticized the content of the U.S. position, but nevertheless agreed to enter the negotiations. How are the United States and the Soviet Union now approaching this problem?

The U.S. decision to resume the talks was in itself a healthy shift in administration policy. The Soviet Union had been urging the American government to do that for a long time. President Reagan offered to rename the talks START, or strategic arms reduction talks. Well, it hardly makes sense to argue about the name, especially since we have always welcomed the idea of reduction. Had the SALT II treaty been ratified, we would already have had 254 fewer missiles than now, and the United States would have had 34 fewer. Both sides would have been well into the SALT III phase, dealing precisely with those significant reductions of strategic armaments, in accordance with the mutual commitment reached at the signing of the SALT II treaty. Instead, we are now facing a more acute question about the positions of both sides at the ongoing talks, whatever their name. Here, the actual U.S. proposal runs against its declared intention to reach a substantive agreement. This proposal is so one-sided that former Secretary of State Edmund Muskie described it as a "secret agenda for sidetracking disarmament while the United States gets on with rearmament—in a hopeless quest for superiority."[26]

To be specific, the American side, exploiting the structural differences between the strategic forces of both countries, offered the kind of reductions that would seriously undermine the main component of Soviet forces —ICBMs—while leaving the U.S. strategic potential almost intact. If we accepted the American terms, we would have to agree to an almost 50 percent cut in the number of our strategic warheads, while the United States would have to renounce only the outdated portion of its nuclear submarine fleet, and would still be allowed to increase the number of its ICBMs. The U.S. strategic bombers, in which Americans have significant quantitative superiority, would not be touched at all. The American proposal would give the United States a free hand to develop and deploy all its most advanced first-strike systems—the Trident II, the MX, the new strategic bomber, and strategic cruise missiles. In other words, this proposal seems to be designed for a unilateral disarmament of the Soviet Union and a devaluation of our previous defense expenditures. At the same time it puts practically no limit on the further American buildup.

But the Americans justify their concentration on the heavy Soviet ICBMs by the fact that they pose a most serious threat to strategic stability.

This argument does not hold. It is based on the old American concept that ICBMs, by virtue of their high accuracy, are well suited for counterforce or even preemptive first strikes, while the main mission of SLBMs, strategic bombers, and cruise missiles is to deal a second, or retaliatory, strike.

This concept, born back in the 1960s, was not so much the result of precise calculations as it was a rationalization for the strategic potential that had been built in the United States by that time. In its details this concept also reflected the specifics of the U.S. geostrategic position and also the outcome of the intense competition between the U.S. Army, Navy, and Air Force.

But in any case, we cannot take this American model for the ultimate truth. The Soviet Union has a different history, a different geostrategic situation, different weapons systems, and a different structure in its armed forces. These natural differences do not at all mean that the USSR is relying on counterforce, or that it is planning preemptive strikes. Besides, it can easily be proven that ICBMs as deterrents are not inferior to SLBMs. The communication with ICBMs is more reliable. A strike against them hits the enemy's territory, and as such would be tantamount to beginning an all-out nuclear war. This cannot escape the attention of those pondering preventive strikes.

In case the ICBMs become vulnerable there is always a launch-on-warning option for the other side—that is, to launch its own missiles while the enemy's missiles are already on their way. The side planning a preventive strike can never exclude the possibility of the enemy's launch-on-warning, and this too strengthens deterrence.

The capabilities of SLBMs and strategic bombers can be estimated in other ways than the ones we have just mentioned. For instance, if a conflict begins as a conventional, nonnuclear war, it would seem safer to concentrate on sinking the enemy's nuclear submarines than on attacking his ICBMs, especially since it can be done without engaging the enemy's territory. There is another question: what would prevent the alerting of strategic bombers to set an enemy guessing about whether they are hiding from a possible attack on their bases, or already approaching the initial lines to launch their accurate cruise missiles? There are such plans in the United States, by the way.

Speaking of these scenarios I have in mind the American strategic concepts, not ours. We reject the concepts of a first strike and a limited nuclear war, considering them not only immoral, but utterly utopian.

There is another factor that I personally find the most important—a factor of time. President Reagan himself, in his Eureka speech, admitted that negotiating an agreement on the basis of his proposal would take a number of years. But what would be going on in the meantime—an unrestrained arms race?

Mr. Reagan said the United States would stick to the SALT II provisions.

It sounds good, but the question then is, why not ratify the treaty itself? It should still not be forgotten that a number of crucial and extremely dangerous military programs are not covered by the SALT II treaty. The United States proceeds to work on them very intensely, and if the situation continues to develop in this way, we will have to take some countermeasures.

That is exactly why President Leonid Brezhnev, in his message to the U.N. second special session on disarmament, proposed that both the United States and the USSR agree to freeze their strategic arsenals for the time of the negotiations, and called on all the nuclear powers to follow the Soviet Union's example in renouncing the first use of nuclear weapons. A realization of this proposal would solve the problem in question, provide a possibility for deliberate negotiations, and would also help contribute to a relaxation of tensions and an improvement of the talks' atmosphere. Unfortunately, the United States responded to this proposal in a very negative way.

But in so doing the United States referred to the existing Soviet superiority.

They referred to a myth, and as I have said in our previous conversations, the real American motive is quite different—the United States wants to achieve superiority first, and only then come to serious negotiations with us. They want to "negotiate from a position of strength." Many Americans freely admit this. But who will concede to negotiate from weakness? It means that we would again have to strive for parity, and to incur again the displeasure of the Pentagon. And so it may go on forever, or more probably until an unrestrained arms race makes a military confrontation inevitable.

Regarding the other talks in Geneva—on the medium-range nuclear weapons—the positions of both sides are still far apart. President Reagan proposed a "zero option" providing for both the United States and the Soviet Union to refrain from the deployment of all medium-range missiles. The USSR rejected this proposal as absolutely unacceptable.

And this is only natural, because in this case, just as in the strategic armaments field, we are being asked to undergo a unilateral disarmament. As I already mentioned, according to the "zero option" proposal, the Soviet Union is to liquidate all its medium-range missiles—both the new SS-20s and the old SS-4s and SS-5s. As for NATO, it is only to abstain from the deployment of the new American missiles in Western Europe, while preserving intact its existing forward-based systems, as well as the British and French nuclear forces.

In Europe today we have a rough parity in the medium-range forces. The "zero option" would drastically change this balance in favor of NATO. Besides, there is a possibility of deployment of the American sea-based cruise missiles in the vicinity of Europe, which would give NATO an additional advantage. Last but not least, we find totally unacceptable Mr. Reagan's proposal to extend a unilateral reduction of Soviet nuclear forces to the Far East area. An arms reduction in this area is a subject apart, which should be discussed, but it is not related to the strategic balance in Europe.

After all, Europe is bristling with nuclear weapons.

Of course. We are for turning all of Europe into a nuclear free zone. All the nuclear weapons—both medium-range and tactical—should be removed from this continent on the basis of reciprocity. But since the West is not yet ready for an immediate realization of this true zero option, we propose to reduce the medium-range systems in two stages, one-third by 1985, and another third by 1990. The bulk of the systems removed from Europe are to be dismantled, while the rest of the Soviet systems are to be placed behind the Urals, from whence they cannot reach Western Europe. Our proposal also provides for an agreement on the adequate verification of its observance.

What about the MBFR negotiations in Vienna?

These have been stalemated for a long time now. In order to overcome the impasse, the Soviet Union introduced, as early as June 1978, proposals going a better part of the way toward the Western position. The Soviet proposals were praised by Western representatives themselves as highly constructive. Later we undertook a unilateral reduction of our armed forces in Europe by one thousand tanks and twenty thousand troops. In the summer of 1980, socialist states came up with a new initiative, suggesting that the Soviet Union cut its forces by another twenty thousand, provided the United States reduced the number of its troops by thirteen thousand. Then there were some new steps forward made by Warsaw Pact countries in the fall of 1980. Yet NATO would not respond.

There are various assessments of the numbers of Warsaw Pact troops. NATO estimates that you have 150,000 more than you say you have. How can any agreement be reached if there are such differences in figures?

First, there's no other way but to accept each other's figures. NATO has been demanding our figures since 1973 as a sine qua non of an agreement. As for us, we accept the figures given by NATO. Generally speaking, this numbers game is nothing but a pretext for delaying the talks. Estimates of military balance have always been political weapons. In 1977 and 1978, when NATO was lobbying for its long-term buildup program, there was a lot of noise about the alleged Soviet conventional superiority in Europe. Now that the program has been adopted, the lobbying is concentrated on Eurostrategic missiles. To make a long story short, I am absolutely sure that if NATO, and the United States in particular, really wanted an agreement, we would have had it already. The same is true for the comprehensive Test Ban Treaty and some others.

The comprehensive Test Ban Treaty is directly related to the problem of proliferation, and Soviet and American interests are especially close in this matter. Some time ago I ran into John A. Phillips, the Princeton Uni-

versity student who was able to devise plans for a workable nuclear bomb.

This particular episode gives powerful evidence of how real the threat of nuclear proliferation has become. It would grow faster in a renewed cold-war climate. You are absolutely correct to observe that nuclear nonproliferation corresponds to both American and Soviet interests, and, I might add, to the interests of all other countries, too.

You mentioned earlier the problem of verification. It was passionately discussed in the United States in connection with the SALT II treaty. Obviously, some senators objected to the treaty because of the unreliability of verification procedures. Why did the Soviet Union not agree to more reliable methods, including on-site inspections?

It seems to me that by the time the SALT II treaty had been truly and seriously discussed in the United States, doubts about verification had largely dissipated. It was proven that the treaty obligations were easily verifiable. One of the problems was rooted in the fact that the administration failed to fully and exhaustively explain to the senators just what the United States would know about our armed forces with the help of the existing surveillance and intelligence means. It failed because such matters are regarded in the United States as some of the most closely guarded secrets. But I think that due to these discussions senators at least realized a truth that had nothing to do with secrets: that without the SALT agreement, verification would be more difficult, rather than easier. The agreement provides for a whole system of verification measures: special counting rules, a ban on interference with each other's technical means, a pledge not to conceal telemetry data, and so forth. The treaty also provides for a special commission to deal with questions in dispute and grievances. Without all this the situation would have been much worse.

As for the question of verification in general, we base our view on the idea that the means and the scale of verification must correspond to the character and scope of arms limitations introduced by this or that agreement. It is the observance of an agreement that should be the object of verification, not the satisfaction of someone's curiosity. After all, we deal with the verification of an agreement, not with facilitating the other side's intelligence activities.

Another important point: the further arms control goes, the more complicated are the questions raised, the more complex the limits—the broader the task of the verification. In estimating whether verification is sufficient, one must always have in mind not just the physical possibilities of violating a treaty, but whether such a violation would be beneficial for the side trying to cheat. One can try to deceive on trifles, but it will hardly result in anything but a great risk of getting caught and the prospect of an international scandal. A violation big enough to have an impact on the military balance would be impossible to conceal. The limitations introduced by SALT II are such that they can be verified by national technical means. It can be different with other treaties. For instance, in the case of the Test Ban Treaty, it was agreed that there was a need to supplement national means by the so-called black boxes placed in the other country. This can already be regarded as a form of on-site inspection. If we have an agreement on general and complete disarmament, then, as the Soviet government declared, we will agree to any forms and methods of control, including, undoubtedly, on-site inspection. I should add that, according to specialists, on-site inspection is far from ideal as a verification method, although in principle we do not exclude it. In many cases, especially where the time factor is of paramount importance, technical means do a better job. And then there are certain things that cannot be verified even with the help of on-site inspection.

But why so much arguing and debating about on-site inspection?

Because this issue can be so easily manipulated by those who are intent on frustrating the progress of arms control. The name of the game is to make demands that you are sure will be unacceptable to the other side. This allows you to kill two birds with one stone: cast suspicions on your partner and cover up your own unwillingness to reach an agreement. And, of course, on-site inspection is probably unique among the issues of arms control as something that got stuck very firmly in the minds of the gullible part of the public. One might call it the Philistine side of arms control.

It is common knowledge that the Soviet Union is painstakingly guarding its secrets and is believed in the West to be overly secretive in general. This lends credence not only to stories about paranoid Soviet attitudes toward the outside world, but also to suspicions as to Soviet intentions, aims, and so forth.

Once again I have to stress that to a great extent such assumptions are the result of political speculations and insidious propaganda. This propaganda created and keeps alive the myth about Western "open" society in contrast to our "closed" society. In reality we are more open, while the West, including the United States, is more closed than is commonly alleged. Many things are kept secret in the United States, not only from us, but from its people, and sometimes even from its own Congress. Attempts at penetrating these secrets or at disclosing them are punished, and the punishment has been getting much more severe of late. On the other hand, there really are differences between the Soviet and the American practices in this sphere. I will not conceal that ours, in many instances, are stricter. There are historical reasons for it. In a country that has been the target of numerous military invasions, and that has lived in a virtual state of hostile siege for a long time, people will naturally be much more cautious about what may be revealed and what should rather be kept secret. Traditional patterns of behavior are not eternal; they are susceptible to change. The same goes fully for the question we are discussing. Détente, growth in trust, the broadening of contacts and of the scope of problems put to negotiations —all of these lead to changes in traditions. Future events will be very important in this regard.

We don't expect Americans to trust us just for our words, even though many Western experts have testified that our record of fulfilling our treaty obligations has been very good indeed. Nothing that has been done so far in Soviet-American relations has been based on blind trust. All agreements have been thoroughly verifiable. The relations have been developing in front of everyone's eyes.

On the other hand, there must be a sense of measure here. No one should expect us to agree to play the role of some kind of international suspect, always ready to respond to every charge and submit to any investigation. It is clear why the United States is interested in portraying us in such a light, as it makes the hoariest accusations against the Soviet Union without any real evidence: mud sticks, and the charge usually rings louder than the disclaimer. But in civilized international politics there should be a rule similar to that in civilized societies—that the burden of proof rests with the accuser.

In concluding our discussion of the arms race and arms control, what should we expect in this area in the future?

I am sure that arms control, aside from its financial and political benefits, is necessary to ensure reliable guarantees against nuclear war. And I would prefer that arms control and disarmament go forward as a result of foresight and rational choice exercised by policy makers. When both sides realize the dangers of the arms race and the benefits of disarmament, that opens the shortest and safest way to a more peaceful world. Another way would be to move back from the brink. From history we can remember times when reason could prevail only after unreason had been able to reign for a while and expose itself fully. Obviously, this type of situation is infinitely more dangerous, and in the nuclear age is even unacceptable.

At this point I would not dare to make a definite forecast. I hope we shall go along the way of arms control and disarmament. However, it looks just now as if arms control is in for hard times—in our judgment as a result of the shift in U.S. foreign and military policies. Everything must be done to overcome these negative trends, for in the final analysis the question boils down to this: either we destroy these armaments, or they destroy us.

Chapter 4 | On Issues of Ideology, Human Rights, and Dissidents

What role does ideology play in relations between Moscow and the Western world in general, and the United States in particular?

Ideological differences between countries with different social systems in our view should not prevent them from having normal political relations. At the same time, the communist parties, while strongly in support of détente and international cooperation, consider ideological differences profound and the struggle of ideas inevitable.

How does one reconcile these two concepts?

The essence of the Leninist concept of peaceful coexistence is that it envisages the parallel and peaceful existence of states belonging to opposite social systems. These systems differ in their economic structures, in the character of their social relations, their values, and their ideals. In today's world the influence of ideologies can't be confined only to those countries where they predominate. Ideologies constantly clash both on the global scale and within many individual countries. This fact of life was not invented by us and it cannot be ignored. To Americans, proud of their pluralist tradition, this should be perfectly clear. But once an ideological struggle is turned into a crusade or a witch hunt, it immediately acquires the potential to arouse and aggravate conflicts. History has presented us with many examples of this kind. Even more numerous are the cases when ideology and ideas in general were only a coverup for actions motivated by other things, like greed, lust for power, and so on. One example could be the messianic pretentions of the Spanish conquistadors.

Ideology and propaganda may also be used as instruments of a certain policy, in particular a policy of subversion and destabilization of other societies. It's true both for times of war and times of peace. The Cold War was a good example, with its peculiar type of ideological struggle succinctly called "psychological warfare." Propaganda of this sort is in our view incompatible with détente and peaceful coexistence. It can only damage relations between countries.

Can it pose a serious threat?

Of course. And this is not only my opinion. International law imposes limitations or bans on certain kinds of propaganda. I can cite quite a few international agreements. One of them, the Roosevelt-Litvinov letters, which served as a formal basis for establishment of diplomatic relations between our countries, was already mentioned.

Then ideology continues to play an important role in international relations?

It certainly does. But we should be very specific regarding these matters. Sometimes an ideological struggle is interpreted so broadly as to include different attitudes toward revolutions and other forms of social change in many countries of the world. Though related to ideology, these attitudes are primarily manifestations of another very fundamental reality, namely the radical social differences between the two systems. And here we are bound to confront very complex problems—political contradictions and even conflicts around many events in different countries. Détente is no guarantee for the status quo. Social and political changes are inevitable. We should learn to live with them so as not to endanger peace and détente.

Shouldn't there be rules of behavior in regard to these changes, particularly for the great powers?

Certain principles and rules already exist. The principle of peaceful coexistence in itself, as was mentioned before, precludes efforts to export revolution, or, for that matter, counterrevolution.

Is it not wishful thinking to try to broaden the framework of cooperation between nations with widely differing systems of values?

No, I consider it a very realistic notion. Certainly, we have differences. But we also have important common interests, the foremost of which is survival. We have to coexist peacefully and keep our differences from jeopardizing the survival of the human race. You mentioned the different concepts of human rights that we have. But don't both societies have a common ground on such a basic human right as the right to live, the right to survive? After all, if that particular right is not guaranteed, other rights lose their meaning.

Is it possible to narrow the gap in the East-West understanding of the concept of human rights?

Why not? I think the gap has been artificially widened by those in the West who want to sow distrust between the two systems. In reality, there is some sort of global consensus on human rights embodied in the 1948 United Nations Declaration on Human Rights, the more recent United Nations covenants on human rights, and the Helsinki Final Act of the Conference on European Security and Cooperation. Most countries of the world are signatories to at least some of these documents.

There may be a consensus all right, but the same principles tend to be interpreted differently by different people.

That's true of any principle. One's interpretation of human rights depends on one's social position, on the body of cultural tradition one belongs to, on the overall historical setting. But before we speak about these differences, I want to make clear one fundamental point. The United States tries to make the following case out of the overall situation in the field of human rights: Americans are the staunchest and almost the only champions of human rights, whereas the Soviet Union and other socialist countries are against them, doing nothing but violating these rights. Both these images are a far cry from reality.

Could you be more specific on this point? It is very important.

Certainly. How can one be against human rights nowadays? It's the same as to be against motherhood. So to do more than repeat political platitudes you have to be concrete and specific. Speaking about the USSR, I would like to stress our deep and long-standing commitment to human rights. It's for human rights that we made our Revolution and then defended it against foreign intervention and a Nazi invasion. More than that—it fell to the Soviet Union to develop a new, broader approach to human rights by including social rights largely neglected before that time, but vitally important for the overwhelming majority of our people and other peoples as well. It took the world community half a century to recognize the significance of those rights in the form of the U.N. covenants.

Would you say that in the field of social rights the Soviet Union is more advanced than the West?

Yes, and this is only natural. At the time of the Revolution in Russia, social rights and freedoms were of prime importance for people who were hungry and lived in conditions of abject poverty, and for the illiterate peasants constituting the majority of the population. These were the right to work, the freedom from hunger and starvation, the right to have a shelter, the right to have land to till, the right to be educated, the right to receive medical care, and so on. And for a country devastated first by World War I, then by a civil war and the intervention of Western powers, the right to live in peace was of the greatest importance. These and many other social rights still occupy the highest places in the set of values of our society. Of course, our constitution guarantees the usual political rights just as well, including freedom of speech, freedom of conscience and religion, freedom of the press, and freedom of assembly, although the understanding of these rights and freedoms here differs from, say, the standard American approach. In general, I am sure that, given a serious balanced approach, there could be a thorough and useful dialogue about human rights. Unfortunately, in the United States and in the West as a whole, this very important and complex question was turned into a symbol of a fierce propaganda campaign against the USSR.

But it is inexplicable to Westerners that a large and powerful nation like the Soviet Union should be so petty in not allowing citizens who prefer to leave to obtain a passport and go.

Well, Mr. Oltmans, every state and government acts in accordance with its own understanding of its interests, priorities, and attitudes toward problems. And you cannot escape here from the influence of historic traditions and historic experiences. There is a great difference in this respect between the United States and the Soviet Union. With the exception of the American Indians, who were forced from their land and almost completely annihilated, Americans are a nation of immigrants or descendants of immigrants, and it is quite logical that other peoples' freedom to emigrate has become sort of a natural right in their minds. But in this country, attitudes and sentiments are different. During its history the Soviet Union witnessed two waves of large-scale emigration. The first wave occurred right after the Revolution and the civil war. These emigrés were, for the most part, bitter enemies of our new society. They had participated in an armed struggle against the new Soviet power, hand in hand with foreign invading forces. Among those who emigrated in the second wave—during and after World War II—were a lot of collaborators with the Nazis and war criminals. As a result, a very definite attitude was formed against those who wanted to leave the country. And the word *emigrant* became almost synonymous to the word *traitor*.

Is this still a widespread attitude?

The situation began to change gradually, first as a result of migration across the borders shared with socialist countries, then through mixed marriages and family reunions and changes in the political atmosphere due to détente. Later, as you know, there was increased emigration to Israel, or, under that pretext, to the West. But this doesn't mean that the traditional attitude has disappeared completely. Speaking frankly, those who emigrate are still far from being regarded as exemplary citizens and patriots. And I think you wouldn't dispute that there are good reasons for such an attitude.

What do you mean?

Emigrating from here to the United States is not like leaving, say, Holland for the United States or the United Kingdom. When somebody leaves this country for the West, it means that he or she rejects the whole set of social values and ideals of the Soviet nation, which were born, developed, and defended through many hardships and ordeals. This also creates certain emotions at the grass roots. The same could be true, to a certain extent, of America. I am sure that a decision to emigrate to a Western European country or Canada would be treated with tolerance. But imagine the reaction of a sheriff from Texas or even an ordinary law-abiding and church-going citizen in a small midwestern town to the news of a neighbor planning to leave for the Soviet Union, Bulgaria, or the German Democratic Republic.

On the whole, whether we like it or not, certain restrictions on emigration and immigration exist in practically every country. The United States, for instance, has severe restrictions on immigration, which is no less a humanitarian problem than emigration.

Only in Utopia will all restrictions cease to exist someday.

Of course, everything is on the move, things change. I firmly believe that the time will come when all restrictions on international migration of people will be lifted. But until then we obviously should treat this matter with a lot of understanding, realizing that it involves some serious problems, which should be reckoned with and not turned into a propaganda trump card. At the same time, I'm sure that our relations and rules concerning emigration are really not the heart of the matter in the campaign for human rights launched a few years ago by the United States.

What do you mean?

I mean that this human-rights campaign has different purposes: to put pressure on the USSR, to arouse anti-Sovietism, to improve the American image around the world, and to restore the foreign policy consensus inside the United States. Human rights themselves were not what the Carter administration cared about very much. The United States often turns out to be the staunchest supporter of authoritarian regimes. And whenever such a regime is toppled—in Kampuchea, Iran, Nicaragua, or Afghanistan —why is Washington so enraged and vengeful?

But no matter how Washington interprets human rights, the problem itself remains vital.

Of course it's important. We in the Soviet Union are for safeguarding and broadening human rights. It's part of our ideology, our laws, our entire outlook. But when the human rights rhetoric is deliberately used to foment distrust and hostility in Soviet-American relations, to undermine détente, it has nothing to do with human rights as such. The noble idea is perverted and abused.

I think Americans should try to understand that if they are so strongly for human rights, this implies they must also be for détente. War and preparation for war, international tensions and crises—these are the factors most detrimental to democracy and social progress. The McCarthyist witch-hunts of the late forties and early fifties would not have been possible without the cold-war atmosphere.

I think it was Harvard University sociologist Daniel Bell who once said that, during the heyday of the Cold War, America was a "mobilized society." By the same token, the CIA and the FBI were set up in periods of tensions to fight an "external enemy." All their methods of operation, subversive activities, and psychological warfare, developed for cold-war purposes, were then turned against Americans themselves, including, as Watergate revealed, even political opponents within the elite. It may be remembered, by the way, that the Watergate "plumbers," when asked in the court about their profession, replied after some hesitation that they were "anticommunists." The same logic is unfurling now that the second edition of the Cold War is being issued from the White House. In a cold war–type situation, governments like those of Chile, South Korea, Pakistan, or El Salvador can afford to do whatever they please with civil liberties and still get American aid and support.

Even if American concern about human rights should be thoroughly political and self-serving, why wouldn't the Soviet Union try to outmaneuver

Washington, "disarm" it, if you will, by changing its mind on some of the sore points that Americans keep pointing to?

To change our minds on some of the sore points would change nothing. One has to realize that in this human rights campaign we deal with an attempt to modify through constant, ever-increasing pressure our domestic order according to Western liking, and at the same time to discredit the USSR before the world public. Specific demands might sometimes look rather modest—to let N or M out of jail (though they were convicted strictly according to the Soviet law), to permit X or Y to emigrate (the reason of refusal being, as a rule, that their former jobs involved access to classified information), to change a procedure of importation and sales of some Western periodicals, and so on. But we have learned through hard experience that with every concession grows an appetite for further demands and pressures. This is quite understandable, because for many organizers of this campaign these demands do not reflect a sincere concern over human rights, but serve as a pretext for stepping up an attack against our institutions and values. There were times when a real war was waged to crush this system. Then came the Cold War, and now other devices, including the human rights campaign, are being utilized.

Are you not exaggerating? Could it be a manifestation of the Soviet paranoid attitude to the West?

Not at all, I assure you, Mr. Oltmans, and, please, don't think that I attach a great importance to this campaign as such; but the point is it can't be viewed in isolation. It should be seen against the background of certain military efforts, foreign policy maneuvers, and other propaganda campaigns. It would be proper to recall, for instance, that in some key American foreign policy documents, like NSC-68, basic changes in our internal structure were put forward as a sine qua non for peaceful coexistence. Many actions in U.S. foreign policy in recent years reflect those guidelines. More than that—somewhere deep in the American political conscience there still lives the thought that we are something illegitimate, created not by God but by the Devil, and that our existence in its present form should be ended somehow.

This is too intangible.

Well, take a specific example—"Captive Nations' Week," celebrated every July by the U.S. Congress. As if this were not enough, the president personally signs a solemn declaration, which has been a routine practice for many years now. But what is its real message? It means, as explained in many U.S. commentaries, that, in the opinion of the United States, the Soviet Union lawlessly holds in its grip fourteen republics, which, therefore, should be "liberated." These include vast territories in Siberia—called DVR—the "Cherkessia," "Idel-Urals," and "Kazakia." I really don't know what all these crazy names mean, but my feeling is that they include the Urals, the Lower Volga basin, the Kuban River region, Don, Northern Caucasus, and some other regions. In other words, we are left with an area extending approximately from Moscow to Leningrad, north to south, and from Smolensk to Vladimir, west to east. I wonder how Americans would react if our Supreme Soviet and President Brezhnev issued solemn proclamations supporting a campaign questioning U.S. sovereignty beyond, say, an area from Boston to Washington and from Baltimore to Detroit, declaring that all the rest should be "liberated"? One could argue that the southern states were kept in the union only by means of war, that others were taken by force from France and Mexico, and that the whole territory originally had been stolen from the most captive nation of all—the American Indians.

But most Americans ignore "Captive Nations' Week." Why do you take it so seriously?

We far from exaggerate its importance. But neither can we completely ignore such things. To finish this theme I'd like to summarize:

We consider the matter of human rights very important. A lot has been and will be done in this area in our country. We know that we haven't reached an ideal situation yet. Who has? The continued progress of democracy remains our basic goal.

Another point: the propaganda campaign launched in connection with human rights by the United States has in fact nothing to do with those rights. We see it as one of the instruments of anti-Soviet policy, and let there be no illusions about our yielding to it. What the West really wants from us in this field is that we help with our own hands to organize anticommunist, anti-Soviet activities aimed at undermining our own social and political system. We aren't going to cooperate in destabilizing our social institutions, just as we would not expect the American government to do so if we were to make such demands on them.

A third point: what makes this campaign look particularly dubious to us is that the United States, in our view, has no right whatsoever to teach others the basics of human rights, because, as is true with many other problems, this one begins at home. It is very difficult for us, for instance, to believe in the value of the American system of free speech when the American news media have become such huge private enterprises, strongly motivated by profit, and catering to the tastes of their owners and the interests of corporate advertisers rather than to the interests of the public.

Denied access to the mass media, you can scream almost anything you want in America without being heard, though sometimes at the risk of being spied upon by the FBI or the CIA, like those young people who were persecuted for their opposition to the war in Southeast Asia. We in the Soviet Union have read about congressional inquiries into the illegal activities of the CIA regarding the Watergate scandal. We know that President Lyndon Johnson used J. Edgar Hoover to spy not only on communists and other radicals, but on respected congressmen as well. Richard Nixon even had a list of enemies drawn up. We know that if the authorities in the United States deem it necessary, they not only harass people, but even kill them. This happened, for example, to leaders of the Black Panthers, a number of whom were murdered in cold blood by the police. Not to speak of assassins who killed or wounded dozens of civil rights leaders from Martin Luther King to Vernon Jordan. And those responsible seldom get punished. Remember Kent State University? And what happened to the American Indian movement? What about numerous black activists sentenced and kept in prison for years on trumped-up charges? You would agree that this can only make us more skeptical toward the United States as a mentor on the subject of human rights.

Yes, but in spite of these alarming examples it is still possible for a dissident CIA agent like Frank Snepp to publish a book on the crimes perpetrated by Americans in Vietnam and elsewhere. Such a publication in the Soviet Union would be unthinkable.

Publication of Frank Snepp's book was possible a couple of years ago. Whether it would be possible now is doubtful. By the way, while Frank Snepp did get his book published, the CIA retaliated through the courts, and he's been severely punished financially. As a result of the legislation passed by Congress in 1980, I'm afraid that he and others like him may suffer much greater hardships. There are numerous indications that the wave of revelations has come to an end. The recent changes in the status of the intelligence bodies and secret police are a throwback to the status quo ante. On the other hand, when you talk about the Soviet Union, you forget that the practices of our security organs underwent very critical scrutiny and revision at a time when the CIA and the FBI were still considered sacred cows. In the fifties, the Soviet Communist Party openly stated that the security organs had violated laws and abused power. There were court proceedings against high officials of those bodies, and those found guilty were severely punished, in some cases with the death penalty. The organs were restructured and put under effective party control. Whenever these matters are discussed by the big Western media, there is a clear double standard applied. No matter what changes occur in our country, no matter what we do, we are accused of being undemocratic. At the same time, violations of human rights in the West are always minimized and regarded as exceptions to the rule.

Without defending the violence in American society, Americans have never experienced anything close to the Gulag Archipelago.

I do not consider it proper, Mr. Oltmans, or in good taste, to refer to the tragic events of our past, so painfully remembered by the Soviet people, using a term that has become a cliché of anti-Soviet propaganda. As I've mentioned earlier, the party took strong measures to correct the situation and to punish those who were guilty. But since you've touched upon this problem, I would like to emphasize that one of the main conditions that made possible the repressions in Stalin's time was the very hostile environment that our country then had to deal with.

The threat from Nazi Germany?

The Nazi threat was perhaps the high point. But the situation was pretty rough even before that. You see, our country lived through a period of intense political struggles after the 1917 Revolution. The counterrevolution would not give up. It was fighting dirty, and it was assisted from the outside on a large scale. Some of our leaders and ambassadors were assassinated. There were repeated military incursions into our territory. Foreign intelligence services were actively operating within the country. We were expecting a big war to erupt sooner or later, and, of course, after Hitler came to power on an anticommunist and anti-Soviet platform, the external situation deteriorated dramatically. Those were the special historical external conditions that made mass repression and crimes against our constitution and ideals possible.

We have not forgotten those tragic events and do not expect others to do so. What we are against are the attempts to interpret our whole history in the light of those events. For us, their meaning even back in those hard times was quite different. We have a lot of truly historic achievements on our record, achievements of worldwide significance. We have made economic, social, and cultural progress at a speed unknown to man before. There has been a rebirth of a people who used to be among the most oppressed and exploited of all the civilized nations. There was the victory over Nazi Germany and the removal of that threat to humanity. There have been a number of tremendously important firsts—economic planning, social developments such as equality of nationalities, equal rights of women, making medical care and education available to the whole population, and many, many other things. There is a lot in our history we can be proud of.

Have you ever tried to compare the costs of progress in different societies?

Well, this is an extremely difficult task. Human history is too complex and multidimensional to quantify. There is hardly any developed methodology for such comparisons. But I have no doubt that the costs of progress in a capitalist society were higher. First, you have to take into account the wars under capitalism. It was only capitalism, with its inherent drive for technology, first of all military technology, coupled with insatiable lust for markets and sources of raw materials, that made wars both worldwide and unprecedentedly devastating. This alone accounts for the loss of millions of human lives. Second, there was colonialism, which preceded capitalism, but which became a worldwide phenomenon and a precondition for rapid development and accumulation of the wealth of most capitalist countries. The cost again was many millions of human lives, as well as brutal exploitation, colonial wars, and political oppression, keeping a majority of mankind in a condition of backwardness. Third, capitalism has not always been associated with liberal democracy. In many countries this social system has taken the most oppressive political form—fascism with its bloody terror, military dictatorships, and other features of ruthless totalitarianism.

But most capitalist countries, including the United States, avoided fascist ways.

It does not mean that they completely avoided terror, cruel repression, and exploitation. The human cost of the United States turning from a small settlement in Massachusetts to one of the two most powerful countries in the world is very substantial. Take the crimes against the black people, beginning with the slave trade and the horrors of southern plantations and ending with the nightmare of life in today's ghettoes. Or the genocide against the Indians. You know, it's still hard for me to understand how the Americans have been able to anaesthetize themselves against any pains of conscience in connection with what they did to the native inhabitants of the continent. I recall these pages of American history not in order to insult Americans. These events should just be remembered in order to help Americans correct what is still possible to correct and to cool down the moralizing passion of some American politicians.

How would you account for the shift of emphasis by the Reagan administration from the human rights issue to that of international terrorism?

One reason is strictly political. It amounts to an admission that the previous human rights policy backfired in the relations of the United States with some of its authoritarian partners. The present administration set upon a course of putting up a global anti-Soviet alliance and had to downgrade all the other criteria for allied relations except the strict loyalty to the cause of the U.S.-led anti-Soviet crusade. They are following an old maxim —"He may be a scoundrel, but he is our scoundrel." It is especially applicable to the recently intensified American ties with cruel authoritarian regimes that nowadays are being urgently, if not too tastefully, rebaptized as "moderately repressive."

So the reasons are purely pragmatic?

I would say that there is also an ideological element involved—namely, a revitalization of the primitive view of the Soviet Union as the Devil's headquarters on Earth, causing all the trouble and manipulating all the anti-imperialist social change in the world by means of terrorism and subversion. The conservatives now in power do not put much soul into their human rights policy since they apparently never really believed in those rights in the first place. But this does not prevent them from conducting a fierce, if hollow, propaganda campaign on the subject.

I'm sure you are aware of the differences between Western Sovietologists in assessing the scope and meaning of changes that took place in your country in recent decades. Scholars like George Kennan and Jerry Hough maintain that the Soviet Union has undergone tremendous changes in the last quarter century, and that the West should alter its traditional perceptions of it. Others, like Richard Pipes or Adam Ulam, say quite the opposite, namely, that the Soviet Union is basically the same as it was back in the days of Stalin: no meaningful institutional changes have occurred.

Well, every country has changed in the last twenty-five years, our dynamic society particularly so. But the heart of the matter is how you define these changes. What is meant by "institutional changes"? We remain a socialist country with an increasingly mature political system in which the Communist Party of the Soviet Union plays a leading role. If it isn't to the liking of Mr. Pipes and some others, they are entitled to their own opinions, just as we are entitled to ours about American political institutions; but there's hardly anything we can do to please them. Domestically, there has been a lot of change in our country in connection with the eradication of the consequences of the personality cult, and as a result of the further development of democracy. In our foreign policy, contrary to allegations of some Sovietologists, there has been much more continuity in the basic goals and methods. And whatever your attitude toward Stalin, you can hardly deny that his foreign policy was prudent, that he was not an adventurist. I think that more serious and knowledgeable American Sovietologists recognize that.

Walter Laqueur argues eloquently that "no intelligent discussion of modern history is possible without a knowledge of the Marxist method." But to many people in Western Europe, societies established on Marxist principles are not very attractive examples. And the same goes for developing lands.

154 THE SOVIET VIEWPOINT

After twenty years of Marxism-Leninism in practice in Cuba, for instance, perhaps only Nicaragua is now partly following Fidel Castro's lead.

Well, the Nicaraguan revolution, as I see it, is taking its own shape. Walter Laqueur may argue for a knowledge of the Marxist method, but as far as he is concerned, he's a violent antagonist of the societies established on Marxist principles. As to the attractiveness of our example, a number of Western European countries have very strong Communist Parties that advocate establishment of a society based on Marxist principles. I mean France, Italy, Spain, and Finland. Communist Parties also exist in other countries, and though they do not yet have large memberships, a considerable part of the population of Western European countries supports the idea of organizing society on Marxist principles.

There is another aspect here. It so happened that countries where Marxist parties came to victory and began building a new society very often faced rather difficult objective conditions. As a rule these were countries that had suffered greatly in the war, like Russia, Yugoslavia, and Poland. Many of them were countries with a backward economy—again like Russia, Bulgaria, Rumania, and others, to say nothing of such underdeveloped countries as Vietnam, China, and Albania. Besides, the West exerted every possible effort to hamper the building of new Marxist societies: pressing the arms race on them, engaging in subversion, economic blockade, etc. Finally, there are inevitable difficulties for those who pave a new way. In such a complicated undertaking there will always be mistakes, and sometimes serious ones. Taking all this into consideration, I'd say that socialism has done the best it could, and it has great attractive power, which will grow. And you will hardly deny that the attractive power of capitalism has declined.

What about Cuba? The 1980 exodus of many Cubans to the United States was portrayed as evidence that the Cuban model of socialism pales before U.S. capitalism.

No matter how it was portrayed by Cuba's enemies, the whole episode, I think, worked in the final analysis not against Cuba but against those in the West who make a business of "defending human rights" in socialist countries. Isn't it indicative that a significant number of those who left Cuba were criminals and malcontents whose absence will only be welcomed by the Cuban people? It is difficult to say what this story has more of, the tragic or the ridiculous. But what it definitely does not amount to is any indictment of Cuban socialism, especially if you take into account the undeniable fact that the United States made a lot of difficulties for Cuba after the revolution, including an economic blockade and attempts to intervene. True, Cuba is still suffering many economic difficulties. But what do you compare her with? Sweden or Switzerland? The true frame of reference here should be Guatemala, Salvador, the Dominican Republic, or Cuba itself before its revolution. Then you will see the picture in a completely different light. Throughout Latin America, respect for Cuba is great and her standing is high.

Whatever else might be said about the achievements of socialism, including its Soviet model, you still lag behind the West in many ways.

Well, in some ways we do. We still have shortages of some goods, and the choice in the stores is more limited than in the West. Services leave much to be desired, and overall living standards are as yet lower than in some other countries. I am not ashamed to admit it.

Your candor is appreciated. Could you elaborate?

I'm not ashamed to admit these deficiencies because they are explained mainly by our difficult history, throughout most of which our people have lived under incredibly hard conditions, having had to limit themselves to bare necessities. This wasn't our fault, for we inherited a backward country and had to go through foreign intervention and an economic blockade after the revolution, then the large-scale preparation for the impending war with Hitler, and the war itself, with its incalculable losses and calamities, and then the Cold War and the arms race forced on us from the outside. As a result of all this, we were faced not only with an inadequately developed consumer goods industry and the consequences of chronic under-investment in agriculture, housing, retail trade, and services, but also with a specific public attitude toward these spheres as matters of secondary importance. Only recently have we begun to overcome this tradition, and this, by the way, has not turned out to be an easy job.

But services are still rather poor.

Well, what would you expect if it is only in the last decade or two that we have begun to enjoy, for the first time in our history, some luxuries of life?

What luxuries?

Whenever one compares the living standards of the Soviet Union and Western countries, one should keep in mind that the Soviet people have enjoyed for decades many of those things that still remain hard to obtain for the average Westerner. I mean free education and health care, guaranteed employment, and so on. Our people are so used to these things that they often forget about them—and for many a person emigrating from this country to the West, the absence of these things comes as a great shock.

At the same time, it is only rather recently that a separate apartment for a single family ceased to be an unheard-of luxury. I'll give you an example that I'm most familiar with—my own. I received a two-room apartment for the first time in 1958, being already a well-established journalist. Before that I lived with my wife, small son, and mother-in-law in a single room thirteen by thirteen feet. In the other nine rooms of that apartment lived more than thirty people, with whom we shared kitchen and bathroom facilities. I wouldn't claim that it was very comfortable. But I can say for sure that we felt no deprivation or unhappiness since everyone around us lived the same way.

You should realize that almost all the people of my generation came to know from their own experience what hunger means—not just the lack of protein or vitamins, but real hunger. And such hardships, which really were shared by almost everyone, created certain modes of behavior. From my childhood years I remember the moral of predominant asceticism: at times it would have been considered improper to put on a golden wedding ring or a tie, even if you had one.

During the Nazi occupation of Holland, we, too, were eating tulip bulbs one at a time. What emotions do these memories bring to you?

I recollect all this with pain, sometimes with a smile, but also with pride, because we were able to bear everything with dignity and live with dignity through a tremendously difficult history. Times have changed, and now it has become a favorite pastime of old people to grumble about youngsters who don't remember the past or properly appreciate what they have. The same is probably true of old-timers everywhere, though. Our people are demanding more luxuries of life now, which is only natural and proper, in my view. It speaks a lot about the changes for the better, and it also means that we'll achieve the goals we have set before ourselves.

Don't you think that some of your problems are not products of a painful history, but have to do with the socialist organization of production?

No, I am sure this is not the case. At the same time, you have to keep in mind that there can be deep differences in values. Every nation must make its choice and, having made it, should not complain about the consequences. For instance, one choice of ours was to have as complete social and economic security as possible, including guaranteed full employment and such employee's rights as to make it almost impossible to dismiss a worker. Naturally, this couldn't help having some impact on the intensity of work, and thus on general productivity. Then, the fact that all our enterprises are practically bankruptcy-proof is probably reflected in the work of the managers. I'm not going to attribute everything to this, and we do our best, while retaining these benefits, to increase the productivity of labor, to develop better moral and material incentives. But the things I mentioned still do have an impact. People do not have to struggle for sheer survival. Is that good or bad? I am sure the overwhelming majority of people in the USSR think it's good.

Is it not too great a price for social security?

We think the price is reasonable. We made this choice and are ready to pay for it. Others are entitled to their own opinions, and we aren't going to try and force them to change their minds.

Such attitudes must have some ideological roots in your country.

That's correct. Communist ideology emphasizes collectivism, which means that there can and should be harmony between individual and collective interests, the latter being just as natural and necessary for individual freedom and development as the immediate interests of the individual. This, by the way, contrasts with the extreme individualism typical of many Americans.

Americans think that individualism helps them keep their freedom.

Well, that's a big philosophical issue that would take us too far away from our topic. Without going into the basic definitions of freedom, I'd confine myself to this observation: individualism has been a potent incentive in American history, but its balance sheet is getting heavier and heavier on the debit side. Americans are paying for their extreme individualism with widespread alienation; social atomization; increasing anarchic patterns in economic, social, and political organization; and escalation of antisocial behavior like crime, drug addiction, violence, and so forth.

Comparing the two social systems, you would conclude that the overall cost-benefit balance is in favor of socialism?

Right. We believe that there can be no real individual freedom without a rational organization of society. The ultimate ideal of communism is the free and comprehensive development of the personality of each individual. This goal can be achieved only in a society organized for the common good rather than for private interest.

But hasn't capitalism achieved some magnificent results, especially in the economic field?

It certainly has. At the same time, assessing the overall economic performance of the two systems, we have to take into account a lot of things: past achievements, rates of progress, capability to perform under duress; and we must also put both systems to the test of solving the complicated problems of the present and future.

Capitalism has shown its ability to produce a lot of things quickly and efficiently, to saturate markets with consumer goods—though I am certain that a system based on central planning and the public ownership of production facilities can and must match capitalism in this respect. But social needs are not limited to cars and pantyhose and chewing gum. Modern society puts an ever-increasing emphasis on education, medical care, environmental protection, conservation of energy and natural resources, public transportation, organizing life in big cities, and so forth. Here, traditional capitalism falters, whereas our system, with all its problems, performs better and more efficiently. And these social needs are becoming more and more important nowadays.

Returning to the eternal topic of perceptions, you don't seem to think much of the average American level of knowledge of the USSR.

Oh, there's still tremendous ignorance. I would refer to what I have seen myself. For example, even among university audiences in the United States, people really know very little of contemporary Soviet literature.

They probably mention Aleksandr Solzhenitsyn.

Of course, that is almost a must, though going a little out of style lately. But I have also heard the names Dostoevski, Tolstoi, and once even Chekhov, who were great writers, of course, but not Soviet ones, strictly speaking.

Gorki?

No, not even once. But if you ask any high school boy or girl in the USSR about American literature, you'll get dozens of names. I am not talking only about classics like Edgar Allan Poe or Mark Twain, or such famous figures of the past as Theodore Dreiser, Ernest Hemingway, William Faulkner, Upton Sinclair, and others. Here our youths are very much aware of contemporary American writers, like Truman Capote, Tennessee Williams, J. D. Salinger, Kurt Vonnegut, Joyce Carol Oates, John Updike, and many others. They have been properly translated and are widely read and known. And this is so not only for American literature, but also for German, French, and British literature, Third World literature, anything of value published abroad. I think the average awareness about America, its national character and history, is higher here than the other way around.

Victor Afanasyev, the editor-in-chief of Pravda, *assured me that the Soviet press prints three times more information about the United States than the other way around. In Hungary it seems to be fourteen times as much. Only when Leonid Brezhnev journeyed to Budapest did the Hungarian capital become swamped with hundreds of Western journalists.*

This is also one of the deep differences between our two systems—the way the press and the media operate. Perhaps we do not always provide immediate responses to political questions or events. But I do feel we offer our readers a rather substantial amount of background, including extensive information on how to interpret or understand the present situation in the United States.

But in the West the Soviet way of journalism and news reporting is often considered unfair and boring.

Well, let us differentiate. Both here and in the West there are good and bad journalists, good and bad news reporting. In this sense, a lot depends on personal abilities and other individual qualities of reporters, editors, and publishers. But there is also a general style, and here the differences are more systemic. Western, and especially American, journalism is skewed toward sensations, particularly negative ones. Normal relations between countries or, for that matter, between individuals, are always much less newsworthy than conflicts and quarrels. In this respect, American journalists obviously have a rough time here when major attention is given to the way our plans for industry and agriculture are fulfilled, cultural events, and so on. Our press does not give much space to catastrophes, incidents, murders, or sex scandals.

I am even ready to sympathize with American journalists in Moscow who by their habitual standards do not find much to report. Perhaps this makes them even more persistent in their morbid interest in dissidents, and in rumors of "what is going on at the top."

But they are really in a predicament. If they produce only what is considered news in the Soviet Union, hardly anybody will publish it.

I understand that, but here there are certain objective complexities. I must also say that there were many attempts on our part to make it easier for Western journalists to organize trips to places of interest, to meet with the heads of some ministries whose work may be particularly interesting for the West, like those dealing with energy. Sometimes it brought good results, sometimes not.

To sum it up, the mission of Western journalists in the USSR is very important, since they are the channel for a great share of information about the Soviet Union that reaches the West. There are still some problems here, some of them rather serious. In my view they can be solved, provided there is goodwill on all sides, including the West and its press. And not only goodwill, but a deep sense of responsibility.

What is your impression of U.S. congressmen when they visit Moscow?

Well, they are persons of different views, backgrounds, and tastes. By itself the development of parliamentary contacts between our countries in recent years has been very important. In general, in spite of all the difficulties we have had during the past few years, these mutual visits have been one of the areas where, in my view, we have succeeded. These exchanges of ideas and opinions during visits have developed to a significant degree. They have almost become an institution, and if they wither now because of the shift in U.S. policy, the resulting deterioration of our relations would be a real loss to both sides.

American lawmakers coming to Moscow seem to make a point of meeting with Soviet dissidents. Some journalists even seem to consider this their first order of business.

It has become almost a routine, a favorite pastime, for U.S. congressmen and many others to meet with dissidents.

A member of the Dutch Parliament visiting Moscow even climbed over a gate in the middle of the night to leave his guest house in order to meet such a person.

I have met with many delegations of the United States and other Western parliamentarians. But frankly, I have not observed their behavior during the night. Sometimes U.S. congressional delegations are preceded by advance men sent by some American organizations to prepare meetings with certain dissidents both in Leningrad and Moscow. When asked by American visitors about the propriety of such meetings, I usually direct them to the head of their own delegation. But sometimes I ask them in return how they would react if an official Soviet parliamentarian delegation visiting the United States set up unscheduled, sometimes almost clandestine, meetings with such groups we might in fact sympathize with, like the Black Panthers, Puerto Rican militants, or Indian activists persecuted by the U.S. government.

What is their answer?

Nothing intelligible, though they proceed with such practices all the same. From those and other conversations I get the impression that many American politicians take part in these activities not because they are truly interested in dissidents or "refuseniks" (which means people denied visas to leave the country), but simply for the record, especially those who have a significant number of immigrants in their constituency.

Anyway, delegations from the Supreme Soviet do visit Washington?

Yes, there were two official delegations, one in 1974 and the other in 1978, headed by the chairman of our Foreign Relations Commission, Boris Ponomarev. There were also smaller groups, the last of them sent in the autumn of 1979.

The question of dissidents continues to cause considerable difficulties in East-West relations. What is your opinion of those people?

The so-called "dissidents" are a small group.

How small exactly?

To the best of my knowledge, in the last decade there have appeared a few hundred such people, including not only strictly political dissidents but also the most active refuseniks, leading members of extreme nationalist groups, and of those religious sects that operate illegally. These are people with diverse demands, programs, and grievances. If and when they become the subject of court or administrative action, it is not as a result of their holding views that differ from the national consensus, as it is often thought in the West. They don't come into conflict with the state because they think differently or "sit apart," which is the exact meaning of the Latin word *dissident.* The problems begin when they choose to break the Soviet law. If and when they do it, the state takes action against them.

A typical feature of these groups in recent years has been their close ties with foreign citizens and organizations. They have relied on foreign media, often actually worked for them, and received various kinds of assistance from abroad, including financial aid in some cases. No matter how the dissidents' motives are pictured in the West, they are perceived here by broad public opinion as people working for foreign interests.

What about the group that monitors Soviet compliance with the Final Act of the Helsinki Conference?

Some people have chosen this cover for their activities. Their real primary aim is to provide foreign media with materials designed to create an impression in the West that there exists in the USSR a widespread political movement opposing the Soviet state and the Soviet society, to arouse and mislead the Soviet public by rumors and messages transmitted via Western media to the USSR. These people are continuously defying our law. Some people in the West might like it. But they, as well as the Soviet citizens engaged in such activities, must realize that they directly challenge the government and the political system as a whole, and they must reckon with the fact that this conflict can't continue without consequences.

What bothers people in the West is that these people are often arrested, tried, sentenced to long terms or sent into exile.

The behavior of these people sometimes becomes criminal according to Soviet law, and crime always leads to punishment. As the head of the State Security Committee said not so long ago, the number of those sentenced in connection with their illegal political activity is now lower than ever in our history. It would undoubtedly be even better if there were no such cases at all. But if the West is moved by humanitarian motives, as it asserts, it must examine, first of all, what it does itself. I am quite convinced, for example, that without the systematic Western support and publicity, without the creation of a kind of halo around the dissidents by the West, as a result of which those people have developed a martyrdom complex and regard themselves as replicas of Saint Joan going to the stake —without all this publicity, most of them would not challenge the law and would not find themselves in trouble.

In other words, you find the West partly responsible for the dissidents' troubles.

The West bears a heavy responsibility. It is Western encouragement and support that make a dissident sure that his every step will get worldwide publicity, and if he goes far enough, may even win him a Nobel Prize. This has pushed some people, perhaps already not quite stable emotionally, toward a test of will with the government, toward brinkmanship with the law. Finally, they cross the legal brink. Sooner or later it ends in human tragedy. That might be exactly the result the Western anti-Sovieteers need so that they can wring their hands, bemoan the "martyrs," and further denounce the Soviet Union.

If the West is truly concerned about the humanitarian aspect, about the fate of some of our citizens, why exploit them in such a way? If, however, the aim of the whole campaign is to do maximum damage to the USSR, why not call a spade a spade and stop shedding crocodile tears? Those running the prodissident campaigns are simply trying to create endless problems for the Soviet authorities, to foster an ersatz opposition inside our country, to create the image of the USSR as a police state, and, finally, to sow seeds of hostility toward the USSR in the West, so as to wreck attempts at lessening international tensions and curbing the arms race. Those activities are actively sponsored by Western intelligence services, as well as by emigré groups and other private organizations.

But if you look at this situation from an American vantage point, the picture would be quite different.

Then I would advise Americans to put themselves into our shoes. How would Americans have reacted if Soviet journalists in the United States had begun to cooperate with members of some clandestine groups like the Weather Underground? Would Daniel Ellsberg have been cleared in the U.S. courts if he had had contacts with Soviet representatives in the United States? What if we had established close contacts with Indians at the particular moment when they were up in arms against the government? We sympathize with them deeply, but would it not have been looked upon as interference in your internal affairs? And would not these people and organizations in such a case have looked like agents of a foreign power?

If the dissidents are so few in number, as you said, wouldn't it be more practical either to disregard them completely or just let them leave the country?

In many cases, this is exactly what is done. But we have found out something, particularly in the case of refuseniks. If we make a step toward such a solution, it is taken as an invitation to greater pressure: new names appear, the noise gets louder. Some refuseniks are apparently incited to act. The Western media take up some cases as "newsworthy," and the whole thing starts anew, but with double or triple the intensity.

What would you say to conclude this discussion of human rights?

I would emphasize again that the issue of human rights, important as it is, should be used for constructive and not destructive purposes. Is it not the most important single right for everyone to live in peace? Given the correct, conscientious approach, debates about human rights should be conducted in ways that do not damage détente. After all, peace and détente are indispensable tools for securing human rights in their broadest meaning all over the world.

Chapter 5 | The Two Giants and the World

It is clear that relations between the Soviet Union and the United States continue to be a tremendously important part of modern international relations. But the whole complexity of the international scene can't possibly be reduced to the Moscow-Washington equation. Almost nine-tenths of the world's population live outside the United States and the USSR. In this age of growing interdependence, the nine-tenths cannot afford to forget about Soviet-American relations; nor can the two giants disassociate their bilateral relations from what's going on in Asia, Africa, and Latin America, not to mention Europe.

Exactly so. The idea of the two superpowers' special rights always has been alien to the Soviet Union. We regard the development of our relations with all the other countries as very important, and we never ignore them because of Soviet-American relations.

So, let us touch upon the problems of other countries and regions in the context of both Soviet foreign policy and U.S.-Soviet relations. One of these is the problem of Soviet-Chinese relations. In the West, a notion has been advanced that, in its policy of détente, the Soviet Union was primarily moved by its fear of China and its growing military might.

This notion is totally unfounded. Quite to the contrary, our policy of détente became one of the reasons for the deterioration of our relations with China. As far back as the late 1950s, the Soviet intentions to pursue détente with the West were bluntly called by the Chinese "treacherous to the cause of revolution."

Would you say there were no other reasons for Chinese-Soviet relations developing the way they did?

Sure, there were other reasons, at least from the Chinese point of view, apart from the announced Soviet policy of détente with the West and, in particular, with the United States. Among those reasons I would mention our refusal to give them the nuclear bomb. Also, quite obviously, Mao saw in the Soviet Union a serious obstacle to Chinese claims for leadership over other socialist countries and the world communist movement, claims that became evident after Stalin's death.

The West, the United States first of all, banked on Mao's anti-Sovietism, calculating that the development of ties with China, and the offer of military aid, would change China into their ally and bring about a drastic shift in the global balance of power. Psychologically, it may have had something to do with a mythology that has surrounded China over the years. This mythology probably received an especially strong impetus at the time of the euphoria prevailing in Washington after Richard Nixon's so-called "epoch-making" trip to the Far East. It is a human weakness to romanticize the exotic and unknown. The Chinese succeeded in playing on this attitude toward the Orient and impressed their American visitors with a certain mystery about the biggest nation in the world. Thousands of years of history, an ancient culture, exquisite cuisine, and human values different from those of the West apparently combined to infatuate and intrigue American visitors almost to the point of overwhelming them. Political platitudes spoken in a very foreign language and in a very foreign way can assume some hidden meaning, charm, and wisdom. Look how cleverly the Beijing leadership nurtured and encouraged this newly found curiosity in the mandarins of the White House, Capitol Hill, and Wall Street.

By the way, China has always occupied a special place in the American mind. Just recall all those missionaries and businessmen who have tried their luck in China since America became a Pacific power.

What about the Realpolitik aspect of the new Western attitude toward China?

I am not trying to argue that lack of relations between the West and China was not abnormal. After 1949, when the People's Republic of China was formed, we did our best to persuade the United States and other Western nations to recognize the new government of China, establish normal diplomatic relations with her, and admit the PRC into the United Nations. But the West balked. What's more, many American sinologists and diplomats who called for diplomatic recognition of China were intimidated and blacklisted during the McCarthy era. Nevertheless, the fact is that the rapprochement between China and the West came only after the Maoist leadership became outspokenly anti-Soviet. Naturally enough, this caused some apprehensions on our part.

But it might have been logical from the point of view of the West, and particularly of the United States, to try to strengthen its position vis-à-vis the Soviet Union by means of improving relations with China.

Well, in a rather open and simple form you have just described the conceptual foundation of this policy—the nineteenth-century balance-of-power game. Its essence is to increase one's own power by putting additional weight on one's own side of the scale.

But is it not quite logical?

Of this I have grave doubts, at least if your goal is to prevent a nuclear holocaust and assure stability in international relations. The concept presupposes a free play of forces. And each participant will of course play at his own risk, as he sees fit, taking into account only his own rules. The historical experience shows that nothing good ever comes out of such games.

Shades of Metternich, Talleyrand, and Castlereagh. It seems that just such principles were codified and even sanctified at the Vienna Congress of 1815.

There's a definite and conscious parallel. But this very parallel also helps us to understand why the old concept is inapplicable in the last quarter of the twentieth century. The world has changed too much. Take just one difference: in the first half of the last century, a miscalculation leading to a disturbance of the balance promised, at worst, another recarving of European frontiers, a replacement of one dynasty by another, or something of the kind. All that was rather limited in scale and frequently reversible. The tide of history could in the long run curb and correct the Realpolitikers of the nineteenth century. So, even if the arrangements of the Vienna Congress did not bring Europe significant stability, they at least could not bring about the destruction of the European civilization.

Today, the balance-of-power concept inevitably leads to a situation where one participant in the balancing act can possess sufficient nuclear capability to destroy one or several of his opponents, and a miscalculation could easily lead to an irreversible outcome. To think of any stability in such an arrangement is nonsense. Even if the worst-case scenario did not materialize, it is hard to imagine how, in such a pseudorealistic world, one could utilize, short of a test by actual war, any advantage of joining hands with one country against the other.

What about a general possibility of war between the Soviet Union and China?

We do not want such a war and are ready to undertake everything possible to avoid it. More than that, we want to normalize our relations with China. As you know, we have continued our negotiations with Beijing whenever possible.

But all Western visitors to China come back saying they were told at all levels of an imminent Soviet aggression.

This was said some time ago. But I would greatly doubt that even then the Chinese leaders were really as afraid of a Soviet invasion as they said, or that they really suspected us of planning a war against them. Even if one were to look at the problem through the eyes of a Western geopolitician, a Soviet attack on China would be an absolutely stupid proposition.

Zbigniew Brzezinski wrote on one occasion that he felt Beijing could make a meaningful contribution to the shaping of a more stable U.S.-Soviet relationship.

Yes, he did write that. But remember that certain illusions concerning the use of the Chinese "card" to intimidate the Soviet Union were, to my mind, an important reason why Washington made its 1979–80 turn off the road of détente to the rough and dangerous path of confrontation. You see, I don't think Mr. Brzezinski has ever sincerely favored stable and normal Soviet-American relations. When he talked of using "the China card" to stabilize those relations, he meant a kind of stability the Soviet Union would never agree to. The real meaning of "the China card"—the poker-game connotation of the term betrays the approach behind it, cynical, deceptive, adventurist—has nothing to do with détente. What in fact is being attempted here is to obtain quick gains for the West from the bad state of relations between us and China. These attempts are made in total neglect of the long-term goals and interests even of the United States itself. Washington seemed to be striving to make a fast political buck during a period of serious difficulties between the Soviet Union and China, disregarding long-term consequences. The American policy toward China has already increased instability and undermined détente, and has worsened the political situation in Asia.

But is that not what the game of international relations is all about? Does Beijing not play the American card as well?

Yes, it did, and in my judgment it has shown itself to be a better player than Washington with its China card.

Chinese-American trade has doubled, and may triple in the 1980s.

Well, a doubling or even a tripling of trade, considering the low level from which this increase started, is not that significant. There was a kind of euphoria in American business circles when the news about the Chinese modernization programs reached the United States and normal diplomatic relations were established. China was almost flooded with delegations of businessmen from the United States, Japan, and other Western nations. Many contracts were signed. But now a more sober mood prevails in the headquarters of Western corporations. The reason is that the plans for modernization have been severely cut, many contracts broken off, many credits not used. The Chinese themselves are looking at the future somewhat more cautiously.

What are the indications of this more cautious approach as you see them? And a broader question—how are the recent changes within China regarded in the Soviet Union?

China's internal situation is an extremely complex matter. I am no expert on this country, and can only rely on estimates of real sinologists. China, as you know, has gone through a very difficult period of almost two decades. The Great Leap Forward and Cultural Revolution undermined the country's economy, led to a grave sociopolitical and moral crisis, and exhausted and disoriented China's Communist Party. Now there seems to be a growing understanding in Beijing that the country's enormous and neglected problems of social and economic development cannot be solved exclusively through reliance on the West and its military aid.

We in the Soviet Union hope that all this will also help the Chinese leaders realize that their people badly need peace, détente, and cooperation with its neighbors, and China will develop its policy accordingly.

What is the Soviet attitude toward the prospect of China's getting sophisticated weapons from the West?

Naturally, we view the expansion and consolidation of military ties between China and the West as a trend toward an anti-Soviet alliance—a trend fraught with many dangers for international security.

*How would you explain the complications in the U.S.-China rapproche-
ment that have emerged under the Reagan administration? One would
have thought that Mr. Reagan would have pursued this accord.*

The Reagan administration's posture on China is rather contradictory. On
the one hand, like its predecessors, it counts on China as a sort of counterweight against the Soviet Union. On the other hand, there is the dogmatic
anticommunism of the Reagan team, for whom the PRC remains "Red
China," existing side by side with "free China"—the Taiwan regime set up
by and allied to the United States.

The traditional stand of American conservatives on China has always
been noted for its skepticism about Beijing's real value for the United
States. The conservatives are afraid that, having traded its anti-Soviet
rhetoric for American aid, Beijing would preserve its freedom of action and
be able to use its increased potential against U.S. interests in the Pacific
and the Third World. According to this logic, the United States should
demand certain guarantees from China and put greater pressure on her. At
the same time they view Taiwan, with its half-million armed forces, as a
reliable ally of increasing strategic importance.

These factors have caused some cooling off in U.S.- Chinese relations.
But it is too early to make any far-reaching conclusions from that.

*President Brezhnev, in his Tashkent speech of March 1982, emphasized
that the Soviet Union is ready to negotiate an improvement of Soviet-
Chinese relations without any preliminary conditions. How is that to be
understood?*

The normalization of relations with our neighbor China has long been one
of the most important objectives of Soviet foreign policy. We continue to
hope that sooner or later this objective will be realized. Leonid Brezhnev,
in the same speech you mentioned, pointed out that, although we have
criticized many aspects of the Chinese leaders' policy, especially in foreign
affairs, we have never tried to interfere with the PRC's domestic affairs or
deny the existence of the socialist order there.

The negotiations on the improvement of Soviet-Chinese relations, should
they succeed, in our view may be of a great long-standing significance for
consolidation of peace in Asia and the whole world. The improvement of
these bilateral relations would cause no damage to other countries.

*Turning to Japan, what is the Soviet position on Japanese claims to the
so-called "northern territories"?*

The Japanese government has been claiming several islands belonging to
the Soviet Union since the end of World War II, when they were returned

to us according to the decision of the Yalta and Potsdam conferences. Japan herself recognized our rights to the islands at the 1951 San Francisco conference. We consider the problem nonexistent from either a legal or a practical point of view.

But this is the heart of the matter: even if justice is on your side, why not yield on the question of a few small islands for the sake of improving relations with a country with which good relations are of such great importance both today and in the future?

We see more in those two or four islands than little pieces of land. We believe that a territorial problem, no matter how small the piece of land in question, demands particularly cautious treatment. In the past, such problems have often enough caused international conflicts and even wars. We have made great efforts to make recognition and inviolability of existing frontiers a norm of modern international relations and a basic principle of détente. We hold that the establishment of this principle helps remove major threats to world peace. Therefore, agreeing to an exemption from this norm in any place, and even on a small point, may very well open a veritable Pandora's box of troubles: many other old territorial disputes would be likely to be reopened, and new ones to emerge. International stability would be further undermined. I am well aware of the sentiments and emotions many Japanese have about this problem, but the Japanese policies have punished themselves here, because it is mostly due to these policies that such emotions were generated. I do hope that in time this question will lose some of its present acuteness for the Japanese and cease to be an obstacle on the way to positive development of Soviet-Japanese relations.

But will the Japanese be ready to take this road if the problem of the islands remains unsolved?

I don't know when they will be emotionally ready to do so. If approached rationally, the problem looks entirely different. You see, I don't believe this question is of any serious importance for the Japanese interests. Japan's major interests lie with guaranteeing her security and economic well-being. None of these interests has anything to do with the islands. All of these interests depend to a large extent on the overall state of relations between Japan and the USSR. And it seems to me that ensuring these most vital interests is of much greater importance than the fate of a couple of islands, particularly if one takes into account the overall economic situation in the world, the growing scarcity of natural resources, difficulties in world trade, and the protectionist wave in the Western countries.

Do you expect the Japanese to follow what you call a rational line of behavior in the eighties?

I do hope they will.

But now the picture looks different. Quite to the contrary, in Japan there seems to be developing a growing hostility to the USSR, including general discontent at the appearance of new Soviet military forces and medium-range missiles in the Soviet far east.

I am aware of this sentiment, as well as of the itch some Japanese feel to join actively in the arms race. But the real cause of the recent deterioration of Soviet-Japanese relations, including the economic ties, was not the question of northern territories, but U.S. pressure to compel Japan to follow the American line. In Japan itself strong doubts are voiced about this policy. Many Japanese realize that, in the context of growing tensions in the world, the Soviet Union cannot help taking adequate measures to provide for its security. And yet I am absolutely sure that the incentives for Japan to develop closer cooperation with the Soviet Union will grow in the 1980s. It is my deep conviction that the Soviet Union and Japan have vast common interests.

You mean economic interests?

Not exclusively. I would even put the main emphasis on the interests of security. Both the Soviet Union and Japan are interested in the preservation of peace and a lowering of the level of military confrontation in the region as a whole. It's evident that due to its geographic position and population density Japan is extremely vulnerable in case of a conflict. And this vulnerability cannot be eliminated by means of arms buildups and military alliances. The only way for Japan to guarantee its own security is to consolidate peace and détente in the region, which will lead to a system of collective security and cooperation.

I was in Japan at the end of 1981, and my impression was that the Japanese were becoming more conscious of the implications of the increased East-West tensions and an all-out arms race for them. And I do hope and expect that with such a great objective interest in peace and détente, a nation that still remembers the horror of atomic bombing will become a much more active participant in the international efforts to insure peace in the world.

The economic aspect is also tremendously important for Japan. There is hardly any other country in the world with an economy so dependent on both peace and international stability. And, of course, there are also very important Japanese interests connected with the development of cooperation with the Soviet Union.

Japan is currently spending about 1 percent of her gross national product on defense. What do you think of the argument that she should have a military might commensurate with her economic potential? In particular, it is argued that as an island nation she should be able to defend her sea-lanes against foreign threats.

Such arguments are based on hopelessly obsolete notions about the utility of military power for economic and political purposes. When Japan tried to enhance her economic position in the world through territorial expansion and militarism she got into a terrible disaster. But look what Japan has managed to accomplish in the last three decades without war and aggression. What would Japan gain now by a remilitarization? An undermined economy? An easier life for her competitors?

As for the talk about defending sea-lanes—the only real defense is peace. Japan was not able to defend these lanes in World War II by military means. To think that she could protect her communications today by creating a big navy is to think in terms of children playing with toy ships.

David Rockefeller's Trilateral Commission aims at a network of close cooperation between Japan, Western Europe, and the United States. Does this triangle policy enhance feelings of encirclement in Moscow?

By itself, the attempt to improve cooperation between Japan, Western Europe, and the United States does not arouse feelings like that in Moscow. It all depends on the political context in which such strengthening of ties takes place. If it should develop in the overall context of détente and go hand in hand with growing cooperation between socialist countries and the states from each apex of the capitalist triangle, as well as with the Third World, there would be nothing wrong with it. But if this increase in cooperation between the three capitalist centers takes place in conjunction with a revival of the Cold War, and if it means strengthening military ties and amassing greater military potential against the Soviet Union or any other country whose policy the West may not like at the moment; if coordination in the economic sphere means participation of all the countries of the triangle in Washington-led boycotts, blockades, or embargoes —then we are definitely against this kind of triangular relationship.

Obviously, the Japanese economy is bursting at its seams. It seems a natural development that Japan should try to penetrate the Chinese market at full force.

Naturally, Japan would like to seize the Chinese market. This desire has deep historic roots. But we talked already about the limitations on trade with the Chinese. Trade is not charity, and I don't believe that Japanese businessmen are searching for a place where they can give away their goods for nothing. Of course, the potential for Japanese-Chinese trade would increase if Japan, which has almost no raw materials, could import them from China. But their development, considering the state of the Chinese economy, will demand huge investments and a lot of time. So, there are prospects, but they will demand efforts and also require a stable political situation in that region and in the world at large.

In 1973, I had a discussion with the then prime minister of Japan, Kakuei Tanaka. Expectations were high at that time for fast development of both friendship with the Chinese and expansion of investment and business. But recently I met with Japan's former foreign minister, Saburo Okita, sometimes called the Robert McNamara of of Japan because of his economic expertise. He had been invited by the present leadership to Beijing as chairman of the Japan Economic Research Center to render advice on financial and economic matters. Minister Okita seemed to caution against overoptimism regarding quick deals and rapid development of trade.

Well, that is exactly what I was talking about. The euphoria is over. The time has come for a more sober and realistic assessment.

Takashi Watanabe, Minister of Finance and former Trilateral Commission chairman in Japan, and also former president of the Asian Development Bank in Manila, assured me that, historically and culturally, the Japanese were naturally closer with the Chinese. He added, "Soviet diplomacy toward us is often 'clumsy.' "

I do not know what Mr. Watanabe means by clumsiness. Perhaps the fact that we did not yield to their territorial claims; but to yield would be much clumsier, I'm afraid. As far as we are concerned, there are also some aspects of Japanese foreign policy we don't like; however, I guess we and the Japanese should not stress the things we don't like in each other's policy, but think more about ways of developing truly constructive and mutually beneficial relations, in which both countries are objectively interested. As for natural closeness between Japan and China, well, taking into consideration the several times those two countries have bitterly fought each other, one could interpret that closeness a bit differently than Mr. Watanabe. In many cases the Japanese were responsible for those clashes; in others, the Chinese were to blame. It is said that Japan was once saved by *kamikaze,* the holy wind that dispersed the hostile navy approaching from mainland China. In our time it is difficult to rely on holy winds. Much more important is a clever, wise foreign policy, promoting peace and international cooperation, removing thick layers of mutual distrust and fear.

Let's switch to Europe now. In 1936, Italian diplomat Count Carlo Sforza wrote: "Either we shall serve the European ideal or we shall perish." What was the origin of the Soviet idea for an All-European conference, which was for a long time a constant theme of the Soviet diplomacy?

We came up with this initiative for the first time as early as 1955. Since then, the Soviet Union and other socialist countries have worked consistently for the convening of a European conference on security and cooperation.

Professor Johan Galtung of Norway has suggested an All-European symbiosis between East and West, turning the entire unit into a political and economic colossus of intertwined cooperation and action.

Actually, the idea is not his. Eighty years ago it was called "the United States of Europe." The idea was sharply criticized by V. I. Lenin, who believed that under the then-existing conditions such a symbiosis would be either impossible or reactionary, in the latter case turning into an alliance of imperialist states united in order to consolidate the system of colonial plunder.

But what is the Soviet position on a united Europe now?

United to what extent? If you have in mind it becoming a kind of new superpower, such a prospect looks rather utopian. We see objective trends in favor of economic integration in Europe, as well as generally in the world, although we recognize the difficulties standing in the way of that process. Suffice it to point out the existing inequalities and the predominance of richer and more powerful nations. One could hardly expect this process to lead in the near future to any unification of European, or even Western European, economies. The other, noneconomic aspects of the problem are even more complicated. Take the growth of national consciousness, particularly evident lately in rather acute forms and unexpected instances: the Walloons in Belgium, the Scots and the Welsh in Great Britain, the Corsicans in France, to say nothing of the regions where the national problem has acquired the characteristics of an open armed conflict—such as Northern Ireland or the Basque country. How can one expect an amalgamation into a superpower of European nations so different in their major characteristics? I've been talking about historic trends. As to the political projects stemming from such unification plans, they look to us rather sinister.

Why?

First and foremost, because, if the projects involve a unification of capitalist Europe only, we cannot help but see in this an attempt to solidify and make permanent the division of Europe into two opposing military-political blocs. And our position, as I am sure you know, is aimed at ending this abnormal situation and ultimately disbanding these blocs, or, at least, their military organizations altogether. If a unification of all Europe is envisaged, then a question immediately comes to mind—on what grounds? The socialist countries are not planning to become capitalist, and, as far as we know, the West does not have immediate plans to become socialist. To try to enforce one's own system on the other side would mean war.

So, after all, you foresee a split in Europe for years to come?

If you have in mind the existence of socialist and capitalist societies in Europe, yes. But this does not mean that hostile relations and tensions are inevitable in Europe. I have already dwelled on our attitude toward blocs. We are for further development of political cooperation to promote arms control and disarmament, and to achieve a greater mutual confidence. We also favor all-around development of intra-European economic, scientific, and technical cooperation; of cultural ties, tourism, and other types of contacts. We are sure that the two parts of Europe can live in conditions of security, close cooperation, and, if you will, harmony, regardless of their different socioeconomic systems.

Speaking in conceptual terms, how would you define the problem of security in Europe?

In the first place, it is a problem of effecting a rather radical change in the whole system of international relations in the region. In Europe, countries belonging to two different social and economic systems meet head-on. And they meet not only politically, but militarily as well. There is no other region in the world where so many deadly weapons have been accumulated, no other region that has become a powder keg that can explode so easily in case of a conflict. Here we face in a particularly clear-cut form the most important, I would say crucial, question—whether peaceful coexistence and cooperation are possible at all. To some degree, Europe has become a testing ground for solutions to the most vital problems of our time.

Willy Brandt left me with the impression that he considers his Ostpolitik as neither having failed outright, nor fully succeeded.

Are there many human endeavors that have been fulfilled completely? On the whole, Brandt's Ostpolitik has undoubtedly brought considerable results. I think that Willy Brandt and his colleagues can be proud of what they have done, since they have contributed to starting détente in potentially the most explosive region, where the conflict between East and West is of a central, rather than a peripheral, nature. It is vital that this move-ment be preserved and developed further. The existing problems and diffi-culties show that political relations in Europe have not been transformed as much as was desirable, and that whatever transformations may have taken place have not yet become absolutely irreversible. But this does not detract from the importance of the positive changes in Europe, to which Ostpolitik has contributed in a very important way.

In spite of these positive changes, former West German Defense Minister Hans Apel has said that talks between East and West really lead nowhere unless they are backed by military preparations.

One would expect exactly such an opinion from a West German defense minister, although it only serves the arms race and incites tensions. And it is military preparations that lead nowhere nowadays. We have three decades of them behind us. Have they helped in negotiations, led to agree-ments or cooperation in a single instance? *Si vis pacem para bellum* is a song mankind has heard for centuries. But in our day and age the ancient aphorism is not working.

The Western Europeans have big economic stakes in détente. There are the human contacts, the feelings of a common destiny, a common cultural heritage shared by the peoples of all Europe, West and East. There are many strong historical ties. Our common struggle against Hitler, shared by the United States, was one experience that brought Europeans espe-cially close together. Soviet people who fled Nazi concentration camps in Western Europe fought in the resistance movements in France, Italy, Belgium, and many other countries. French officers fought in our air force.

The Soviet army played a decisive role in the liberation of Europe, which is understood by the Europeans better than by the Americans. The graves of Soviet soldiers who gave their lives to defeat the Nazis are strewn all over the continent. All in all, peace and détente receive a much higher priority in Western Europe than in the United States. In a way, Western Europe on some occasions was virtually dragging the Americans into dé-tente, and now it is resisting, sometimes timidly and inconsistently, the American attempts to revive the Cold War. I don't mean to say that cold-war hangovers have evaporated from all Europeans minds. There are forces in Western Europe that are afraid of détente and would prefer a tenser atmosphere between East and West.

What forces do you have in mind?

Well, for one thing, every Western European country has a military-indus-trial complex of its own, with much the same attitude toward détente as the American one. Then there are people who are concerned about domestic instability in their countries and scapegoat détente as a major reason for that instability. To them, a climate of renewed East-West hostility and polarization looks like an effective means to discipline those struggling for social change in Western Europe, to bring about national unity on the issue of an outside threat, whether such a threat exists or not. One should also mention anticommunism. In Western Europe, particularly in those countries where communists are a strong political force, anticommunism takes different forms than in the United States. But it is there as a considerable factor for increased international tension.

Finally, there is a traditional factor for tension in Europe: the German imperial syndrome. Of course, it's weaker now than forty years ago or seventy years ago, but there still are people in West Germany, including very influential sections of the power elite, who think that Germans should have another try at hegemony in Europe and other parts of the world. They chafe at the existing limitations on German military activity.

So what are other Europeans—Europeans anxious for peace and détente —to do?

The same thing as anxious Russians and anxious Americans: understand that military power alone does not guarantee security, and that a durable peace requires détente, arms limitations, and broader cooperation between East and West. Besides, the Europeans should not yield to fears about their alleged defenselessness, spread by proponents of a continued arms race. All that deterrence can give, it gives also to the Europeans. Because a war in Europe will inevitably become a world war, and a nuclear war. This is a political reality of today's world. I am sure this is well understood in the Soviet Union. One could only wish it would be understood in the West, too.

But isn't the unprecedented rise of the peace movement in Western Europe proof itself of this understanding?

Exactly. This movement has grown out of genuine and powerful grassroots feelings among millions of Europeans who have sensed the futility of arms racing and military confrontation. No wonder all this happens in Europe—a continent devastated by wars and still saturated with modern armaments. Hence, the vitality, the persistence, and the political impact of this movement, for there is nothing so strong as an idea taking hold of millions of people.

The initial response of high American officials to this movement was a clumsy attempt to write it off as a Soviet propaganda plot, but they have ultimately had to recognize the new European climate.

Granted, the 1949 model of a Soviet threat to Western Europe looks odd today; but there still exist fears of a Soviet military action—say, in response to a crisis in Eastern Europe.

Yes, current NATO thinking has evolved in this direction. They've got to have a credible image, to keep at bay the force of reasonable doubt in the public mind. But I wonder whether people would find credible this latest product of the NATO brain trust. Just think of it. They say they have to defend Western Europe from a possible Soviet attack, which might result from some event in Eastern Europe the USSR might not like. If there's any logic in this, it can only be based on the assumption that Western Europe would have a lot to do with events in Eastern Europe—otherwise, why expect any hostile reaction to the West from the Soviet Union? To put it simply, NATO seeks to defend its intention to meddle in the internal affairs of East European states. Does such an intention have anything to do with the real interests of Western Europe, of Europe as a whole? The West has to accept the fact that socialism is here to stay in Eastern Europe.

What would you say in this respect about Poland? Have not the recent events there demonstrated a serious discontent with the existing conditions?

There is discontent, of course. But it is not centered on the whole social system. It has to do with things not inherent in the system—mistakes, economic difficulties, corruption, and other misdeeds of certain officials.

And there were other factors involved. From the very beginning of the events in Poland, the United States, with certain circles in the West, did their best to turn these events into a major international crisis. I am sure that the extreme positions taken by some Solidarity leaders and other opposition figures were inspired by a firm belief—cultivated from the outside—that they would be thoroughly supported by the United States and NATO in putting pressure on the Polish government, as well as on the USSR and other socialist countries.

Of course, Poland is going through difficult times. But this does not conceal the obvious fact that Poland, which in the past was one of Europe's poorest countries, has achieved a great deal under socialism. And it will find a way out of the present troubles as well.

You have said that Washington tries to use increased international tensions to strengthen its relations with its allies.

Yes, it is trying to do that. One can even assume that quite a few American politicians did not like détente and preferred an atmosphere of tension for the very reason that tension helps shorten the reins and "discipline" the allies, as well as the folks back home. As to the effectiveness of this tactic,

I would say that it's working to a limited extent, and in the short run, while at the same time exacerbating the long-term problems between America and Western Europe, creating and increasing both open and hidden tensions in their relations. As a matter of fact, we are already witnessing it.

You mean that if a new cold war has "ersatz" motives, it can only bring about an "ersatz" unity in the West?

Yes, the world has changed since the 1950s, and no matter how strong the nostalgia in Washington, it can't make time run backward. Having become much stronger economically and less dependent on the United States politically, the allies now demand that their interests be taken into account.

I realize the great significance of the European peace movement, but I must tell you that many citizens in Europe are annoyed and bored, if not puzzled, by the endless talk about unimaginable dangers and missiles soaring through the skies at the speed of sound, carrying their unholy loads of destructive power.

The annoyance is explainable; this talk has been going on a long time, but it's impossible merely to wave off the importance of the problem of survival. You cannot get annoyed with survival. If you allow a more general comment, I do not want to create a false impression of being some sort of Eurocentrist, but to all of us this continent is very dear. "All of us" includes Soviet citizens living not only on this side, but also beyond the Urals, as well as Americans, most of whom have deep ancestral roots in Europe. It is extremely important to preserve this continent and secure fair conditions for its future existence. It is up to the Europeans themselves, in the first place, to take care of that. But the same issue should be present, as one of the most important problems, in Soviet-American relations. The latter cannot be separated from Europe. Europe has been both the hotbed of the Cold War and the birthplace of détente.

The European issue is not merely a question of altruism of the two superpowers toward Europeans. It is the question of self-preservation for both the USSR and the United States.

What would be, from your point of view, the most desirable situation in Europe in terms of international relations?

I would say enduring security and extensive cooperation. To reach these, it is necessary to end the abnormal situation of the continent being split into two opposing camps armed with powerful nuclear and conventional weapons and spending billions and billions on military needs. Therefore, we favor disbanding both military blocs, or, as a first step, dismantling their military organizations. The Warsaw Treaty Organization's Charter contains a special article according to which the organization would disband if NATO ceased to exist.

And while trying to reach that goal you want to get the United States out of Europe?

What makes you think so? We are realists and don't set before ourselves unattainable goals. Besides, reaching the positive goal I referred to is unthinkable without American consent—more than that, without the active participation of the United States in the process of détente and disarmament. Finally, we want détente, security, and cooperation, not just in Europe but around the world. I would say that it is difficult to imagine a stable system of international relations without stable relations between the United States, Western Europe, and the Soviet Union. I would repeat that our goal is good relations with Western Europe, good relations with the United States, good relations with all other countries.

Summing up our talk of things European, I would like to stress that Europe, after all, is becoming too small and crowded for all the hostilities and confrontations pressed on her from the outside.

China, Japan, India, and Europe are important for Soviet-American relations, no doubt. But in connection with the trials and tribulations of détente over the past five years, different places come to mind—Angola, the Horn of Africa, Afghanistan, and, of course, the Middle East. The evermore dynamic events in the Third World are creating problems for any rapprochement between the United States and the USSR. In turn, increased tension between the two superpowers complicates dealing with the pressing problems of developing lands.

Indeed, the world has been changing rapidly, and some developed countries are finding it more of a problem than others. But I do not think it justified to regard the Soviet Union and the United States in similar terms as regards their policies toward developing countries. Let's look at the basic facts in the Third World. For generations, this part of the world has been a colonial or semicolonial backyard of the capitalist West. If one is to look for any outside forces responsible for the dismal state of those hundreds of millions of people in Asia, Africa, and Latin America, the responsibility lies squarely with the West.

And Russia.

Russia got out of the colonial club in 1917. Before that, Russia had its own colonies, which were ruthlessly oppressed and exploited. It was one of the main tasks of our Revolution to provide for a political liberation and an economic and cultural rebirth of those parts of our country.

Evidently, the Central Asian republics of the Soviet Union have come a long way since 1917. At least that was my impression when visiting there.

In a very short time span those peoples have passed from medieval backwardness to modern civilization. What's no less important, their ethnic heritage has not only been preserved, but has flourished. So we think that to the extent that we had been directly responsible for the plight of colonial peoples, we have done our duty to redress the wrongs.

Does that mean that you are not going to assist developing countries anymore?

No. We do so now and we shall assist them in the future as much as we can. But we also believe that those who owned and exploited colonial empires, embezzling their wealth and resources, carry a special responsibility. The West's private corporations continue to invest in those countries in order to squeeze superprofits out of them.

But don't many developing countries themselves do everything possible to attract foreign investments, private or public?

You are right; they do need substantial investments, capital funds, technology, know-how, skilled manpower, etc. And the multinational corporations have enormous resources the Third World could use. The big question is, on what terms and in whose interests? When a private corporation invests in a Third World nation, the main corporate goal is to obtain a rate of profit it can't get in a developed country because of higher labor costs. This in effect means superexploitation of developing countries. There lies one of the reasons for conflict between them and the West.

Obviously, different developing countries have different attitudes toward multinational corporations.

That's true. Some Third World regimes are totally or nearly totally subservient to multinational corporations, allowing them to play a free hand in exchange for a payoff. The results are usually the same—the country is bled white, popular discontent builds up, sooner or later a coup d'état or even a revolution follows, and the new regime tries to strike a more equitable bargain with the corporations. But renegotiating a bargain is always a rather painful process. In many cases the corporations, aided by the governments protecting them, try to destablize the new regime or to buy it off. So, developing countries learn to be on alert, as well as to develop other options.

Like turning to the Soviet Union?

For many developing nations, relations with the Soviet Union play an important countervailing role, permitting them to increase their bargaining power in dealing with the West, and to obtain better terms from the multinational corporations. Had there not been the Soviet Union and other socialist countries as an alternative to capitalism, a substantial part of the Earth's population would still live in colonies.

But can there ever be a working détente with this competitive approach to Third World nationalism?

Nothing of what we do in the Third World is inconsistent with international law and U.N. Charter resolutions and declarations. Besides, even the West has realized by now that the old system of relations with developing countries is hopelessly obsolete. It has been repeatedly recognized by the international community that developing countries are entitled to a fair share of the world's resources. All the developed nations have a vital interest in solving this global problem—this is the essence of the work for a new international economic order. The Soviet policies in the Third World are aimed at helping find a solution. Why it should be inconsistent with détente, I can't see. Of course, it is possible to turn the Third World into an arena for a power struggle between East and West, but the problems of developing countries can also be regarded as an additional incentive to global cooperation. We would prefer the latter option.

What about Angola?

All right, let us begin with that country, and remember some basic facts that are now almost forgotten in the West. The crisis in and around Angola flared up in 1975. The major political force in that country was, just as it is now, the Popular Movement for the Liberation of Angola (MPLA). It had been engaged in a war for liberation from Portuguese rule since the early 1960s. The U.N. General Assembly supported that struggle by adopting a series of resolutions and urging all nations to render assistance to liberation movements against colonialism in every way. The MPLA sought help from the United States but got a cold shoulder. So they turned to the Soviet Union, and we gave them considerable material aid, to say nothing of moral and political support. All that was strictly in accordance with the U.N. mandate. As a matter of fact, other countries were also helping the MPLA, Sweden among them.

In 1974, a revolution took place in Portugal. The new Lisbon government declared its intention to withdraw from all its colonies, including Angola. The MPLA was recognized by most Angolans and by Portugal as the leading political force of the emerging nation. However, the United States,

China, South Africa, and Zaire were actively interfering in Angolan affairs and supporting two rival movements—FNLA and UNITA. The CIA was pumping money and arms into these two political factions, which even in colonial times had devoted almost all their energies to fighting the MPLA rather than the Portuguese colonial rulers. South Africa invaded the Angolan territory, at one point almost reaching the nation's capital. Faced with foreign aggression, the Angolan government, formed by the MPLA, asked the USSR, Cuba, and a number of African nations for help. That help was given. Cuba even sent some military personnel there. But contrary to Western predictions, Angola has not been turned into a Soviet colony or military base. It might be proper to recall here that most of the Angolan oil is still extracted by the Gulf Oil Company of Pittsburgh, Pennsylvania.

And the Cubans are still there.

As a matter of fact, they are ready to withdraw their personnel step by step, and they even reached an agreement with the Angolan government to do so. But each time the withdrawal had to be postponed in the face of attacks by South African troops and their separatist proxies within Angola. With the danger of this aggression removed, the Cuban personnel would leave, as was emphasized in the Cuban-Angolan statement of February 1982.

You are certainly aware of the fact that this situation is seen quite differently in the West; events in Angola are regarded as a major reason why détente has been replaced by a new period of international tensions.

That is why I tried to refresh the whole episode in our memories.

All right, let's get down to Ethiopia now.

In Ethiopia there was a similar situation in the sense that, had there been no foreign aggression against that country, there would have been no need for Soviet military assistance or the Cuban military presence. It was the Somalis who started a war against Ethiopia. Personally, I am convinced that they never would have attacked their neighbor had they not been led to believe that they would have the support of the United States and some other nations. By the way, when we maintained friendly relations with the Somalis, they never dared interfere in Ethiopian affairs, let alone claim part of the Ethiopian territory. We never gave the Somalis any reason to count on our support or assistance should they decide to commit an act of aggression. And this despite the fact that Ethiopia remained a pro-Western monarchy at the time. If it had not been for the help from the Soviet Union and other socialist countries, Ethiopia, the oldest independent nation on the African continent, would probably have been dismembered and there would have been an enormous death toll among the civilian population.

But why were the Somalis led to believe that they would get support?

Because Washington wanted to destroy our friendship with Somalia and take advantage of the strategic position of that country, particularly its Indian Ocean port of Berbera.

But it was the Soviet Union that was accused of wanting a naval base at Berbera.

Just at the time we were accused of such plans we agreed to negotiate with the United States an agreement banning foreign military bases in the Indian Ocean. But the talks have been broken by the United States, and Berbera is now an American naval base.

Cuban Vice-Premier Dr. Carlos Raphael Rodriguez explained to me in great detail in his office in Havana the motivation of the Cuban government for their steps in Africa. He might have convinced me, but Washington feels absolutely differently.

Sure they feel absolutely differently. I believe they would have preferred to see South African troops in Angola, or the dismemberment of Ethiopia, just to keep any socialist influence off. I'd like to emphasize that the Cuban assistance to various African nations has not violated any norms of international law. Both the MPLA and the Revolutionary Council in Addis Ababa not only had every right to ask for help, but they had every reason to do so. And the Cubans were wholly within their rights to comply with those urgent pleas.

What Washington above all objected to was that the Cubans seemingly acted on behalf of and in the name of the Kremlin.

Cuba is an independent, sovereign state not inclined to act on somebody else's instigation or blindly follow somebody else's will. It was their own decision to help the Angolans. And we backed their actions because we sympathized with the cause the MPLA was fighting for, namely, the complete independence and territorial integrity of Angola, which was jeopardized by the South African military intervention, white mercenaries, and the CIA.

The constant irritant of Cuba as a Soviet ally on the doorstep of the United States is a new experience in American history.

Yes, it is new, just like many other things the United States will have to learn to live with. An increasing number of countries around the United States are pursuing independent policies. I don't see, however, why an independent state should necessarily be an irritant.

When talking with Dr. Carlos Raphael Rodriguez, it was clear to me that once Washington lifted its blockade, the Cuban government would be ready to resume normal relations with the United States.

We think such a normalization is possible and long overdue. We are all for it.

A few more general questions on Latin America. Now that there's been a new series of revolutions in Latin America, highlighted by Nicaragua, what do you expect in that region in the coming years?

In Latin America, the United States has laid probably more mines under its own policies than in any other area of the world. Since the early nineteenth century, when the Monroe Doctrine was proclaimed, the United States has regarded Latin America as its own plantation. It's not often recalled, by the way, that, while claiming American hegemony in the Western Hemisphere, President Monroe also pledged American noninterference elsewhere. In no other region does the United States have its way to the extent it does in Latin America. Exploitation by U.S. corporations is most direct there, U.S. political interference most crude, and the overall approach most shortsighted.

On the other hand, Franklin Roosevelt tried a good-neighbor policy and John Kennedy launched the Alliance for Progress.

The hard line that normally predominates in U.S. policy toward Latin America inevitably begets discontent, resistance, and radicalism in the region. Periodically, Washington tries a more reformist, conciliatory approach, gives in on some secondary points. But these modifications of methods have not changed the essence of American policy there, which is to preserve Latin America as an object of neocolonial exploitation. Therefore, reform regularly fails to satisfy the Latins, and Washington goes back to the hard line, using military force and installing pro-American juntas.

I wouldn't exclude that we are witnessing just such a return to the hard line in the whole region. The immediate reason might be the revolutions in the Caribbean and Central America. Just as the Dominican Republic was invaded in 1965 to prevent a "second Cuba," the United States is getting militarily involved in El Salvador to prevent "another Nicaragua." The CIA has stepped up its subversive actions against those regimes in the area Washington considers dangerous, and the American support of Britain in its war with Argentina over the Falklands demonstrated Washington's intention to keep the big stick over the Latin Americans' heads.

Do you see a danger of international complications in this region?

The eighties and nineties could, if U.S. policies remain what they are at present, turn out to be rather stormy for the Western Hemisphere.

After all, we were never nearer to a war than during the Cuban missile crisis of 1962.

Well, the increasing social turmoil in Latin America should not necessarily make that continent a crisis zone in international relations—a zone that would become a theater of military confrontation between East and West.

Going back to Africa, you don't regret the aid given Angola and Ethiopia?

As a matter of fact, today more than a few Americans sympathizing with the cause of African liberation recognize that that assistance played a constructive role in Africa.

Let us assume that Soviet and Cuban assistance did help the peoples of Africa, but damaged détente, if only by creating additional reasons for doubting Soviet intentions and charging the Soviet Union with expansionism.

Our assistance to Angola and Ethiopia was, indeed, used as a ground for such charges. But in fact, I think that détente, provided it is deep enough, could help avoid situations where military assistance is required to solve problems like those faced by Angola and Ethiopia.

What would have been different with a deeper, better-developed détente?

If there had been more trust in Soviet-American relations in 1974–75, if the questions of military bases and foreign military presence in the Indian Ocean had lost their importance by coming under the regulation of peaceful agreements, the United States might not only have refrained from fostering false illusions with Somalia, but might even have provided a restraining influence on them. Thus, there would have been no conflict. In Angola, too, many problems could have been solved by consultation and negotiation. Détente cannot deprive the peoples of former colonies of their right to struggle, including armed struggle, if necessary, for their liberation. But détente, a calm international environment, a strengthening of trust between countries—all can help prevent situations when episodes of liberation struggles are turned into international conflicts and even confrontations between great powers.

No doubt, the liberation of Zimbabwe was an event of historic signifi-
cance. But it has been definitely overshadowed by developments in the
Middle East, the Persian Gulf, and Southwest Asia. For a couple of years
now, everyone's attention has been focused primarily on "the arc of insta-
bility," as Mr. Brzezinski called it.

In the Soviet Union we often use the term "the Middle Eastern knot" when
we talk about these problems. Indeed, the issues in the area are tangled
and tied into a complex whole involving many conflicting interests. The
knot has to be untied if we are to remove a major source of danger to world
peace. Unfortunately, in the last few years we've seen quite the opposite
tendency. New issues have appeared, making the situation even more
complicated and explosive, among them, increased American dependence
on the Middle Eastern oil. There are illusions growing in Washington about
U.S. ability to solve the problems created by this new situation by means
of force.

Apparently, you disapprove of the Camp David approach?

We interpret it as a dangerous diversion off the road to a comprehensive,
peaceful settlement in the region, a renewed drive for American
hegemony in the Middle East, an attempt to evade one of the central
issues, which is the right of Palestinian Arabs to self-determination. Despite all the disappointment resulting from the United States backing out
of its previous commitment, we still believe that the cooperation of the
USSR, the United States, and some other countries is vital to resolve this
very complicated and important problem. This would be in the interest of
not only the two great powers, but oil-importing and oil-exporting nations, including the peoples of Palestine and Israel. As for the Camp
David Accord itself, the fact that that approach doesn't work is becoming
more and more obvious. The underlying idea was obviously that if other
nations supported the separate deal, the United States wouldn't lose anything. If they did not, the U.S.-Israeli-Egyptian-Iranian axis would be
strong enough to provide for American interests without any confirmation at Geneva or wherever.

And then Iran fell out of the game.

Right. And the expected support for Camp David from more conservative
Arab regimes like Saudi Arabia and Jordan wasn't forthcoming. The deal
was falling apart at the seams. This may also explain why the United
States is using every pretext to build up its military forces in the Middle
East, the Persian Gulf, and the Indian Ocean. We're witnessing a massive
militarization of American policy in the area.

Do you think the United States will succeed in imposing its will this way?

I doubt it very much.

Why?

The bottom line is what one Middle Eastern leader described this way: "Oil burns." Before Washington gets anywhere near the hegemony it is seeking, the tensions and conflicts that will inevitably arise from such a policy are likely to disrupt the energy supply to the world economy.

"Oil burns" can be an epigraph to the Iran-Iraq war.

Yes, if you take its energy dimension. But this war underlined many other things—in the first place, the dangers of general instability in the region and the possibility of new conflicts that can escalate into serious crises, especially with the smoldering ashes of the old conflicts nearby.

The latest conflagration in the Middle East, the Israeli invasion of Lebanon, added some new features to the situation in that area. Israel is more isolated now, while international sympathy with the PLO has increased. At the same time, Lebanon's tragedy, the cruelty of the war, and the roles played by Israel and the United States have had an impact on the position of the conservative Arab states. The Fez conference was able to come up with a joint Arab approach to the problem. Yet another new feature has been the change of attitudes toward the Mideast problem in America and in Israel itself. The bloodbath in Lebanon staged by Begin and Sgaron opened the eyes of many Israelis and Americans to some key realities of the Mideast crisis.

Why are there no diplomatic relations between the USSR and Israel? Do you intend to restore them?

The diplomatic relations between the USSR and Israel were ruptured during the Six Day war in 1967. That was our reaction to Israel's aggression and its unwillingness to relinquish territorial gains. The restoration of diplomatic relations is possible in the context of the settlement of the Middle Eastern crisis along the lines of the well-known resolutions of the U.N. Security Council.

You are not questioning, then, the right of the state of Israel to its existence?

No. We've repeatedly made official statements that the guarantee of the rights of all the states in the region to existence and security, including the rights of the state of Israel, should be an integral and absolutely necessary part of any settlement of the Middle Eastern crisis.

There are speculations in the West concerning the attitude of the Soviet Union toward terrorism, especially in connection with the events in the Middle East.

We are against terrorism.

But you maintain friendly relations with Arafat, and terrorism is often connected with the PLO.

We've always supported the Palestinians and their struggle. This does not mean that we associate ourselves with each step or action of every extremist splinter group driven to despair. As to Yassir Arafat, we see him as the most prominent and influential political leader of the Palestinians. And this view is shared by an ever-increasing number of world political figures, including some Western leaders. Speaking of terrorism in its most pronounced form, we should recall that Begin used to be an active terrorist himself. But this does not prevent him from being accepted in the West.

The USSR is being accused of striving to preserve in the Middle East a situation that can be called "neither peace nor war."

We are as much for détente there as everywhere else in the world. Even if we had thought that a "controlled tension" situation, which is what is usually meant by the phrase "neither peace nor war," corresponded to our interests, we would not have favored it. For we understand perfectly well that a situation of tension cannot be controlled indefinitely in such an explosion-prone region as the Middle East. Therefore, a "neither peace nor war" policy would be tantamount to an acceptance of war. Actually, the Camp David policies, intentionally or not, are fraught with such a danger.

What about the recent resurgence of orthodox Islam in Asia?

I would not overestimate the role of any religion as an independent force in social and political life. The activization of Islam is a reflection of growing social tensions and political turmoil in Asia. Religion in general, Islam in particular, retains considerable ideological and sometimes political strength. But I think "the Moslem world" is about as much of an abstraction as "the Christian world." Different social groups and countries in Asia are using religious slogans to pursue different, sometimes mutually exclusive aims. Evidently, the awakening of the broad masses in Asia to active political life is giving a new content to the Islamic religion, which, like any other religion, must constantly adapt to changing circumstances in order to survive.

You are certainly aware of the puzzlement in our part of the world as to why the USSR risked so much in goodwill, especially in Moslem and Third World nations, by using military force to uphold the regime existing in Afghanistan.

Since you have raised the question of Afghanistan once more, I would like to make a general remark. I am not counting on persuading American or other Western readers to subscribe to the Soviet point of view on the problems connected with the events in Afghanistan, to support the April 1978 revolution there, to take Babrak Karmal's side, or to back the Soviet decision on rendering military assistance to the Kabul government. You see, it's not a matter of just knowing the facts, but of attitudes toward them. And those attitudes are determined not only by information but by class, ideological and political sympathies, and interests.

Then what would be the use of discussing these topics?

It seems to me that it still might be useful so that Americans and other Western readers have a clearer idea of the Soviet point of view. All the more so because so many lies about the real state of affairs have been spread in the West.

Why then did the USSR decide to risk so much by intervening militarily in Afghanistan?

We've sent our military contingent there for two closely interrelated purposes: to help the government formed after the revolution in Afghanistan ward off aggression from the outside, and to prevent the turning of Afghanistan into an anti-Soviet base on our southern borders. The contingent was sent after repeated requests by the Kabul government. And there is an important legal side: the assistance was given according to the treaty signed in 1978 between the USSR and Afghanistan. We do not plan to stay in Afghanistan permanently, or to turn it into some kind of a springboard for actions or threats against other countries. The troops will be withdrawn as soon as the reasons that led to their being stationed there disappear.

You said the Soviet aim in sending troops was to help the revolutionary regime. But the regime was headed by Hafizullah Amin, who was killed on the arrival of Soviet troops and replaced by Babrak Karmal, who denounced Amin and changed Kabul policies quite abruptly. It looks strange and contradictory.

Please remember that we are talking about a revolution, and any revolution is a most complicated historical event, with its rapid changes, sharp and unexpected turns, a constantly shifting balance of forces, people changing sides overnight. I've already spoken of the reasons for the Afghan revolution that started in April 1978. The government formed immediately after the revolution and led by Noor Muhammad Taraki received broad support. Babrak Karmal was among the other top leaders. Hafizullah Amin was also close to the top. The revolutionary government started a broad program of social change concentrating on land reform, development programs for ethnic minorities, women's rights, and education.

These policies encountered resistance. Why?

Because they went against the interests of the old ruling classes deposed in 1978—forty thousand big feudal landowners who had to give their land back to their peasants. Before the revolution, 70 percent of all the land belonged to them. A rather typical thing in any revolution—people do not want to yield their power and privileges, and they use any methods to restore the status quo ante. The deposed privileged groups provided the backbone of the counterrevolution in Afghanistan. But they would not have presented such a great danger had it not been for the outside support.

Some opposition is inevitable in any revolution, but it definitely would not have grown into a serious threat to the new government had some of that government's policies not led to broad discontent.

There were mistakes made by the new government. Mistakes are inevitable in any revolution and are particularly understandable in such a backward country. The biggest mistake, to my mind, was to try to do too much too fast—in Marxist language, a typical leftist deviation. Serious mistakes were made in the area of relations between the state and the Moslem clergy. Most of the clergy was written off as a counterrevolutionary force; some were persecuted, some mosques were closed. And, of course, the situation was seriously aggravated by Hafizullah Amin and his group.

You named him as one of the leaders of the Afghan government?

Yes. As a matter of fact, Amin's personality had a lot to do with the difficulties of the Afghan revolution. He was a power-hungry plotter, an unscrupulous intriguer using the revolutionary upheaval to get to the top and become a dictator. History has seen such figures more than once. In September 1979, Amin staged a coup and killed President Taraki. Later he was accused by the government of direct treason.

If the USSR didn't approve of Amin, why did it agree to his request for Soviet assistance?

It was not done for Amin personally. It was done to save the Afghan revolution.

That sounds rather evasive. Amin was the leader of the country at that particular moment.

He usurped the leadership position. But despite Amin's repression and intrigues, there remained many people in the party, even some in the government, who resisted his policies and tried to do what was possible to retrieve the heritage of April 1978. And they removed him from power just on the eve of the execution planned by the Amin group of a large group of imprisoned revolutionary leaders.

But why did you permit the exile of Karmal and the crimes of Amin?

What do you mean "permit"? We assisted the Afghan government and advised them, but could not dictate the way the Afghan revolution proceeded. It could not have been and was not a Soviet-controlled process. As to the problem you mentioned, we had cautioned the Afghani leaders many times and given them advice, but it was they who had to make decisions, as it was their revolution.

Has the government of Babrak Karmal succeeded in strengthening the position of the revolutionary government?

They moved rapidly to bring the government's policies back on the right track. They freed fifteen thousand political prisoners jailed by Amin, punished those responsible for repression, and declared a general amnesty for those who had fled the country. They restored religious freedom and adopted sound economic policies. In foreign affairs they are trying to normalize relations with their neighbors, particularly with Pakistan. I think the key to the political settlement in the area would be an agreement on closing the bases of anti-Afghan terrorist activities on the Pakistani territory and banning the transition of armed groups through the border. Then the Soviet troops could be sent home.

That brings us to the other Soviet motive in sending its troops to Afghanistan. Was it perceived in Moscow that a possible defeat of the revolution there represented a danger to the USSR?

Yes, it was. We had reason to believe that the United States and some other countries intended to turn Afghanistan into a base for hostile actions against the Soviet Union. Our border with Afghanistan is twenty-five hundred kilometers long. It was a very friendly and quiet border for several decades.

What do you think would have happened in Afghanistan if you had not sent your troops there?

Don't think, please, that it was an easy decision for the Soviet Union to make, and that all the possible negative reactions were not taken into consideration prior to this. The Soviet government came to a conclusion that, without assistance, the government of Afghanistan would not be able to save the revolution and repel attacks from abroad, and that further development of events in the area might create a threat to the security of the Soviet Union. To Afghanistan itself it would have meant the triumph of the counterrevolution, with all its logical attributes—terror, bloodshed, rage of reaction.

What specific threats to your security did you expect?

Afghanistan might have been turned into an anti-Soviet stronghold, which could be used for the establishment of military bases on our borders and other hostile activities.

Military bases?

Why not? There used to be U.S. military bases in Iran, and they are now searching all over the region for a substitute. Why not Afghanistan?

According to a widespread Western view of the Soviet motives for sending troops to Afghanistan, the USSR was trying to get direct access to a warm-water port and Middle Eastern oil.

That is baloney even from a purely military viewpoint. Both the Persian Gulf and the Indian Ocean are already close enough to the Soviet Union. And had we planned to get even closer, we would never have chosen Afghanistan, with its very difficult terrain, as a springboard. As an American friend of mine put it, it would be like Californians attacking Oregon through Nevada. But the most important thing is that the kind of push toward warm seas that the West ascribes to the Soviet Union would invite

World War III. Contrary to the American propaganda, nobody is going to see Soviet tanks or soldiers on the shores of the Persian Gulf or the other warm seas.

What will the developments be around Afghanistan now?

We believe that a political solution is possible. Therefore, we fully support the proposal put forward by the Afghan government concerning normalization of the situation in the area. Kabul is ready to talk with its neighbors on normalizing their relations. In 1981 we also proposed to combine talks on the international aspects of the situation in Afghanistan with the broader talks on peace and security in the Persian Gulf area. I am sure that if Afghanistan's neighbors and the United States adopt a constructive position, it will be possible to achieve a settlement, including the withdrawal of Soviet troops. Afghanistan was and will remain nonaligned. But we do not want it to be hostile to us, and I think this concern is justified.

In the West it is maintained that the Soviet Union was afraid that the establishment of a military Moslem regime in Kabul could spark trouble among the Moslems in Soviet Central Asia.

Now, look, this is really incredible. Just compare poor, illiterate, backward Afghanistan with Soviet Central Asia, Azerbaijan, and other formerly Moslem parts of the USSR. They are prosperous, confident, and happy. Can anyone seriously believe that the obscurantist, repressive theocracy that the counterrevolution wanted to install in Afghanistan would present an ideological challenge to the Soviet Union? I've been elected to the Supreme Soviet of the USSR from the Republic of Azerbaijan, which has a large Moslem population. I've been representing a district of that republic for several years now, and I can tell you on the basis of firsthand experience that Islam presents no political problems to the Soviet Union. Those believing in Allah are free to worship. There are mosques, and the Moslem clergy is respected.

But do you feel in retrospect that the USSR misjudged Western reaction to the Afghan events?

Well, you can never foresee reactions of other nations to a particular event in all detail. There are always both pleasant and unpleasant surprises. But in general, I think we had evaluated the situation correctly. You see, we acted on the premise that American policies had changed. We came to this conclusion before Afghanistan. I think it could also be expected in Moscow that the United States and some other Western countries would use the events in Afghanistan as a pretext for an anti-Soviet campaign. I think that, having launched this campaign, Washington was overreacting terribly, contrary to everybody's interests, including those of the United States. This overreaction can to some extent be explained by the feverish attempts of the Carter administration to find a way out of its own difficulties, like those in Iran and the Middle East. In this connection, the events in Afghanistan seemed to present an opportunity to portray the United States as a force that might be useful to the Moslem world. This has not come true. To some extent, it was a mere explosion of emotions that some people in the Carter administration could not control.

Returning to the general question of how events in the Third World influence U.S.-Soviet relations, one hears more and more often today in the West that clashes in the Third World have become the main factor undermining détente.

Yes, it is quite a widespread point of view. But I have serious doubts about it. It is very important to see why it has gained such wide acceptance. I think the first reason is that the great powers realized long ago that a direct confrontation between them would be extremely dangerous, even suicidal. Therefore, they avoid direct clashes on the central lines of their relations, and this creates an impression that the major source of danger now is the Third World. Second, the situation in the Third World is very volatile, indeed. Third, some great powers, and here, alas, I have to point to the United States again, are exhibiting an unusual interest in the Third World for strategic considerations. In case there might be a conflict with the Soviet Union and other socialist countries, the West wants to have bases and well-protected communications lines in the Third World. Fourth, developing countries are of great interest to the United States and its allies as sources of raw materials, primarily oil.

In other words, you confirm that the Third World is now the main source of danger.

No. Far from underestimating the importance of developing countries, I would still like to point out that the course of events there, particularly the gravity of conflicts and their impact on the international scene, to a very great extent depend upon the state of Soviet-American relations. Take the Yom Kippur war of October 1973. In the context of détente it was possible to localize this conflict and even to work out a basic framework for a comprehensive settlement in this area. I simply shudder at the thought of what might have happened if that war had occurred in a climate of tensions, even such as exists now. So, I think that what I said leads to a different conclusion, namely, that much depends on the political situation in East-West relations, that is, relations between socialist and capitalist countries, between the Soviet Union and the United States. If those relations should be ruled by a cold war, the Third World will become one of its most dangerous battlefields. But if the ideas of détente should gain an upper hand, the Third World could become a major sphere of cooperation among all economically advanced countries. They can cooperate in facilitating a speedier development of the Third World, in creating workable security systems in its various areas, in using its resources sensibly, all with due regard to its peoples' interests and aspirations.

The Third World nations are not going to make their history either for the West or the East. They will live and develop for themselves. A majority of the population on our planet lives out there, and those people are entitled to the same rights and opportunities for self-realization as the Europeans and Americans. What's more, they know it, and they are determined to struggle for a better life.

Many Western experts insist that without establishing certain rules of the superpowers' conduct in the Third World, perhaps even some sort of crisis-management mechanism, there is no hope for détente in the future.

Well, the idea of bilateral cooperation in crisis settlement and prevention was present in détente from the very beginning. On the Middle East, for instance, a kind of crisis-management mechanism was emerging in the form of the Geneva conference, and it is through no fault of ours that this approach was abandoned. The same idea is inherent in the broad program of the demilitarization of the Persian Gulf area, put forward by President Brezhnev in December 1980 and again in February 1981. Another Soviet proposal has been to ban the use of military force. We do not have an idea of the superpowers playing the global-policeman role, but we are sure that détente will remove a lot of the flammable stuff that feeds crises, and that joint efforts in crisis management and prevention may in turn become important components of détente itself.

Do you believe that East-West cooperation is possible in the Third World despite the existing difficulties?

Of course, the difficulties are tremendous, but if we succeed in securing a durable peace and in preserving and strengthening détente, such cooperation could become feasible. The situation is unparalleled in history and requires unusual wisdom from the economically advanced nations.

Do you expect America and Russia to increase or decrease their role in the world by the end of this century?

If developing countries succeed in their economic affairs, the share of all industrialized nations in the world gross national product is likely to decline. Generally speaking, the world scene by the end of the century is going to get increasingly diverse—politically, culturally, and philosophically. This would be an appropriate and healthy development. But in the foreseeable future, the two great powers will continue to play a major role, if only because of the physical dimensions of their power. The important thing is that their military and economic potentials do not give them any special rights or privileges, only special responsibilities. They are responsible to all of mankind for avoiding nuclear war and keeping normal and peaceful relations between themselves, as well as for taking a constructive part in the solution of those problems that the world at large is facing.

Chapter 6 | A Few Words about the Future

Now, after many hours of discussion and many months of work, I would like to ask you the same question that I asked you at the beginning: is Cold War II possible?

I would not take back a single word of my first answer to this question. But I could add a few words.

This is precisely why I have repeated my question.

In addition to all I have said already, Cold War II would be different in the sense that it would be sort of a phony cold war—a *drôle de guerre froide,* as the French would say. It would be phony because, unlike Cold War I, it would hardly be backed by conviction. The conviction of Cold War I was wrong, based on misplaced fears, prejudices, and ignorance; but it was there as an important psychological factor.

This time, one would have to have a very low opinion of people's mental capacities, Mr. Oltmans, to expect Europeans to believe in the 1980s what your family did in the 1940s when they left for South Africa. Even the Americans seem to me too sophisticated to be easily drawn into the kind of a state that characterized them in the late 1940s and early 1950s. It is difficult to believe that their prophets could once again become people like Senator Joseph McCarthy or Representative Parnell Thomas, those oracles of Cold War I who later were recognized as simple crooks, or, to put it a different way, crooks whom the Cold War helped turn into oracles. Indeed, it would be a phony cold war, with very few people believing in its aims and rationale. What is even more substantial, against the background of the experience of détente, not very many would agree to consider such a war the only alternative to a hot war. And it would be a phony war in the sense that the United States would start it without the wherewithal to win it. It could not win Cold War I, when its position vis-à-vis the world was incomparably stronger than now. There is absolutely no way for the United States to win such a war in the last decades of this century. But the fact that there are Americans who are still trying to start it portends great dangers to world peace and stability.

How do you visualize the future of Soviet-American relations?

Whether there will be any future at all depends on whether there will be at least minimally decent relations between the USSR and the United States. In terms of what would be the most desirable future, I would say without any hesitation a future characterized by peaceful coexistence, détente, arms limitation and disarmament, broad cooperation, and increased mutual confidence. But, I am sorry to say, at this moment we do not seem to be heading for such relations. There is a rising concern, shared by some Americans, too, that the United States has set upon a course providing for an intensified arms race. It attempts to strengthen its military alliances. It tries to demonstrate a greater readiness to use military force wherever it deems it necessary. If it goes on this way, the situation is likely to get worse before it gets better.

Can it get any worse?

Unfortunately, it can. Lately, Washington has done almost everything, short of direct military hostilities, to spoil the political atmosphere, heat up the rhetoric, rupture economic and cultural ties, and freeze arms-control talks.

Would you rule out any bold new initiatives, unexpected actions, or turns of events that could bring about significant improvements in the world situation, including Soviet-American relations?

Of course, such initiatives or turns of events cannot be ruled out. What's more, I am sure that the Soviet Union will be coming up with such initiatives, as it has done in the past. But an improvement of relations requires goodwill on both sides, and I am far from certain that we can expect such initiatives from the other side. Of course, you asked about unexpected things, those that cannot be forecast at present. In case there are pleasant surprises, we shall welcome them, naturally.

Forecasts will always then be imprecise, for life is full of surprises.

Certainly. This is why forecasts based on a simple extension of current trends into the future almost never come true. Here is a good example: I have heard of one of the very first attempts to forecast the development of urban problems, undertaken by the Parisian authorities in the middle of the last century. The authorities asked the experts to prognosticate the major problems awaiting the capital of France in the twentieth century. The experts pondered and replied: horse manure. They predicted that Paris would literally be buried in it, given the rate of development of horse-driven transportation at the time. I don't think we should follow the example of those early futurologists. We have to consider the possibility of surprises, including positive and negative ones. Also, one of the major arguments in favor of détente is that it creates additional guarantees in case of bad surprises, making both peace and the international system more durable. That is why it is so bad that we have entered the 1980s with international relations so gravely darkened by the relapse to enmity and elements of the Cold War.

So, again the crucial question: what can be expected of the coming years?

If we manage to break the present trends—and I hope we do—there can be a return to more stable relations, which would make a lot of things possible: firm guarantees of peace, disarmament, fruitful and mutually beneficial cooperation, and so forth. If we do not reverse these trends we shall have serious problems for years to come. The worst of them is that we shall be faced with a strong possibility of an all-out arms race, leading to probably the most dangerous period in the history of mankind. Political developments will be augmented by trends that work independently of whomever has been elected. I have in mind, first and foremost, the acceleration of scientific and technological development, which can produce many new types of deadly weapons, as well as heighten the danger of nuclear proliferation.

As Richard Barnet points out, by the year 2000 as many as one hundred nations will know how to acquire nuclear weapons.

Quite conceivably. And some of them may actually decide to acquire them if the rest of the world just sits back and counts. Recent trends in nuclear proliferation are very alarming indeed. There have been reports that South Africa and Israel have exploded a bomb, and that Pakistan may soon follow suit. Here we come to another very strong factor for a low predictability of events in the 1980s—an increased number of participants in world politics.

When do you expect an improvement in Soviet-American relations?

In the long run, it is almost inevitable, for in a very real sense there is no acceptable alternative to détente. But if a significant improvement should come very soon it would be a pleasant surprise. I can say for sure that the later such a turn of events should come about, the greater time and effort it will take to restore what has been so hastily destroyed.

If we are talking about the possibility of bringing back détente in the near future only as a pleasant surprise, then the prospect for Soviet-American relations and for the international situation as a whole in the 1980s must look rather gloomy.

Let me clarify. We are at a crossroads in Soviet-American relations now. A decision has to be made on which way to go—to greater tensions, into the trenches of another cold war, or to negotiations, détente, and cooperation. And much will depend on what will be done in the near future. Unfortunately, we have entered this decade in a very complicated situation. The hard fact of life is that the current trends in the foreign policies of the United States and some other countries can only have a very negative impact on the world situation.

We are cautious in giving a final assessment of these policies, in taking what the Reagan administration says and does for its last word. But the time is coming when we shall have to do it, just as all other countries will have to, because it affects them as well. The United States is acting as if it feels offended and angry not only with the Soviet Union, but with other countries as well—adversaries, allies, neutrals—angry with the whole world. This is a very bad, very dangerous attitude not only for other countries, but for the United States itself.

But one must also see the opposite trends that are operating now and will certainly continue to operate in the 1980s. These trends stem from very real and, I would add, more and more compelling interests of the two countries and the world at large—such interests as securing peace, decreasing the burden of the arms race, and developing cooperation. Looking at the long-term trends, I remain certain that positive and realistic tendencies will become much stronger again and will be even more relevant to the real problems we all face.

Why are peace and coexistence even more relevant in this decade?

I would not deny an emotional involvement in my judgment here: I wish it to be so. And it is not just my personal attitude. I am sure all Soviet people think likewise, as well as most Europeans and Americans. But there is more to it than just emotions. My analysis leads me to a conclusion that a policy that aims at a return to cold war cannot be too durable; its goals are neither relevant to the vital interests of any country, including the United States, nor attainable. The military buildup and the jacking up of the arms race are said to be necessary to provide for U.S. national security, but the fact is that it is the arms race that presents the major threat to security. The idea of seeking military superiority is just as preposterous, for there is no way that America, or anyone else, for that matter, can achieve it.

The revival of interventionism is just as senseless and dangerous. I do not believe that even the best imaginable rapid deployment force could have prevented the Iranian hostage situation. Besides, the United States will hardly be able to create a bigger or better expeditionary force than the one sent to Vietnam.

Neither do I consider realistic the NATO program for a steady increase in arms spending for years to come.

Do you expect the West to go bankrupt because of that program?

No, but providing both guns and butter will be increasingly problematic. America, like many other countries, is facing lean, not fat, years. The present trends in the American economy are very indicative in this respect —slow growth, rising unemployment, declining productivity, difficulties on the world markets, stagnation, and even a decline of living standards. The economies of some American allies are also entering a difficult period.

If you add to this economic squeeze the growing global problems involving resources, environment, food supplies, and so on, you realize that even trying to sustain the present habitual standard of living in the United States, Western Europe, Japan, and other industrialized nations will become an increasingly difficult task. In these circumstances many things become luxuries one cannot afford.

What luxuries do you have in mind?

First of all, an unlimited arms race. A new massive military buildup can be financed, if at all, only by deep cuts in social expenditures, as the Reagan administration is finding out. Such a redistribution, aside from its negative economic effects, is bound to have explosive political consequences.

Another luxury none of us can afford anymore is the present high level of tension and the absence of cooperation. If we are to provide for our survival, and for a decent life on this ever smaller and more complex planet, we will have to change our behavior. I am afraid Earth is too fragile for increased international rivalry. Cooperation is becoming the sine qua non of both survival and decent existence.

Do you mean that it is the very problems and difficulties faced by the two countries and by the planet as a whole that will work as a strong impetus to better relations and cooperation between the Soviet Union and the United States?

For some reason or other, dangers and difficulties turn out to be stronger and more effective stimuli for cooperation than abstract considerations of mutual benefit. In the face of Hitler's aggression it took the Americans, the British, the French, the Dutch, and others a rather short time to become our allies. I am fully convinced that should our planet be invaded by some creatures from outer space with hostile intentions, we would again become allies overnight.

Whenever there is a specific, palpable common enemy, particularly a deadly enemy, cooperation gets very easy. Unfortunately, when the threats are not so clearly embodied and personified, it is vastly more difficult to cooperate, even if those threats are no less serious than the guy with the gun aiming at you.

Which dangers could ultimately bring East and West closer together?

Well, one obvious danger is the danger of war, which we have already discussed at great length. Another is the aggravation of such global problems as the supply of energy and other natural resources, the problems of food, environment, and Third World poverty. One can dispute the precise estimates of the Club of Rome and other experts, but I think they are talking of some real problems. The population of the globe is expected to grow from 4.5 billion to over 6 billion by the year 2000, which means that we shall have to build as much in the coming two decades as used to be built in centuries. Pressures on natural resources will grow immensely, particularly on the energy resources. Food supply will become more difficult. If the present tendencies hold, the number of people seeking jobs will grow to a billion by the end of the century.

And you expect the imperative of finding solutions to these problems will be a powerful incentive for building détente and cooperation?

Yes. To borrow a phrase from former President Carter, these threats can be regarded as a moral equivalent of war, in the sense that they demand a maximum mobilization of efforts and necessitate cooperation among all nations—the Soviet Union and the United States in the first place.

Threats and fears do remain strong forces for sensible deeds.

Well, mankind is still in its formative stage, so it's understandable. Besides, the threats are real, not mythical. As to fear, it does remain one of the strongest human emotions. The important thing is not to let it be misplaced, misdirected. I would very much prefer that people be moved mostly by compassion and love, but we are not yet mature enough for it.

You don't expect me to believe that you consider such feelings important for Soviet-American relations?

No, and not because of any cynicism. Maybe things will change in the future, but now we are talking not of love, but of a rational and accurate perception of one's own interests. As a Russian, I do not have to love America to advocate good Soviet-American relations. It is enough for me to be a deeply convinced Soviet patriot, for such relations are in the interests of my country. The same is true for Americans. There is no need for them to love the Russians or the communists, or even trust the Russians, in order to favor good relations with the USSR. Suffice them to be good American patriots and love their country. Certainly, if after a while this rational calculation and self-interest is compounded by some nice emotions, that will only help. But right now it is another luxury we can do without.

But will the Russians, the Americans, and all others be sensible enough to avoid these threats?

In a long-term prospect, I think they will—that is, provided they survive in the meantime. I think this problem was very aptly formulated by a well-known Soviet scientist, Nobel laureate Nikolai Semënov. He believes that, according to the criteria and measures of both organic and inorganic nature, mankind has not yet emerged from its early childhood. When it grows up and matures, there will be no problem it will not be able to solve. The danger is that it may make some really bad, incorrigible, irreversible mistakes in childhood. Semënov sees two such mistakes as possible: a nuclear war, and an irreversible breakdown of the balance between man and his natural environment.

What would you forecast for mankind—doom or prosperity?

You see, any forecast of social and political developments is inevitably value oriented and problematic to one extent or another. It is not like forecasting weather or earthquakes. We are participants in events; we make forecasts in order to be better able to influence them, to manage them if we can.

The program of action implied in my forecast is détente. The connection between it and the prevention of war is self-evident. As to the global problems, détente itself does not solve them, but without détente it is pointless even to think of beginning to solve them.

But how do you get back on the road to détente? When will the two sides be mature enough to understand its necessity?

I can assure you that in the Soviet Union the awareness of the necessity of détente and normal relations with the United States has not disappeared.

Professor Dieter Senghaas of the Frankfurt Institute of Peace and Conflict Studies recently observed that no one in the world really knew what Moscow was thinking.

I find this an ignorant statement. It is widely accepted that Soviet foreign policy is more consistent and predictable than the policies of many other countries. It is not difficult at all to learn what they think in Moscow. Besides, we maintain the kind of relations with virtually all countries that allow them, in case of need, to ask questions. This is what I would answer Professor Senghaas.

He may have had in mind the most recent period, since late 1979, when the deterioration of the world situation led to breakdowns in the dialogue and to overall weakening of contacts.

Any deterioration of this kind inevitably has such consequences, and not just because of the complications in contacts. It seems to me that tension always has a profound emotional impact on people's minds and on their ability to perceive and understand. A person driven by emotions such as hatred and jingoism is a poor partner for a dialogue.

Some people think that international relations resemble a pendulum, or a tide—after a high comes a low, so we just have to wait a bit.

Conventional wisdom would suggest that, just as in a family quarrel, we should sit back and wait for the passions to subside and only then make peace. But the logic of political life does not follow conventional wisdom. According to conventional wisdom, détente could not have even begun. In the early 1970s, not only did passions rage, but there was a war in Vietnam. American boys were being killed, many by Soviet-made weapons. Soviet boys were dying in Haiphong and Hanoi, hit by American bombs and mines. American behavior was outrageous, from our point of view, in Vietnam, in the Middle East, and in other places. At the same time there were many things in our policies that Washington did not like. The first summit was hanging by a hair. And yet détente did start. But what if we had waited for more favorable conditions? What would we have gained?

Do you think this is the way the question stands now, too?

Yes. It would make no sense at all to wait for the situation to become more favorable for a return to détente. The current trends are such that the situation cannot possibly calm down by itself. Rather, one can expect that if we just do nothing but wait, the tensions will be building up. In other words, time is running out for all of us.

Yes, but someone must take the first step.

I don't think this is how we should look at the situation now. At this point the problem is not that, out of unwillingness to chicken out, or fear of being rejected, or just caution, no one dares say the first word. We did say it, and would be willing to do it again, but the way it looks from Moscow, the U.S. government simply has not wanted any easing of tensions.

Would the situation change if the Soviet Union made a step toward the American position and, say, started withdrawing its troops from Afghanistan?

If you imply a political solution to the problems of Afghanistan, we are all for it. This is our official position. The Afghan government also favors a political solution. But if you have in mind the withdrawal of our military contingent from that country without any settlement, what would it bring? Confirmation that one can talk with the Soviet Union only in the language of threats, blackmail, and pressure? I have serious doubts as to whether it could open up any opportunities for bringing Soviet-American relations back to the road of détente. Besides, the reasons that made us send a military contingent there must be removed. In general, I think it would be futile to put forward some preliminary conditions for normalization of relations between the two sides.

What other specific steps might be taken to bring Soviet-American relations back to détente?

I do not think, Mr. Oltmans, that you and I are well enough equipped to discuss specific diplomatic measures. Provided there is a mutual intent to return to détente, finding a way of making the first step in this direction would not be too difficult. Did we not once witness a Ping-Pong competition chosen as a first step toward a serious restructuring of relations?

True enough. But there may be another question: since, in your view, it was the American side that spoiled these relations, should they also make this first step toward their improvement?

Generally speaking, it would be quite logical, particularly since on many questions the ball is in their hands. But I do not think the Soviet Union wants to turn this question of who should be the first into a principle. Quite the opposite: during 1980 and 1981 we made a number of steps that could be considered invitations to the American leaders to normalize our relations.

For instance?

For instance, a proposal for an immediate beginning of negotiations on limiting intermediate-range nuclear weapons in Europe in conjunction with the U.S. forward-based systems there and our new proposals on Vienna talks. The United States finally came to accept the former, although it took a lot of effort not only on our part but on the part of the American allies as well. I would also mention some of the recent initiatives proposed by the Twenty-sixth Party Congress here in the Soviet Union: there was a proposal to move ahead with SALT talks and introduce some specific arms-control measures—for instance, to limit the deployment of the new U.S. "Ohio" and Soviet "Typhoon" class submarines. There was a proposal to extend the sphere of confidence-building measures to the whole European part of the USSR on a basis of reciprocity from the West. And there was a proposal to resume an active Soviet-American dialogue on all levels, including a summit meeting.

If and when we get back to détente, I think it must be a Détente II, free of some of the weaknesses of its predecessor, but preserving and advancing its strong sides.

Could you outline those weaknesses?

For one thing, during Détente I arms limitation fell far behind the progress in the political sphere. To put it more exactly, the arms race continued and even intensified despite the political progress, the improvements in the atmosphere between us, and even the partial agreements on arms control. That doomed détente to great difficulties, as L. I. Brezhnev had warned as early as 1973. This movement in two opposite directions at once could not possibly continue for long. Hence the lesson: the problems of arms limitation must receive attention and be solved faster and more radically. And there should be no attempts on either side to keep or gain or regain military superiority. There simply has to be much more restraint in military programs.

Another valuable lesson of Détente I was that it was not some geological era that took thousands of years to develop—it was a situation that opened up some possibilities that had to be grasped quickly. It is important to keep getting results. I would compare the process of détente with riding a bicycle: the faster, the steadier, and no standing still.

Another observation: I have noted that our Western partners, Americans particularly—and I am talking about some very influential political and academic circles—began, under a not unseemly pretext of desiring more tangible results, to exhibit growing skepticism. From almost the very first steps of détente, they somewhat downgraded the importance of the overall atmosphere of relations.

Well, but you have said yourself that the downgrading of more general issues could be motivated by a simple desire to gain tangible results in specific spheres.

Could be. But unfortunately, such a desire is often unfounded and impossible to realize. It seems to me that those people, in fact, underestimated the scale of work to be done to create a firm foundation for relations, to bridge the gap of asymmetries in political thinking and approaches, or simply to learn to understand the other side better. As a wise American friend of mine put it, to assume the worst when evaluating the other side, and to exclude all lesser possibilities, could actually invite the worst.

I'd like to point to yet another vital problem: the importance of work in creating mutual understanding and building confidence. This importance should be realized not just by the government, but by the media as well. Détente is in the interest of a great majority. But it means that one must create for it the broadest possible, enlightened, vocal, and politically active constituency.

None of it is easy.

Right. But only these things can make détente, or Détente II, if you will, durable enough. The experience we have now in Soviet-American relations shows unmistakably that to clear out the backlog of the Cold War, exhibit restraint, work for mutual understanding, seek solutions that would be mutually acceptable, make compromises—in short, to do all that détente requires—is excruciatingly hard work, demanding great effort, patience, wisdom, and political courage. It demands much more of these qualities than does the Cold War, with its emotional fits. I am sure that détente is the only appropriate yardstick to measure and test political leaders in a nuclear age.

Today, a correct choice of policy is important as never before. In fact, the options are not many. In the final analysis, eternal remains the truth voiced many centuries ago by Plato: "Everybody must live his life in peace, as long and as well as possible."

May I ask you a personal question? We have covered a wide range of problems in our discussions. How do you look upon them as a human being, as Citizen Arbatov?

I think I shall repeat what I once wrote for *Newsweek*. It is very personal, but I am sure that this thought is shared by most Soviet people of my generation.

My father went to war when he was eighteen. I also went to war when I was eighteen. Both of us were lucky—we returned home. And I am very glad that my son, who is now thirty-one, did not have to fight in a war. For there will be no homecomers from the war threatening humanity nowadays. And there will be no winners.

Do you sympathize with the young people of today who are pessimistic about the future, having lost hope for a saner and more peaceful world?

Antonio Gramsci defined the best combination of pessimism and optimism in human temperament as pessimism of the intellect and optimism of the will. I think he meant that people should be able to see, to recognize all the threats and adverse trends, but be determined to overcome them and achieve a better world. Unfortunately, we often see quite the opposite mix, when people shrink from really hard, critical scrutiny of reality and find themselves helpless and despondent in crises.

Personally, I would hate the idea of entrusting the fate of the world to a generation that has lost hope. To be sure, some of today's challenges are unique in the magnitude of their danger to mankind. But I am certain that mankind does have the means to cope with these challenges. The crucial element is the will to do it.

I don't think all the youth of today is pessimistic. As to those who are, I can understand them to some extent. They do encounter serious problems and deep disappointments. And they should not be blamed for it. I see a great responsibility here for the older generation. We must leave them not only hopes for a better life on this planet, but the planet itself.

Chapter Notes

1. On the Ordeal of Détente and the Value of Accurate Perceptions

1. *Pravda*, 13 January 1980.
2. Speech on 19 February 1980 to members of the American Legion in Washington, D.C.
3. Henry Kissinger, *The White House Years* (Boston: Little, Brown, 1979), pp. 1256–57.
4. *New York Times*, 10 October 1980.
5. *Playboy* February 1980.
6. *Moscow News*, 21 January 1979.
7. *The New Republic*, 1 November 1980, p. 21.
8. *San Francisco Chronicle*, 2 December 1979.
9. *New York Times*, 10 February 1980.
10. *Newsweek*, 25 January 1982, p. 12.

2. On the History of Soviet-American Relations

1. Telegram of the People's Commissar on Foreign Affairs of the Russian Soviet Federal Socialist Republic to ambassadors abroad. Sept. 10, 1920. No. 520. "Dokumenty Vneshnei Politiki SSSR" (Documents of the Foreign Policy of the USSR). Vol. 3. Moscow, 1959, pp. 176–77.
2. *Foreign Relations of the United States, 1933,* vol. 2 (Washington, D.C.: Government Printing Office, 1949), p. 806.

3. C. L. Sulzberger, *A Long Row of Candles* (New York: 1969), pp. 307–8.
4. Quoted in D. Yergin, *Shattered Peace: The Origins of the Cold War and the National Security State* (Boston: Houghton Mifflin, 1977), p. 315.
5. Anthony C. Brown, ed., *Dropshot: The American Plan for World War III Against Russia in 1957* (New York: Dial Press, 1978), p. 45.
6. Thomas Etzold and John Lewis Gaddis, eds., *Containment: Documents on American Policy and Strategy, 1945–1950* (New York: Columbia University Press, 1978), p. 431.
7. Ibid., p. 402
8. Ibid., pp. 423–24
9. Ibid., pp. 435–36
10. Ibid., 434, 389
11. Kissinger, *The White House Years*, p. 113
12. Ibid., p. 530.

3. On Peace and War, the Arms Race and Arms Control

1. *New York Review of Books*, 6 November 1980, p. 24.
2. L. I. Brezhnev, speech on 25 April 1978, Leninskim kursom, vol. 7, p. 300.
3. L. I. Brezhnev, speech in city of Tula on 18 January 1977, Moscow 1977.
4. *Pravda*, 25 July 1981.
5. L. I. Brezhnev, Leninskim kursom, vol. 7, p. 312.
6. *The Progressive*, April 1980, p. 46.
7. *Pravda*, 25 July 1981.
8. *Nuclear War Conference* (Washington, D.C.: Anderson Pub., 1978), p. 163.
9. *Scientific American*, October 1964, p. 35.
10. *Washington Quarterly*, Autumn 1979, pp. 5–6.
11. *Public Opinion*, May-June 1978, pp. 58–59.
12. *New York Times Magazine*, 1 November 1981, p. 79.
13. *The New York Review of Books*, 17 December 1981, p. 31.
14. *Common Sense in U.S.-Soviet Relations* (Washington, D.C.: American Committee on East-West Accord, 1978), p. 46.
15. Ibid., p. 59.
16. *Whence the Threat to Peace*, Moscow, 1981, p. 7.
17. Department of Defense Annual Report FY 1982, p. 43.
18. *Washington Post*, 18 October 1981.
19. "The SALT II Treaty." Hearings before the Committee on Foreign Relations, United States Senate, Ninety-sixth Congress, part 3 (Washington, D.C.: Government Printing Office, 1979), p. 75.
20. "Air Force," December 1979; also "The Military Balance, 1979–80," International Institute of Strategic Studies, London.

21.   *New York Times Magazine,* 9 December 1979, pp. 46, 47, 55.

22.   Alain Enthoven and Kenneth Smith, *How Much Is Enough?* (New York: 1971), p. 123.

23.   Arms Control Today, vol. 8, no. 9 (October 1978), p. 5.

24.   P. Dickson, *Think Tanks* (New York: 1971), p. 106.

25.   Joseph A. Pechman, ed., *Setting National Priorities: Agenda for the 1980s* (Washington, D.C.: The Brookings Institution, 1980), p. 286.

26.   *International Herald Tribune,* 14 May 1982.

Index